THE
WITNESS

The fighting had ended but for
Sandakan's most notorious prisoner
the war was not over

THE
WITNESS

TOM GILLING

ALLEN&UNWIN
SYDNEY · MELBOURNE · AUCKLAND · LONDON

Allen & Unwin
83 Alexander Street
Crows Nest NSW 2065
Australia
Phone: (61 2) 8425 0100
Email: info@allenandunwin.com
Web: www.allenandunwin.com

 A catalogue record for this
book is available from the
National Library of Australia

ISBN 978 1 76087 927 3

p. 9 image courtesy of *Rochdale Observer*; p. 283 image courtesy of Ben Sticpewich
Set in 11.5/17 pt Minion Pro by Midland Typesetters, Australia
Printed and bound in Australia by Griffin Press, part of Ovato

10 9 8 7 6 5 4 3 2 1

For Richard Walsh

CONTENTS

CONTENTS

GLOSSARY

AASC   Australian Army Service Corps
AGH   Australian General Hospital
AIB   Allied Intelligence Bureau
AIF   Australian Imperial Force
AMC   Army Medical Corps
AWGU   Australian War Graves Unit
CO   commanding officer
GHQ   general headquarters
HQ   headquarters
IJA   Imperial Japanese Army
MO   medical orderly
MT   motor transport
M&V   meat and vegetable
NCO   non-commissioned officer
NEI   Netherland East Indies
OC   officer commanding
POW   prisoner of war
QM   quartermaster
SOA   Special Operations Australia
SRD   Services Reconnaissance Department
W/T   wireless

Introduction

The story of the more than 2400 Allied servicemen who died as prisoners of the Japanese at Sandakan in Borneo is among the most tragic of the Second World War. More than a thousand men died on three brutal forced marches from Sandakan inland to Ranau, a distance of around 260 kilometres along rough jungle tracks. Three-quarters of the dead—and all six death march survivors—were Australian.

A 30-year embargo imposed by the Australian Government on evidence given at the war crimes trials came to an end only in the late 1970s. Peter Firkins' *From Hell to Eternity* (1979) was the first book to make use of newly opened files that included harrowing personal testimony from Sandakan survivors. Valuable investigative work was done by authors Don Wall, Athol Moffitt and others in the 1980s and early 1990s. Lynette Ramsay Silver's *Sandakan: A conspiracy of silence*, first published in 1998, expanded significantly on their findings and remains an important reference work.

Hell on Earth (2013) by Michele Cunningham, whose father was a prisoner of war at both Sandakan and Kuching, fills in some gaps and disagrees with Silver on several points. Drawing on the memories of his father, one of the six survivors, Richard Wallace Braithwaite's *Fighting Monsters: An intimate history of the Sandakan tragedy* (2016) is a perceptive study of the experience of both the prisoners and their gaolers. While neither book enjoyed a wide readership, both have added to our knowledge and understanding of what happened at Sandakan.

Paul Ham's *Sandakan: The untold story of the Sandakan death marches* (2013) did attract a wide readership, although the subtitle might have puzzled readers familiar with the subject. Ham's lively telling suffers from some surprising errors and misreadings of evidence that undermine its usefulness as a reference.

Each of the authors mentioned above makes extensive use of witness statements and interrogation reports taken from the six survivors after the war ended. These statements underpinned the prosecution of scores of Japanese prison camp guards in war crimes trials conducted in late 1945 and 1946.

The authors also draw on tape-recorded interviews made by historian Hank Nelson and ABC broadcaster Tim Bowden in the early 1980s for their radio documentary series *Prisoners of War: Australians Under Nippon*. Four of the six death march survivors—Keith Botterill, Dick Braithwaite, Owen Campbell and Nelson Short—were interviewed for the series. Of the four, Bowden considered Braithwaite and Campbell to be the 'most reliable'. He found Botterill 'very edgy and nervous'. The other two survivors, Bill Moxham and Bill Sticpewich, had died by the time Nelson and Bowden made their radio documentary.

After the commanding officer and the doctors, Sticpewich (pronounced 'Stipperwitch') was perhaps the most prominent Australian POW at Sandakan; he was certainly the most notorious. Everybody knew him, and few liked him. Asked in 1983 what he felt about Sticpewich, Dick Braithwaite told Bowden:

> I don't have any feelings about him ... I personally didn't like the man ... he didn't do anything to me personally, I heard he did do things that were unconventional, to say the least, and not in the best interests of the other prisoners, but this is only hearsay, I don't know ... he certainly didn't go out of his way to endear himself to people.

Dick Braithwaite was a scrupulous man, unwilling to accept as fact something he knew only as hearsay. Others did not hesitate to accuse Bill Sticpewich of being a collaborator, a 'white Jap'.

Sticpewich, who died in 1977, was the single most valuable witness to what happened to the Australian POWs at Sandakan and on the forced marches to Ranau. He not only saw everything but also remembered it, and he told what he knew in a series of statements and statutory declarations made directly after the war and in evidence he gave in person at the trials of Japanese and Formosan war criminals.

In every trial in which Sticpewich appeared as a witness his evidence was critical to the prosecution; Japanese officers and guards who had revelled in mistreating POWs had good reason to fear his testimony. Small wonder, then, that after Sticpewich made his escape from Ranau a search party was sent out with orders to shoot him on sight.

Yet for a guard found guilty of war crimes, a favourable 'character reference' from Sticpewich (in the form of a comment annexed to his statement of interrogation) could make the difference between a harsh and a lenient sentence.

Captain Athol Moffitt, the peacetime Sydney barrister entrusted by the army with prosecuting the Sandakan commandant, grasped at once the qualities that would make Sticpewich a crucial witness.

[H]e is one of the six survivors and the brightest of them—that should be enough. He got on the right side of the Japs and can speak quite a lot of Japanese—being very handy as a carpenter and good at fixing machines he made himself invaluable to the Japs. He had the run of the camp and got a little extra food from the Jap leavings. He also poked his nose into things and can now tell us all sorts of things as to what food they had and what medicines they had etc. At the same time he was a member of the secret organisation run by that hero Capt. Matthews to get food and medicine in and wireless news out to the civilians and also doing some espionage work.

'Got on the right side of the Japs . . . run of the camp . . . extra food . . . espionage work': Moffitt was perhaps too naïve to see that those words could also be put together to tell a different and darker story.

Chapter 1

HE SMILES A LOT

———⟫●⟪———

The Second World War had been over for four months when Captain Athol Moffitt, from Lismore in New South Wales, first set eyes on Captain Hoshijima Susumu of the Imperial Japanese Army. Six apocalyptic years of fighting had cost the lives of perhaps 60 million people. Among the dead were 2428 Australian and British prisoners of war at Sandakan in Borneo, where Hoshijima was commandant. In a makeshift courtroom (in reality a tent set up in a coconut grove) on Labuan, an island off the coast of Brunei, Hoshijima was going to answer for their deaths.

The commandant was marched into court by Gurkha guards from Nepal. 'I saw Hoshijima for the first time today,' Moffitt wrote in his diary. 'He is about 5' 11" and very powerful build and his face is more sadistic than I expected. He smiles a lot in a hard evil way—looks a smart man.'

Born six weeks before the outbreak of the First World War, Moffitt was a barrister when the Second World War began. After enlisting in the 2nd Australian Imperial Force as a private, he served in the artillery before being seconded to prosecute Japanese soldiers accused of war crimes.

Hoshijima was six years older, a graduate in applied chemistry from Osaka Imperial University who had gone to work for the Dainippon Celluloid Company and was researching the properties of aluminium when he was called up for military service. In a statement tendered to the court Hoshijima recalled that 'during the 10 odd years I was in school I was the leader and representative of my class. I was also chairman of the students committee.' He asked for this information to be 'take[n] into consideration' by the court 'when you judge my character'.

During his time in the army, Hoshijima claimed to have 'always done the work of a person one rank higher than myself'. During his school years and the years he spent in uniform he had 'never been once punished for breaking any regulations' but instead had 'always been rewarded and praised for my work'. The reason for this, he said, was that he had been 'sincere in all the things that I have done' and had also 'done everything to the best of my ability'.

The court at Labuan was open to the Australian press, but Moffitt would later say that he was unable to remember seeing a single journalist. The reports of Hoshijima's trial that appeared in Australian newspapers were largely drawn from summaries made by Moffitt himself for his military superiors.

In his diary entry for the previous day, Monday, 7 January 1946, Moffitt recorded that he 'only had a few drinks . . . in view of the big job tomorrow'. Now, on the first day of the trial, Moffitt expressed his 'determin[ation] . . . to see the slaughter of those lads is avenged'.

Another Australian soldier had also travelled to Labuan determined to see Hoshijima punished. He was William Hector 'Bill' Sticpewich, a warrant officer in the Australian Army Service Corps. Six years older than Moffitt, Sticpewich was the same age as Hoshijima. Of the six death march survivors, Sticpewich was the only one well enough to give evidence at Hoshijima's trial.

Moffitt already had in his possession a written statement running to fifteen closely typed pages given by Sticpewich to Captain J.G. Ruse at Morotai on 7 October 1945. While this and later statements contained detailed descriptions of atrocities committed by Hoshijima and his guards, Moffitt worried that on their own they would not be enough to prove Hoshijima guilty.

On Sunday, 6 January, two days before the trial was due to begin, Moffitt wrote in his diary, 'Sticpewich arrived today so all is well'. Moffitt spent the morning with him and was excited by what he heard, finding Sticpewich's first-hand account of events 'more convincing' than his written statement. Hoshijima had four Japanese lawyers on his defence team but, after talking to Sticpewich, Moffitt predicted they would 'cause me little worry'.

Moffitt considered Bill Sticpewich a 'typical Aussie—fairly rough but hail fellow well met with a ton of resource and personality'. There could be no argument about Sticpewich's 'resource': he survived more than three years as a prisoner at Sandakan and Ranau when almost 2500 men died. But as to his being a 'typical Aussie': not everyone agreed with that.

Chapter 2

SPEED DEMON

———⊰⊱———

Bill Sticpewich was born on 4 June 1908 in Carrington, New South Wales. When he joined the army in 1940 he described himself as a certified meat inspector, but ten years earlier Sticpewich had been one of the pioneers of Australian speedway racing.

Originating on small dirt tracks before the First World War, speedway racing became popular in the Hunter region of New South Wales, where Bill and his brother Charlie were introduced to it. By the late 1920s there were professional speedway teams in Europe. Having cut their teeth on local tracks, Bill and Charlie left Australia to try their luck in France and Spain before moving on to England, where the money was better. Bill, who was known as 'Stippy', captained the Rochdale team in 1930 while his brother rode for Wembley.

ROCHDALE SPEEDWAY
SATURDAY, MAY 10th, 1930, at 7-30 p.m.
The First Appearance in this Country of
BILL STICPEWICH (Australia) "The Speed Demon," the holder of all the New Zealand Track Records.
GINGER LEES, fresh from his triumphs in Copenhagen and Hamburg, and who last night Cleared the Board at Liverpool.
SMILER "LES" WOTTON, the Liverpool Captain, who put up such a great show against Burton.
A. B. DREW, the original conqueror of "Sprouts" and who is now riding better than ever.
I. RASSMUSSEN, the Magnificent Danish Star, who is over here on a Trophy collecting jaunt.
In the Golden Sash and Golden Helmet Races; also Team Trial Match, Reds v. Blues.
Note New Prices: **1/- All Round** (Stands Extra) EXTENSIVE CAR PARK
SEASON TICKETS at 25/- are still available.
The Usual Fleet of MOTOR COACHES will run direct to the Track

Advertised by promoters as the 'most Hectic rider of all time', Bill was an aggressive racer with a knack for escaping serious injury. On 6 June 1930 the *Halifax Evening Courier* reported an 'exciting spill' involving two drivers, Austin Humphries and Dick Fletcher:

This pair and W. Sticpewich were racing abreast around a bend when the first-named came to earth. The New Zealander [sic] escaped narrowly, but Fletcher was not so fortunate, and he was thrown violently, machine and rider completing several somersaults before coming to rest on the green. It was remarkable no one was badly injured.

In 1930 Bill and Charlie returned to Australia via the Panama Canal and New Zealand. According to the Sydney *Referee*, 'the Sticpewichs . . . had only dallied a short space in Spain. Not even long enough to get the hang of cuss-words like "sapristi" and "caramba". When they strike trouble, as they did on Saturday night, they expressed themselves in fluent Australian.'

While the establishment *Sydney Morning Herald* noted merely that 'Bill Sticpewich rode under engagement to several English promoters' and

was 'reasonably successful', the *Labor Daily* was more effusive, declaring
him a 'very hot number to be reckoned with' owing to his having 'plenty
of experience in every kind of riding and on practically every kind of
track both here and abroad'.

By the mid-1930s Bill was building and racing midget cars. As the
track record holder with five firsts and one second place in six starts,
he was celebrated by *The Telegraph* in Brisbane as the 'star' of a meeting
at the Exhibition Speedway. In the night's most exciting race Sticpewich,
coming fast on the outside of the field, 'narrowly missed crashing' into an
overturned car.

More significant, perhaps, than the newspaper's account of Bill and his
great rival Jean Reville 'racing abreast at breakneck speed' was a photograph of Sticpewich and his midget racing car above a caption that read:
'Bill Sticpewich, on left, points out the front wheel drive, universal joints
and brakes of his interestingly laid out 3½ h.p. racing car, which holds the
Exhibition track record.'

Sticpewich was an unusually talented mechanic who could fix anything, from car engines to wrist watches. In a Japanese prisoner of war
camp, skills such as those were worth a great deal.

Chapter 3

TEARS IN THEIR EYES

⟶⟫◆⟪⟵

After being called up in September 1941, Hoshijima was stationed for a while in the northern part of French Indo-China as commander of an engineering company. According to a character reference given at his trial by Lieutenant Colonel Sago Takuji of 37th Japanese Army HQ, when one of his subordinates fell seriously ill Hoshijima went out of his way to see and comfort the officer, travelling several times to Hanoi more than 160 kilometres from his station and 'extend[ing] his endeavour to supervise the construction work stipulated to this officer before he [fell] sick and complet[ing] the work for [the] merit of the officer'.

From French Indo-China, Hoshijima was sent to build an airfield in western Borneo before being posted to Sandakan in mid-1942 to manage construction of a new airfield that would enable Japanese aircraft to refuel when flying between Japan and the newly conquered territories of Singapore and the Philippines. The Sandakan aerodrome would also be a refuelling stop for Japanese aircraft flying to and from Java and other islands in the Netherlands East Indies.

Hoshijima almost died before he could take up his new post. In the Balabac Strait just off the tip of north-east Borneo, the ship carrying Hoshijima to Sandakan was torpedoed and sunk by an Allied submarine. According to a statement by Sergeant Watanabe Katsumi, who had served under Hoshijima in the 4th Independent Engineering Regiment and later joined him at Sandakan, the Japanese who escaped from the sinking ship expected to be machine-gunned in the water. They were surprised when the Allied submarine 'disappeared into the darkness of the night without making any firing upon us who were floating in a small rowing boat'.

When Sergeant Watanabe and others asked Hoshijima why the submarine had not fired on the survivors, he 'explained to us that the American or British observed the international Laws of War and showed us their humanity and justice of which they were proud'.

For two days the survivors were lost at sea before they reached an island. 'During these two days of turmoil,' Watanabe wrote, 'having only a small amount of ration just enough for one meal and a bottle of water for each man, Capt. Hoshijima divided his own ration and water among his men taking no food nor water for himself.' As well as sacrificing his rations Hoshijima insisted on doing much of the rowing himself, 'taking an oar away' from an exhausted man: 'Without taking a nap nor rest during more than 40 hours he encouraged the men while he coxed or rowed . . . it was his leadership which made us do our best and saved our lives.'

According to Watanabe, the engineering company assigned to the aerodrome at Sandakan was disbanded in October 1942. The men separated from their 'beloved' Captain Hoshijima with 'tears in their eyes'. Some were sent back to Japan, some to Java. Watanabe was assigned to a unit in Kuching in Sarawak, on the north-west coast of Borneo.

Bill Sticpewich remembered Sergeant Watanabe well. He told Australian war crimes investigators that Watanabe 'came to Sandakan about Aug 42 his duties were Cpl [corporal] in charge of camp work parties etc administration':

> Was responsible on one occasion for sending all PsW who could move ... to the airport to work and belting some who protested meaning the doctors and the medical orderlies who wanted to care for the sick. The sick were left for the day without any attention. Other occasions striking PsW with stick and making them go to work.
>
> On one occasion he struck an Indian milk vendor down with a shovel, cutting about the head, the shoulders for no reason at all. He was transferred to KUCHING.

For a while Sergeant Watanabe's colleagues in Java continued to write to him 'longing to become [Hoshijima's] men over again'. Watanabe also missed him after he was sent to Kuching: 'However far we departed from Capt. Hoshijima,' he wrote, 'we could not forget him a moment.'

Chapter 4

A GOOD SOLDIER

Bill Sticpewich was 32 years old when he enlisted in the army on 19 June 1940 at Kelvin Grove, Brisbane. His medical fitness was assessed as Class I and he was described as having brown hair and blue eyes. Under the heading 'distinctive marks', his service and casualty form mentioned a 'right side hernia scar', a scar on his left shin and a 'lump' from a broken right hand.

Sticpewich's career in speedway and midget car racing was over but the practical and engineering skills he had acquired meant he was initially assigned to a technical unit. By the first week of August he had been promoted to acting sergeant. In October he was promoted again, this time to warrant officer, but in March 1941 he was court-martialled on charges relating to the theft of two beds from an army depot in Brisbane the previous December.

After the beds had been 'souvenired' from the depot, two detectives from the Queensland police were sent to investigate. Sticpewich allegedly told four private soldiers: 'The beds are pretty hot. You know what to do.' The men then loaded the beds into a van and got rid of them in nearby bushland. It is unclear just how much Sticpewich knew about the original theft, described by one of the privates as a 'good joke'. It is possible they stole the beds without telling him, knowing that as a warrant officer Sticpewich would be held responsible.

The private soldiers gave evidence implicating Sticpewich at a preliminary court of inquiry, but before the court martial could take place all four insisted on withdrawing their statements in the presence of Sticpewich and an officer. According to Major Maplestone: 'At 0815 hrs [on 14 January 1941] Sgt-Major Sticpewich paraded Ptes Nott, Murray, Prescott and Lang before me. Sgt-Major Sticpewich said to me: "These men wish to retract their statements made to the Court of Inquiry".'

At Sticpewich's court martial Private Murray was asked about his retraction:

Q: Was it at the accused's instigation that you retracted your statement?
A: Not altogether, we had a conversation and decided it was the best thing to do.

Private Murray told Maplestone that Sticpewich 'did not explain what he meant by saying "you know what to do"'. Sticpewich might have been suggesting the privates return the stolen beds but it seems more likely he was urging the opposite: to get rid of them.

Sticpewich was eventually court-martialled on two different charges: 'Conduct to the prejudice of good order and military discipline'; and 'Neglect to the prejudice of good order and military discipline'. At his court martial Sticpewich was acquitted of the first and more serious charge but found guilty of the second in that he 'failed to cause the delivery up to the proper authority of two tubular metal stretchers and two fibre mattresses, public property, which it was his duty to do'. He was fined £5.

The official report on the court martial, dated 14 March 1941, drew attention to the fact that 'although the Court found that the accused had a prima facie case to answer, he did not give evidence on oath, or make any statement in his defence'. In a statement to mitigate punishment, his defending officer told the court that Sticpewich had paid for the stolen beds, that he had not been involved in taking them and that the 'whole matter' was a 'practical joke by the men'. He then stated, 'Accused feels his position keenly as W.O. [warrant officer].'

During the court martial Maplestone was asked whether Sticpewich was a 'good soldier' and whether he displayed 'soldierly qualities'. To both questions the major answered 'Yes'. His service record shows that in March 1941 Sticpewich was 'released without prejudice to further arrest' and marched out to East Command. He sailed for Singapore a few months later as a member of the Australian Army Service Corps. Described by some as the army's 'grocers' and 'truckies', the unit was responsible for procuring, storing and distributing consumables such as food and petrol and transporting troops, stores and ammunition.

'Procuring, storing and distributing': before long Sticpewich would be carrying out the same tasks as a prisoner of the Japanese.

Chapter 5

ARRIVAL

———◆———

On 7 July 1942, just over a month after Hoshijima had saved his comrades from their sinking ship, a party of 1494 Australian prisoners of war embarked from Singapore's Keppel Harbour on the tramp steamer *Ubi Maru*, bound for Sandakan. The prisoners were designated B Force. Their commanding officer (CO) was artillery officer Lieutenant Colonel 'Alf' Walsh of the 2/10th Field Regiment. Walsh had been forced to take up the position of CO 'at short notice' when the Japanese decided not to allow his superior, Brigadier Harold Taylor, to lead B Force. Putting a senior infantry officer like Taylor in charge of such a large force would have constituted a serious risk for the Japanese; Walsh, who was not well liked by his men, was a much safer bet. In his evidence to the Australian war crimes commission, Walsh commented simply that Taylor was 'not acceptable to the IJA'.

Billy Young, who had joined the army at the age of fifteen, reckoned that when the Japanese asked for a working party to go to Sandakan the Australian officers at Changi were told it would be 'something of a picnic, with no work required'. According to Young, the large number of officers and NCOs who signed up to go to Borneo was proof that they had fallen for the story.

The *Ubi Maru* was one of the hell ships used by the Japanese to transport prisoners: a 'dirty stinking screamer of a steamer', in Young's words. Conditions on board were atrocious and the Australians, packed shoulder to shoulder inside the ship's three fetid cargo holds, were given little to eat or drink. Water for the prisoners was carried in two tanks, one about 8 feet (2.4 metres) square at the forward end and a smaller one aft. After three days the latter was dry and the men in the rear hold had to risk punishment by scrounging or stealing water from tanks reserved for the Japanese troops.

Sticpewich, not for the last time, found ways to escape the deprivations endured by his mates. 'At first we did not get sufficient water,' he told Captain Ruse, 'but I was on the forward end and managed to get sufficient for my needs.'

Twice a day the Australians were given meals of limed rice (rice to which lime juice had been added in a futile effort to stop it spoiling). Half a century later Billy Young still recoiled at the memory of 'soggy green rice. Sour, sticky, putrid, lime green rice . . . A witch's brew of toads, and snails, and puppy dog tails, couldn't have been any worse. The rice had gone off well before the lime had, so leaving us with a lethal brew of limed rice stew.'

Thanks to the spoiled lime rice, dysentery was rampant, with men clambering up steel ladders to squat over the drop toilets that hung precariously over the side of the ship. As the ancient cargo vessel lumbered around the northern coast of Borneo, the men below decks found it difficult to breathe. Many of the sick were too weak to make the climb and the hold became awash with excrement.

Nine days after leaving Singapore the *Ubi Maru*, as Billy Young put it, 'collapsed' against the old timber wharf at Sandakan.

The pre-war capital of British North Borneo, Sandakan was a pretty colonial town on a narrow coastal plain above which loomed a jungle-covered escarpment. Photographs from the 1920s show white-suited Europeans in pith helmets walking down open-sewered streets lined with timber buildings. A few bitumen roads stretched back into the environs.

While half the prisoners remained on board the *Ubi Maru*, the rest were taken into Sandakan town. After being given weak tea and a cup of the despised green rice they were led up the hill to the Anglican church, a dour bluestone edifice that would be almost the only large building in Sandakan to survive the war intact. The church was not big enough to accommodate the whole group, so some prisoners had to be herded back to the ship while the rest slept in whatever space they could find.

The next morning the men who had been kept in the hold were brought into town. After a head count and more lime rice, every man capable of walking was marched uphill to the crossroads and from there along the road to the site of the old agricultural station near the 8-mile peg. Around twenty bedridden men went on ahead by truck. From the main road a turn-off to the right led to the camp, a noticeboard outside reading 'No 1 Prisoner of War Camp, British North Borneo, HQ Kuching' (also known as 8 Mile Camp and No. 1 Camp).

The former agricultural station had been intended to house Indian troops before the war, but after Pearl Harbor it was turned into an internment camp for Japanese civilians. Other ranks slept on wooden floors in Japanese-built *atap* (palm-fibre) huts, 45 or 50 men to a hut, while the officers lived 30 to a hut in the original three-roomed wooden huts built by the British. Other huts served as sickbays and a cookhouse. 'Wooden buildings and palm huts, leaky roofs. No fittings or furniture' was how Nelson Short summed up the accommodation.

All the huts were alive with bugs and lice. According to Lieutenant Rod Wells, 'You could catch up to 100 [lice] a night without any trouble.' Richard Braithwaite, whose father Dick was a member of B Force, described one of the newly built atap huts collapsing as the men were moving in. Prisoners had to leap out of the way as the hut tumbled down the hill.

Spread over a couple of hectares, the camp was surrounded by a cyclone-wire fence topped with barbed wire, with sections of concertinaed barbed wire sandwiched between more barbed-wire fences. The whole camp was overlooked by two timber guard towers. Outside the gate was the main guardroom, while seven sentry boxes were placed at regular intervals around the perimeter. At night the fence was illuminated by powerful electric lights.

Sanitation facilities were not so impressive: 'Sanitation would have been all right if the buckets, in the first place, would have fitted the latrines,' Colonel Walsh told the war crimes commission. 'The latrines had been built by the authorities in British North Borneo. They [had] an opening at the back where the receptacle would go in, but the buckets the Japanese provided for us would not fit.'

The quality of the water at the camp was very poor: 'muddy and full of bacteria' according to one prisoner. 'We were warned by our own doctors . . . not to drink the water unless it was treated.' Artillery Sergeant Walter Wallace, a former prison officer who would become one of very few POWs to escape from Sandakan, remembered a pond containing fish that 'we soon learned not to touch on any account as they ate the mosquitoes . . . Outside the camp on the north a large area of ground, about a mile [1.6 kilometres] in length and half a mile wide had been cleared of all timber and undergrowth. On the west there was a narrow clearing, then jungle. On the south was the road by which we had come, and on the east I could see nothing but thick jungle.'

The camp had one outstanding natural feature: a huge mengaris tree

(*Koompassia excelsa*) that was known to everyone as the 'Big Tree'. In his official report of events at Sandakan compiled after the war had ended, Major Harry Jackson wrote that the tree 'was to attract many a PW's eye for the next few years', but this hardly does justice to the profound impression the Big Tree made on the minds of the men who saw it.

Soaring above the parade ground where the hungry and bone-tired prisoners assembled for the evening *tenko* (roll call), the tree acted as a meeting place for prisoner-run activities such as lectures, church services and singalongs. Wallace remembered it as the 'biggest tree I have ever seen. It must have been over two hundred feet [61 metres] high, a wonderful guide to aircraft should any ever decide to pay a visit to the camp.'

In his interview with Tim Bowden, Dick Braithwaite said the Big Tree 'played an amazing part in the exchange of ideas. It was like the Kings Cross of the camp . . . after the evening meals you'd sit there and watch the beautiful sunsets . . . the people that could walk from the hospital would walk over there and chat and hear the news of the day, what had happened to so-and-so; who had died and what was being done out on the . . . airfield.'

Native bees often made nests in mengaris trees and honey from the Big Tree was collected for the patients in the camp hospital. When his toothbrush wore out, Dick Braithwaite made a new one by cutting down the bristles from a clothes brush and fastening them together with fuse wire. To avoid cutting his mouth on the tied-off fuse wire, he moulded beeswax over the sharp ends. 'That brush lasted me all the prison camp days and was as good when I got out . . . as when I first made it.'

The Big Tree's buttressed roots made a useful hiding place for valuables; Richard Braithwaite mentioned 'rumours of much treasure hidden in its folds'. Lieutenant Tony White told Braithwaite that he kept a pistol hidden there.

Billy Young recalled the tree 'command[ing] the area around the parade ground' where the prisoners would 'muster for work each morning, and where we would receive whatever admonitions the then "other master race of the world" would wish to give out, to us slaves'.

Chapter 6

MIND GAMES

It was several days before the Australians had their first sight of then Lieutenant Hoshijima. Major Jackson's report described him as being 'six foot, evil, English speaking'—perfunctory epithets that might say more about Jackson and his mission than they do about Hoshijima, whom he had never met. Besides interviewing witnesses and finding out what had happened to the Sandakan POWs, the purpose of Jackson's 1946 trip to Borneo was to identify locals who had helped Australian prisoners and reward them for their efforts.

Each of the six Australians who escaped from the death marches—Private Keith Botterill, Gunner Owen Campbell, Bombardier Dick Braithwaite, Private Nelson Short, Lance Bombardier Bill Moxham and Warrant Officer Sticpewich—had vivid memories of Hoshijima, who was in charge of the camp when they arrived but had not yet been appointed commandant. (He was formally appointed commandant a month after the prisoners' arrival, on 17 August 1942.)

Speaking to ABC broadcaster Tim Bowden, Dick Braithwaite described Hoshijima as 'a character in his way':

> He was a tall man for a Japanese . . . close to six foot . . . and he liked to ride round on this old horse . . . someone said it was an old Queensland racehorse . . . he used to ride that horse around and . . . you'd be working on a working party and next thing you'd look up and there he'd be sitting on his horse, just up above you, watching you. He used to sneak around a lot and if anything wasn't going according to his liking, trouble started immediately.

In another interview Braithwaite told Bowden and historian Hank Nelson that he viewed Hoshijima as a man 'without a single humane bone in his body'.

Keith Botterill described Hoshijima to Bowden as 'big—about 6 foot. [He could be] kind or vicious, depending on his mood. He gave the officers permission to build a garden outside and work a garden, and then he'd turn around and gouge a man's eyes out.'

In his book *Fighting Monsters*, Richard Braithwaite devotes two pages to what he called Hoshijima's 'mindgames':

> Well-educated and somewhat narcissistic, Hoshijima was a tall (about 1.8 metres) man, full of confidence, and proud of the number of languages he spoke. He spoke English well but chose to have the interpreter, Osawa, translate his speeches on parade. He would then correct poor Osawa's mistakes. On one occasion, Osawa translated Hoshijima as saying 'hundreds of years' and Hoshijima hissed at him, 'centuries'. An Australian officer, Lieutenant Peter Bell, smirked at this byplay and was immediately king hit by Hoshijima for his perceived disrespect.

In the beginning, before Japan's worsening military position caused conditions in the camp to deteriorate, Hoshijima mainly acted the martinet, although he could be ferocious when crossed. Another member of B Force, Tony White, told Richard Braithwaite that in the early days he and other Australian officers regarded Hoshijima as a 'good officer'.

Braithwaite quotes the opinion of Hoshijima's superior and the Kuching-based officer in charge of building the aerodrome, Captain Yamada Masaharu, that Hoshijima was 'meticulous . . . [but] not very flexible . . . he was a very earnest officer, and was also knowledgeable about construction, besides being commandant. In that sense, we all respected him. Among all the officers who were at Sandakan, he was the best.'

Owen Campbell remembered him as a 'good stamp of a chap to look at . . . about six foot in height. He didn't wear glasses . . . dressed mainly in white.' In a statement he gave after the war Campbell accused Hoshijima of bashing prisoners 'on four or five occasions within my own knowledge':

Capt [Hoshijima] would stand a PW to attention and then 'king-hit' him, knocking him down. He would then stand the prisoner up, stand him to attention again and then knock him down again. He would do this repeatedly. He always used the heel of his hand and hit very hard. A mate of mine said it was like a horse kick. [Hoshijima] was about six feet tall and a fine physical specimen.

Hoshijima's message to the members of B Force on that day in July 1942 was the same message he would give to other groups sent to Sandakan. Nelson Short, who arrived in July 1943 with E Force, remembered it like this:

[T]here was 500 of us, and . . . he gave a speech to us, he said that . . . we'd come there to build an aerodrome at Sandakan and we would work and if anybody escaped, well, there'd be five or six pulled out and shot if anybody escaped. And the war would go 100 years and . . . we would work there until our bones rotted under the tropical sun of Borneo. Which was pretty right, in the finish, I mean to say, they all did. But that was the speech, and he says, you're here to build an aerodrome and that's it.

In his book *Hidden Horrors* Yuki Tanaka notes that Hoshijima was originally sent to Sandakan in his capacity as an engineer to 'oversee construction of the airfield', adding that he 'had no expectation of being made camp commandant'. In other words, his responsibilities were, first, to get the airfield built and, second, to manage the POW camp. In keeping with those priorities, Hoshijima delegated most of the day-to-day running of the camp to his subordinates. 'His principal task was the construction of the airfield,' Tanaka writes, 'and the POWs were the raw material with which he was to complete that task. Their welfare was doubtless a secondary issue for him.'

Tanaka goes further, suggesting that not only was the task of managing the POW camp secondary to the task of completing the aerodrome but also the tasks were inherently contradictory, since 'the imperatives for the construction of the airfield were often against the best interests of the prisoners and their welfare'.

During the interrogation that preceded his trial, Hoshijima admitted that having responsibility for the aerodrome construction as well as the POW camp made him 'very irritable' and caused him to 'beat the prisoners to make them work harder'.

Working underfed prisoners to exhaustion and forcing sick men to do heavy manual labour was self-defeating in the long run as it reduced the number of men available to work. This was one of the lessons learned from the Siam–Burma railway. If pursued ruthlessly enough in the short term, however, it could achieve results, albeit at the cost of many lives. Hoshijima's first obligation was always to the airfield.

Chapter 7

A SIMPLE LIFE

———⟫•⟪———

Hoshijima allowed the prisoners a few days to fix up the camp before putting them to work. They began by building a road from the camp to the site of the new aerodrome just over 2 kilometres away. Once the road was finished, work started on clearing and levelling the ground in preparation for the aerodrome's two runways. The Australians soon set about sabotaging the few pieces of machinery the Japanese had brought with them, ensuring the job would have to be done almost exclusively by hand with axes, picks, shovels and baskets. Not everyone agreed with the sabotage: Braithwaite writes that it made the prisoners' lives harder by creating more manual labour while provoking the Japanese to be more aggressive.

While the bulk of the prisoners worked on the aerodrome, a few were assigned to other duties such as collecting timber for cooking and for the boiler used by the Japanese to generate electricity. The men assigned to the aerodrome set off at around 7 am and knocked off around 5.30 pm. In the beginning some locals were allowed to run food stalls where the prisoners could buy fruit and fried pancakes containing small pieces of meat, known as 'doovers'. Tony White recalled Major Frank Fleming buying a few of these pancakes and stashing them in his officer's hat to distribute among the men.

Food at the camp was barely adequate. At first there was enough to eat but the diet was unbalanced and deficient in protein: it was more than a month before the Australians received their first issue of fish. For a while they were given dried or fresh fish roughly three times a week, the amount varying from about 150 pounds (68 kilograms) to about 250 pounds (113 kilograms) shared between 1500 prisoners. If fish was not available there might be beef, pork or dugong. Lentils were sometimes mixed with the rice and they were also given some vegetables.

The hard manual labour involved in building the aerodrome made life more difficult at Sandakan than it had been at Changi, but most prisoners managed to adapt. These men learned to live with the physical exhaustion, terrible food and the random brutality of the guards. Ways were found to work less hard without incurring beatings and inadequate rations were supplemented with food scrounged from outside the wire.

The lax security arrangements that prevailed in the early weeks were soon tightened, but it was still possible—albeit very dangerous—for prisoners to slip out of the camp at night. Some contrived to steal rice from a food dump beyond the wire, boring through the wall and drawing rice from the bags before plugging up the hole with a bit of wood. When the Japanese found out what was happening they brought in dogs and tethered them around the catwalk that ran the perimeter of the swamp. As Dick Braithwaite told Tim Bowden:

Our fellows started going through the wire and bringing the dogs in . . . And of course they ate them . . . And I remember one Jap guard who spoke a bit of English and [he] said to me, 'Oh, our dogs, they go.' And I said, 'Oh yes, probably crocodiles . . . in the swamp over there' . . . some evenings after that, we'd see them watching over their shoulders rather than watching the camp.

In a speech to Japanese guards at Kuching Major Suga, the officer in charge of all prisoner-of-war camps in Borneo, declared that prisoners 'must be taught to put up with a simple life and to feel thankful for that'. Suga did not prohibit beatings for prisoners who broke the rules, although he counselled the guards at Kuching to 'strike the happy mean between harshness and leniency'. Prisoners—both officers and men—had little recourse against arbitrary violence. In his evidence to the war crimes commission Captain Jock Britz described an attack on the camp's senior medical officer, Major Hugh Rayson, by a Japanese doctor:

[Dr] Yamamoto punched Maj. Rayson, cutting his face badly and blackening both eyes. He then beat Maj. Rayson about the head with the victim's wooden clogs, which were then lying on the ground. While being beaten, Maj. Rayson was forced backwards several times onto a barb-wire fence, causing severe lacerations to his back and shoulders.

There was no apparent reason why Yamamoto should have thus treated Maj. Rayson and this particular Japanese seemed to go berserk after working himself up into an A1 frenzy.

Maj. Rayson was forced to remain in his bed for several weeks after the beating and to my mind was severely shocked mentally as a result.

Not everyone was cowed. Six weeks after B Force's arrival at Sandakan something happened at 8 Mile Camp that made an instant legend of its commanding officer, Lieutenant Colonel Walsh.

On 2 September 1942 work parties were cancelled and all prisoners were ordered to the parade ground. There were many more guards than usual and machine guns had been mounted on the roof of the guardhouse. According to Walsh, 'there were about 150 fully armed Japanese soldiers, there were hand grenades etc. and we were absolutely corralled like a mob of sheep'.

Three or four tables had been set up on the parade ground, and on each table was a book several inches thick with a typed oath at the front followed by blank pages awaiting signatures. Following a number of brave but unsuccessful escape attempts from Sandakan, Hoshijima had been ordered by 37th Army HQ in Kuching to demand that all prisoners sign a pledge not to escape. Hoshijima's interpreter Osawa stood on one of the tables and read out the document, which consisted of three clauses. Dick Braithwaite remembered them as follows:

> I promise to obey the orders and regulations of the Imperial Japanese Army.
> I promise not to escape.
> If any of us should attempt to do so, we request that you shoot them to death.

After Osawa had read out the oath there was a 'bit of a pause and a certain amount of tension in the ranks'. Hoshijima called Colonel Walsh over and ordered him to read out the oath again, after which Walsh declared, 'I am not ordering anyone to do anything, but I personally refuse to sign this document.' Walsh could hardly have done otherwise, having already told the Japanese military police, the Kempei-Tai, that he had no authority to order prisoners not to escape since under Australian Army regulations each man had a duty to escape if he could.

At once Walsh was put under arrest and marched through the gate with his hands tied behind his back. 'A Japanese guard and about 20 other ranks loaded their rifles,' Walsh recalled, 'and there was a certain amount of glee, laughter and chatter amongst them.' Some of the Australians, thinking that Walsh was to be executed, called out for him to sign, but the colonel refused. Dick Braithwaite told Tim Bowden:

> There was silence except for the birds and the jungle noises that were drifting in . . . there was a dead silence and . . . a sort of feeling of menace, that something was going to explode. The guards were surrounding us and . . . we more or less turned, half turned automatically to face the nearest guards to us and they had that feeling too, because the fellow near me, he was shaking. Now we would have been massacred, no doubt, but we would have taken some of them with us, and possibly the people who survived it would have been executed.

In the midst of the stand-off Major John Workman spoke to Osawa, whom Walsh considered to be 'quite an intelligent interpreter', and suggested a change in wording so that the last clause read 'I promise not to escape and if I do I know that I will be shot'. Workman called out to the men that the oath was meaningless in any case because they were being made to sign it under duress.

The revised wording was acceptable to Walsh and he signed. The rest of the prisoners then lined up to sign, most of them under jovial false names such as 'Phar Lap', 'Ned Kelly' and 'Bob Menzies'. For the next six hours the Australians were kept on the parade ground while the guards searched the huts for paper and writing implements, which Hoshijima had been instructed by 37th Army HQ to confiscate.

Similar pledges not to escape were demanded from prisoners of war in other Japanese camps, but showdowns such as the one at Sandakan were unusual. Escape attempts continued, since most men did not consider themselves bound by oaths they had been forced to sign at gunpoint.

Walsh's defiance made him a hero to the men of B Force. 'We didn't have a great deal of time for Colonel Walsh,' Dick Braithwaite recalled, 'but our admiration for him knew no bounds after this incident.'

'The whole camp is very proud of Col. Walsh', Private Tom Burns wrote in his diary, the only one discovered among the remains of 8 Mile Camp after the Japanese incinerated it in 1945.

> The guts he showed was fair dinkum Aussie spirit and I know if ever the time comes we will be with him to the last man, for he showed plenty of courage. I do hope the opportunity will soon come and we will make up for the dreadful treatment we are receiving at the hands of the Japanese. They are forever beating our boys who work at the drome. There are several chaps carrying large scars on their backs where they have been hit with the butt of the rifle. The general state of health of the troops is bad. We are all suffering from malnutrition. Most of the boys have sore throats and sore eyes and lips and dysentery is still very bad and we have averaged a death each week since we came to Borneo. I have lost over three stone through sickness and lack of good food . . . I think the condition of the camp hospital is shocking. The sleeping quarters are just alive with bugs and crabs and all classes of skin complaint are mixed up with other disease.

A month after the signing incident Colonel Walsh was transferred to Kuching along with several other Australian officers. There, according to author Don Wall, Walsh 'kept to himself, ate alone for three years, and generally was not popular'. The transfer to Kuching saved his life, as no Australian officer survived the death marches.

After the war Walsh was made an Officer of the British Empire in recognition of the courage and leadership he showed that day. Tom Burns felt that it was 'lucky for the Japs' they didn't shoot Walsh since the enraged Australians would have taken revenge and 'there would not have been a Japanese alive in this area of the prison camp'.

To some of the prisoners the incident must have felt like a victory: they had signed on their own terms and showed Hoshijima the meaning of Aussie spirit. But Hoshijima had the signatures he wanted, and he had gone to the brink to obtain them. There was a lesson in that for the Australians.

Chapter 8

SMART OPERATOR

After the fall of Singapore in February 1942 Bill Sticpewich was classified initially as 'missing' and sometime later as 'prisoner of war'. As far as his service record goes, the two and a half years he spent as a prisoner at Sandakan are a blank: he was one of hundreds of Australian soldiers who, by the middle of 1943, were listed by the army simply as 'interned Borneo camp'.

In 8 Mile Camp everybody knew 'Stippy'. Keith Botterill told Don Wall that the 'Japs only knew a few people. They knew Sticpewich, Captain Cook and a few [others]. They knew them by name. All the rest, no. [You had] . . . a little Jap number . . . You never had a name.'

Richard Braithwaite describes Sticpewich as one of the 'smart operators, good at looking out for themselves, but tending to sail close to the wind with the Japanese—and everyone else'. His father Dick remembered Sticpewich being 'something of a bully' who 'picked wrestling fights with young blokes who were receiving much less food than he'.

Wall, himself a former POW and survivor of the Siam–Burma railway, knew or at least knew of Sticpewich when they were prisoners together at Changi. Wall described him to Tim Bowden as 'not a popular person. He was known not to have any friends—close friends . . . Sticpewich was a loner. [He] was only interested in anyone that he could benefit from . . . [He was] a bit of a dealer.'*

Being a loner in a Japanese POW camp was unusual: every prisoner needed a mate he could depend on when he was sick. If Sticpewich did not have a mate it could only be because he was able to manage without one.

It did not take Sticpewich long to realise that life at Sandakan was going to be very different from life at Changi, where POWs were nominally under the control of their own officers and therefore less susceptible to beatings by the guards. Albert Thompson, a corporal in the Royal Australian Engineers, wrote in his diary that at Changi there was 'no scraping and bowing, no lashing and no interference whatsoever'. Prisoners were not worked to death at Changi, but at Sandakan being worked to death appeared to be their sole purpose. Hoshijima had said as much in his welcoming speech.

Sticpewich set about creating a job for himself that afforded him some independence and a degree of protection from the violence of the guards

---

* Don Wall's remarks about Sticpewich should be treated with caution. He told Bowden, 'I only saw him once in the early days in Changi—I didn't go to Borneo—so I can't comment on Borneo except for the information that the survivors gave me, and they weren't impressed.' However, Wall did repeatedly comment on Sticpewich's time in Borneo and his comments were nearly always hostile. To Bowden's question 'What was he doing for his fellow prisoners?', Wall bluntly answered, 'Nothing,' adding that Sticpewich 'concentrated on' ingratiating himself with the Japanese. While Sticpewich certainly spared no efforts to ingratiate himself with the Japanese, the assertion that he did nothing for his fellow prisoners is, as we will see, simply untrue.

and from the demands and privations experienced by other prisoners, a job that would enable him to get a bit more to eat and at which he wouldn't have to work too hard. He told the judges at Hoshijima's trial: 'I did carpentering. I was in charge of the technical department and area master for No. 1 area. That was a Japanese appointment.'

Sticpewich's technical party consisted of carpenters, engineers, plumbers, electricians and drivers. Housed in a large workshop built outside the gates of No. 1 Camp, they did everything from repairing watches for the guards to manufacturing buckets to fit the latrines. By making themselves indispensable around the camp they avoided having to work at the aerodrome.

As chief of the technical party, Sticpewich was in a position to barter with guards and to cultivate friendships that would be key to his survival. 'I was on a parole of limits which allowed me to proceed with reason throughout the whole of the camp areas including the surroundings of the Japanese barracks,' he told the war crimes commission. 'I have done work for all guards, at some time or other.'

In a typewritten statement he called 'Prelude to the Sandakan–Ranau march: War crimes and events' (hereafter 'War crimes and events') Sticpewich described the work of the technical party without actually acknowledging that he belonged to the party and was its leader. The members of the technical party, he wrote, were 'more fortunate than other P.W.s as they were cared for by the Jap Q.M. to whom they were responsible. He did them well and supplemented their rations to such an extent that they had an extra meal a day of as much as they could eat of sweet potatoes, tapioca, greens, sugar, salt and at times meat and fish.'

Extra food was not the only advantage Sticpewich had over his fellow POWs. According to Braithwaite, he was the only prisoner outside the officers' lines to have a mosquito net—a precious luxury in such a malarial place.

Chapter 9

NERVOUS WRECKS

——⇒•⇐——

While Sticpewich kept himself busy with odd jobs around the camp, hundreds were put to work with shovels and hoes at the aerodrome. Some had threadbare clothing while many wore nothing but loincloths. As Lieutenant Rod Wells told the war crimes commission:

> In the beginning they all had [boots], but after the first wet season, in November 1942, the excessive water and mud, which was more or less a quagmire all the way out, absolutely rotted the boots off the men, and no replacements were issued . . . A large number were working in wooden clogs with leather straps over them . . . made by themselves . . . towards the end of my stay I should say 25 per cent or 30 per cent of the men were bare-footed.

Daily rations of 15–16 ounces (425–450 grams) of rice per man per day and stew containing 'native greens' but little or no meat were barely enough, even when bolstered with 'black-marketing with the natives on the aerodrome'. The men 'went down rather rapidly, although they managed to survive', Wells told the commission. As the officer in charge of a wood-collecting party, Wells ate with the Japanese guards and saw the difference in rations. The Japanese, he said, 'had infinitely more':

> The rice was of a better quality and they had more of it. The cooking for the Japanese was much better. We had to improvise to cook our own food. We had only one small cookhouse for 1500 men, with the result that the first rice for the morning meal was cooked about 12 o'clock at night, and . . . it was not very fresh in the morning. The Japanese got fish, vegetables and numerous other delicacies which were denied to us.

Walter Wallace, who escaped with seven other Australians in June 1943 and eventually returned to Australia by submarine, gave a bleak description of the conditions he had endured at Sandakan: 'Sugar and salt were never heard of, and soap in very small blocks was issued on rare occasions. Men were going to work bootless, shirtless and in lots of cases [with] just a piece of cloth around the waist. Sickness increased at one stage to over 300 bad cases with little treatment and even patients were bashed from time to time.'

In his evidence to the war crimes commission, Nelson Short told Justice Mansfield: 'We had no boots to work in . . . I worked on the drome all the time in bare feet. I had tropical ulcers on both feet and even now my toe, which was nearly hanging off, gives me trouble.'

The only treatment Short received for his ulcers was hot water. After the supply of bandages brought from Changi by the medical officers ran out, Captains Picone and Oakeshott improvised bandages out of old shorts and even banana leaves. 'I had beriberi in the legs for which I received no treatment,' Short told Justice Mansfield. 'I also got dermatitis and scabies, though I did not get malaria. I had the itch in the camp. No treatment was given for the scabies. The men, generally, with beriberi and scabies got no treatment at all as there were no medical supplies.'

As construction of the aerodrome fell behind schedule, more and more men were forced to join the working parties. Officers were initially allowed to supervise work at the aerodrome, but after October 1942 they were forced to do manual labour themselves. '[R]oad parties of 200 to 300 were sent out to make roads, wood cutting (40) and transport drivers (12) were also required,' Wallace wrote in his report.

When the number required (400 to 600) could not be made available due to illness, guards went through the camp and turned men out of hospital, also doctors and padres ... Rain or sunshine, Sundays included, work had to continue. Ju-jitsu was practised on the prisoners, a lot of men becoming nervous, always fearing a bashing for no reason.

One of the most notorious bashings occurred at the aerodrome on 17 February 1943; the victim was Private Jimmy Darlington. A former concrete worker from Barraba in New South Wales, Darlington was the eldest of fourteen children. On his attestation he named Molly May Madigan as his next of kin, defiantly describing her as his 'unmarried wife'. Darlington was renowned as the best boxer at Sandakan: on the voyage out from Australia he had won the boxing competition, defeating champions from Victoria and Queensland.

At Sandakan he worked as one of the camp cooks. According to Richard Braithwaite, Darlington was 'often given extra food by his admirers' in the POW camp, which he always shared with others from his home town. A 'gentle and generous' man, he was fiercely proud of his Aboriginal heritage. Don Wall wrote that before the incident on 17 February Darlington had told friends that 'if a guard hit him without good cause he would flatten him'.

The story of the bashing of Jimmy Darlington became part of the folklore of Sandakan, told and retold by the few who witnessed it and by the many who heard about it afterwards. Nearly every Sandakan survivor told a version of it to the war crimes commission. In brief, a Japanese guard nicknamed 'Mad Mick' decided to wash his underpants in a 44-gallon cooking drum at the aerodrome cookhouse. When one of the cooks remonstrated with him, Mad Mick knocked him down and started kicking him. Darlington was set upon when he tried to intervene. Putting all his ring craft to use, Darlington dodged a punch, straightened up and threw a right hook that flattened his attacker, smashing his jaw. Other guards standing nearby immediately laid into Darlington with sticks and rifle butts.

Darlington was half dead by the time the bashers had finished with him. Guards dragged him to a pile of split firewood near the cookhouse and forced him to kneel on a platform made of the sharpest logs. More firewood was wedged behind his knees and the crooks of his elbows and his body was trussed with ropes soaked in water. As the ropes dried they contracted, cutting off the circulation to Darlington's hands and feet, which began to turn black.

Left all afternoon to bake in the hot sun, Darlington was revived with a bucket of cold water whenever he passed out. Eventually he was thrown into the back of a truck and taken to the 'cage': a low wooden structure built on Hoshijima's orders with a 3-foot (900 centimetre) ceiling and atap roof but no protection from mosquitoes. Sticpewich described it as being 'something like a circus proprietor would keep a baboon in'. Delirious from his bashing and denied medical attention, Jimmy Darlington lay there all night, unable to sit up, screaming in agony and 'begg[ing] the guards to kill him'.

Allied officers protested to Hoshijima but they were ignored. Somehow Darlington survived. Hoshijima had him transferred by boat to Kuching, where he was interrogated by the Kempei-Tai before being tried and found guilty of striking a guard. Sentenced to six months at the Outram Road Prison in Singapore, he never returned to Sandakan.

Richard Braithwaite suggests the brutal treatment of Jimmy Darlington was symbolic of the power struggle within the camp: 'It was obvious [the guards] were trying to kill him slowly and cruelly, so everyone would be taught the lesson that even the best fighters could be broken by the Japanese.'

At Hoshijima's trial Athol Moffitt drew special attention to the bashing of Jimmy Darlington. The case was 'quite typical', he told the court. While forced to kneel on a 'sharp triangular piece of wood', Darlington was 'beaten . . . with sticks. He was kicked in the crutch. His arm was broken and he was rendered unconscious, bleeding from the head, face, arms and legs. His arms were tied and he was placed in the small cage unconscious . . . Hoshijima admits he was present, saw it and did nothing to release him until the next day.'

Sticpewich did not mention Jimmy Darlington in the fifteen-page statement he made to Captain Ruse at Morotai, although he described several other savage beatings. After speaking to Moffitt, however, Sticpewich was able to give a detailed account of the incident to the judges, implying that he had witnessed the bashing himself when in fact he did not see Darlington until the latter was brought back from the aerodrome to be put in the cage.*

---

*   For once Sticpewich's memory for dates let him down: he told the court the incident took place not in February 1943 but 'as far as I can remember in early 1944'. The judges appear not to have noticed.

By the time Hoshijima stood trial for his actions as commandant at Sandakan, Darlington had been safely repatriated to Australia. Outram Road Prison was an atrocious place but it spared Darlington from being sent on the death marches; his near-fatal bashing at the aerodrome probably saved his life. After the war ended Darlington was discharged from the army 'at own request' on compassionate grounds, having served a total of 2007 days. Tragically, he died in a house fire in 1976.

Chapter 10

THE BASHER GANG

———⟶●⟵———

Working conditions at the aerodrome became more brutal. To enforce discipline and ensure work quotas were met, Hoshijima recruited a 'basher gang' of young Formosan conscripts under the command of Lieutenant Moritake.

Formosan conscripts were often treated with contempt by Japanese soldiers. As soldiers of the Imperial Japanese Army the Formosans had expected to enjoy the same status and privileges as Japanese soldiers but found instead that they ranked below the lowliest Japanese private. 'When we Formosans became ill we were sent to a hospital in Sandakan,' one guard complained. 'The treatment for us was not adequate but it was available because the Japanese in the hospital used to receive good attention. The PWs received even less than we did.'

Treated as inferiors, Formosan guards inflicted on the POWs the same violence and humiliations they were forced to endure from their Japanese masters. A staff officer, Lieutenant Thom, told the war crimes commission about a 'gang of special bashers' who were given the 'special task' of administering 'brutal beatings to officers and O/Rs [other ranks] at the drome'. The bashers had nicknames: 'Black Prince', 'The Bull', 'Speedo'.

In a statement made at Labuan in December 1945, Formosan guard Ikeda Yoshio testified that 'Captain Hoshijima employed a special gang of bashers [at the aerodrome] for keeping the PW working hard. One or two of these were very cruel.' Another guard, Nakano Ryoichi, stated there were 'certain of the Formosan guards that used to beat the PWs for their own pleasure. This was known to the officers and NCOs who made little attempt to interfere.'

Hoshijima's bashers took particular pleasure in beating officers. Captain Ken Mosher told the war crimes commission that it was 'standard practice to beat, with rotan, hoe handles or fists, men and/or entire parties at Sandakan especially Dec 42–Feb 43 when 4 Jap soldiers . . . were specially employed . . . under direct orders of Hoshijima . . . to beat and bash. I personally was assaulted with the implements named and by all four.'

Lieutenant Washington gave evidence to the commission that on 29 December 1942 all 40 members of an officers' working party were 'singled out for a beating' by the basher gang. Washington said:

> For no particular reason the officers' party was stood to attention with arms extended for 35 minutes and slashed across chest, shoulders and legs with Malacca canes. On many subsequent occasions various officers were beaten. Working on the same aerodrome were Chinese civilians and coolies and it is my opinion that this display was given mainly to humiliate us before the civilians and to break our morale.

Private Tom Burns wrote in his diary: 'They lined up all our officers and belted them across the backs with a thick cane. Gee it makes one's blood boil to see them get away with it.'

Chapter 11

ESCAPE

—————————

On 28 March 1943 E Force, comprising 500 Australian prisoners of war and the same number of British, departed Singapore's Keppel Harbour on a tramp steamer bound for Kuching in Sarawak. The British remained at Kuching, but for the Australians it was only a transit stop. After a few days helping unload cement from the cargo ship *Taku Mara*, the Australians—still caked with cement dust—were transported 800 nautical miles around the coast to Sandakan. As there was not enough room for them at the main camp they were disembarked at Berhala Island, a picturesque island at the mouth of Sandakan Bay where first Japanese civilians and later Europeans had been interned at the old quarantine station.

Hoshijima delivered his standard welcoming speech, the same one he had given their predecessors in B Force, warning the Australians against trying to escape while vowing to work them until their bones rotted under the tropical sun. The chances of a successful escape from Sandakan were, in any case, vanishingly small. While no officers had so far tried to escape, several other ranks had made a break. In every case the fugitives had been betrayed by local people, recaptured and sent to Singapore's Outram Road Prison. Although unsuccessful, these escape attempts earned the Australians a reputation as prisoners of 'bad heart' who were more troublesome than other Allied POWs.

Richard Braithwaite's suggestion that the Japanese were 'not . . . too bothered' by the early escapes since the fugitives were 'quickly re-apprehended' is contradicted by Major Jackson's report, which stated that the escape of eleven Australians on 31 July 1942 'annoyed Lt Hoshijima a great deal' and that 'the remaining PW paid for it in many unpleasant ways'. Jackson's assertion is corroborated by Sticpewich's evidence to the war crimes commission. After four men from Sticpewich's own unit escaped and were recaptured, 'the 1500 of us were mass-punished. They cut off our meat and fish supply for a week and reduced the vegetable supply. All we had to eat was the 17 ounces of rice per day and a few vegetables.'

According to Dick Braithwaite, the threat of reduced rations for those left behind became a consideration for those contemplating escape: 'When you thought about escape you thought, well, there'll probably be a dozen blokes die in the prison hospital if you go, because of the repercussions, and they didn't muck around, your rations were cut immediately, in half or more, maybe [cut] out altogether for days.'

While the 500 men of E Force waited on Berhala Island, new huts were built at 8 Mile Camp. Hoshijima was determined to keep the two groups apart, later ordering the members of B Force to keep their hair cropped short so they could be easily distinguished from the men of E Force, but the trouble he anticipated had been brewing under his nose long before the arrival of E Force.

A civilian underground centred around Dr Jim Taylor, the Australian-born district surgeon and principal medical officer of the British North

Borneo Company, had for several months been smuggling food and medicine to the prisoners at 8 Mile Camp. Taylor worked at Sandakan hospital and was able to manipulate hospital inventories to supply the camp doctors with life-saving drugs and equipment such as the anti-malarial Atebrin, quinine, ether, sterilised bandages and surgical instruments, as well as extra food for the sick.

Dr Taylor also passed on intelligence about Japanese troop dispositions and sent chemicals needed to operate a secret wireless set built at the direction of the intelligence officer, Captain Lionel Matthews. The receiver allowed the Australians to obtain accurate news that contradicted propaganda from Hoshijima and his guards about Japanese victories. In his official report on the events at Sandakan, Major Jackson wrote that 'although Capt. Matthews was careful in the disposition of the news, many of his brother officers and PW helpers were not so discreet. In fact, as time went on many of them became extremely careless and it was only luck that prevented the Japanese from discovering the secret in the early days of the receiving set.'

While the officers and men of E Force waited to be transferred to the mainland, members of Sandakan's civilian underground maintained the flow of contraband and acted as messengers and couriers between Berhala Island and 8 Mile Camp. These civilians were instrumental in the conspiracy that led to the escape of eight Australians, including four officers, on the night of 4 June 1943 just hours before E Force was to be moved to the mainland.

The escape was discovered the next morning. The fugitives had split into two groups, with three men attempting to paddle by dugout canoe to the island of Tawi-Tawi in the south-west Philippines while the four officers and Walter Wallace hunkered down on Berhala Island to wait for a boat.

The Japanese soon concluded that the escapees must have had local help, which for Hoshijima would have been a disturbing development.

Previously he had been able to rely on local collaborators to catch
absconders, and the near certainty of betrayal by locals meant that
senior Allied officers at Sandakan actively discouraged escape attempts.
When the Berhala Island escapers put their plan to the commanding
officer at 8 Mile Camp, Major Fleming, he rejected it and urged them
to stay. Adding to Hoshijima's concern was the sheer size of the escape
group and the fact that it included four officers: Captain Ray Steele
and Lieutenants Rex Blow, Charlie Wagner and Miles Gillon. The mass
breakout and its apparent success would have been a serious humiliation for Hoshijima.

On the morning the escape was discovered, Hoshijima personally visited the former watchman of the island's quarantine station,
Mohammed Salleh, offering the old man a huge reward for help in
capturing the escapees while oblivious to the fact that Salleh himself
had helped facilitate the escape and would continue to play a vital role
by supplying food to the group still hiding on Berhala Island. According to Major Jackson's colourful account, presumably obtained from the
watchman himself:

> Salleh went out of his way to tell the Commandant just how much that
> money would mean to him, he went on to say that he hated the white
> man anyway and would turn them over to the Japanese even if there
> wasn't any reward. The Commandant was very impressed with Salleh's
> loyalty. The wizened little watchman had every reason to be proud
> of his acting ability. The Japanese continued to visit the island three
> times daily in order to find out if Salleh had anything to report. The
> answer every time was the same, 'I am sorry that I have not seen
> the white men, I wish I could, I would love to have the reward.'

Salleh was among those arrested and tortured by the Japanese military
police, the feared Kempei-Tai, in the spasm of retribution that followed

the Berhala Island escapes. The end of the war cut short his twelve-year gaol sentence.

For three weeks the five escapees hid on Berhala Island, keeping out of sight of Japanese spotter planes and moving to stay ahead of Hoshijima's dog teams. Launches circled the island day and night to prevent the Australians escaping by sea. Throughout this time members of the Sandakan underground kept the group supplied with food while arranging for them to be smuggled off the island by native boat. Eventually all eight of the Berhala escapees made it to Tawi-Tawi, where they joined the Filipino guerrillas fighting against the Japanese.

With the Berhala eight safely away, other prisoners began plotting their escape from Sandakan. Once again the underground played a central role in preparing for the escapes, stockpiling food, medicines, currency and other necessities for use by the fugitives. At the same time senior Allied officers inside the camp and key members of the underground were discussing something much more dangerous: an armed guerrilla uprising against the Japanese occupation force timed to coincide with a breakout of prisoners.

Lieutenant Wells told the war crimes commission that Captain Matthews had made contact with Colonel Suarez, the leader of the Filipino guerrillas on Tawi-Tawi. Suarez had responded by sending machine guns, rifles and ammunition to be used 'in the event of any Allied move in the vicinity of Sandakan'. The Sandakan insurrection was to be part of a larger revolt that would include an uprising at the major town of Jesselton (now known as Kota Kinabalu), 300 kilometres to the west.

In his report Major Jackson described the would-be revolt as being 'very much in the early stages'. While weapons and ammunition had been buried at 'strategic spots' close to 8 Mile Camp, few POWs had more than a vague idea of what was being planned. However, the mass escape of eleven prisoners the previous year followed by the escape of the Berhala eight in June 1943 put the Japanese on the alert for any sign of an uprising.

After a petty business dispute betrayed the workings of the Sandakan underground, the Japanese began rounding up its members. During a search of the camp the guards found news summaries hidden by Lieutenant Wells in a pair of rolled-up socks that confirmed the existence of a secret wireless. As Jackson reported it, the commandant 'pulled Lt. Wells out of a working party . . . "Lt. Wells," said Hoshijima, "you are a very stupid boy for writing those things" . . . he then struck Wells heavily around the face and head. He twisted a handkerchief that Wells had around his neck and besides nearly choking him he continued to give him a severe bashing.'

Hoshijima demanded to know where the radio set was. After initially denying its existence, Wells led Hoshijima on a wild goose chase around the camp, which gave time for the receiver to be hidden. According to Sticpewich, the receiver had been secreted in a false-bottomed cabinet in the technical workshop and by the time Wells took Hoshijima to the spot it was gone. To save the precious receiver Wells eventually allowed Hoshijima to find the less valuable transmitter, correctly guessing that the Japanese would not know the difference. Two Japanese officers claimed to have seen Captain Matthews returning from the latrines 'about 11 o'clock' the previous night with a shovel. Hoshijima found freshly turned earth nearby and, according to his own account, '[after] digging at this position I found the radio'.

Sticpewich told Captain Ruse that he had been 'implicated . . . because of the discovery of a false compartment to a home-made cabinet in my room, which actually had been used to keep the wireless in'. That the radio was not there when Hoshijima came looking for it was due, Sticpewich wrote, to his having 'moved the set and hidden it elsewhere and filled the false compartment with fish and fruit . . . Later the wireless was dug up in the officers' lines where it had been hidden under my instructions.' Even if, as Lynette Silver asserts, Sticpewich 'played no part whatsoever in the building or working of the wireless', he was evidently trusted with its safekeeping and had the authority to move it.

According to Sticpewich, 'a number of the officers were removed from the camp because of their connections with the wireless and other things which had been discovered as a result of the Japs finding Lieut. Wells's diary'. At 5 pm the next day Sticpewich himself was hauled in for questioning. In his statement to Captain Ruse, he said that he was 'accused of being an accomplice in the working of the set and was told that they knew all and was asked to admit my guilt. I refused to do so and repeatedly told them I knew nothing'. Between interrogations Sticpewich, Sergeant Davidson and Private Pickering were tied up and made to stand out in the rain. At 1.30 am they were thrown into the cage with three officers and Sticpewich's future escape partner, Private Reither, who 'undid us'.

Unlike the officers, Sticpewich, Davidson and Pickering were not sent to the Kempei-Tai for further questioning, which invariably involved torture. During their four days in the cage they were alternately given normal rations and salt and water and were 'not bashed'. Although not allowed to bathe or wash, the three men were let out twice a day to use the latrine.

As in the affair of the stolen army beds, Sticpewich was very careful not to incriminate himself. Having seen Sergeant Alf Stevens viciously bashed and kicked by Lieutenant Moritake and then dragged off by the Kempei-Tai after admitting his involvement with the wireless, Sticpewich continued to plead ignorance. Stevens was eventually taken to Kuching, found guilty at trial and sentenced to six years penal servitude.

After three nights and four days Sticpewich, Davidson and Pickering were released from the cage and told by Moritake and the interpreter that 'we had been found guilty of certain crimes and that we had been temporarily punished for these crimes, that we were being sent back to camp and that in future we were to be of good behaviour'. Sticpewich, a stickler for detail and documentation, asked what exactly he had been found guilty of and was told by the interpreter, 'Never mind. They think you are guilty and that is enough . . . They punish you and that is our custom.'

Captain Matthews and eight members of the civilian underground were eventually executed as a result of what became known as the 'Sandakan incident'. Many others, including Lieutenant Wells, were permanently maimed by their Kempei-Tai torturers.

The wireless affair showed Sticpewich that for all his efforts to ingratiate himself with the Japanese his privileges did not amount to impunity. He never went back in the cage.

Chapter 12

FLYING PRACTICE

The Sandakan incident and Jesselton uprising caused the Kempei-Tai to question its ability to maintain security within occupied Borneo. The war was turning against Japan, and news of Allied victories had begun to circulate among the civilian population. Japanese defeats and the prospect of the Allies moving to reconquer Borneo weakened morale among the Japanese forces. According to Yuki Tanaka, '[B]oth regular troops and the Kempei-Tai [became] increasingly suspicious, aggressive and paranoid in their relations with the local population.'

Thanks to the secret wireless, information about Japanese defeats had been able to circulate, at least in a limited way, around 8 Mile Camp, heightening Japanese fears of a prisoner uprising. The risk of such an uprising was more acute at Sandakan than at other camps due to the unusually high proportion of officers among the POW population.

Of the roughly 1500 soldiers sent from Singapore as B Force, 143 were officers—one for every ten men. If non-commissioned officers were included the ratio fell to one in three. The Japanese believed removing the bulk of these officers would reduce the risk of an uprising as, in Tanaka's words, 'the Japanese believed that enlisted men would be more or less incapable of mounting any active resistance without leadership'. Nelson Short put it more bluntly in his interview with Tim Bowden: 'The Japs thought they were taking away the brains of the camp—in case there was a mass escape.'

Since the arrival of B Force in July 1942 Hoshijima had done everything he could to reduce the number of Allied officers at Sandakan. Tony White told Richard Braithwaite he thought the presence of so many officers at 8 Mile Camp 'caused Captain Hoshijima to have sleepless nights'.

The signing incident in which Colonel Walsh initially refused to sign a no-escape pledge had given Hoshijima an excuse to start weeding out potentially troublesome officers. In the last week of October 1942 both B Force's lieutenant colonels, four majors and a captain were transferred to Kuching. On 10 June 1943, less than a week after the escape of the Berhala eight, they were followed by the remaining seven majors, one captain and nine lieutenants.

The removal of the officers robbed the prisoners of some protection against violence from the guards, which had dramatically increased with the arrival of a new group of guards in late April 1943 to replace the old soldiers who had been at Sandakan from the beginning. The new guards, conscripts known as 'kitchi' (a reference to their small stature), were younger and more vicious than their predecessors. Where these conscripts came from was something of a mystery—a 'moot point', Dick Braithwaite told the war crimes commission. Japanese guards told Private Lance Maskey, who understood the language, they were Chinese, although the conscripts invariably claimed to be Japanese. Braithwaite said that he 'often' asked them where they were from and they would always reply 'Osaka, Kobe, Tokyo or some other place [in Japan].' While Silver described them as 'Formosan conscripts . . . who had been recruited into the Bushido Youth Corps', Dick Braithwaite felt it was 'hard to say just what they were'.

According to Sticpewich, the old soldiers 'had seen action and were inclined to be more easy with us and were rather lax in enforcement of orders. The kitchi guards, however, were new men and treated us brutally. They seemed to be bad characters and would bash us on the least provocation.'

Sticpewich's recollection of benign treatment by the old regime is more likely a reflection of his own privileged position in the camp than of the experience of prisoners toiling at the aerodrome. By his own account he was 'not allowed' to take part in the heavy work at the aerodrome due to his being on the 'administration staff and technical staff' of the camp. He recalled only two occasions when he had to join a working party at the aerodrome, both times 'to make up the necessary number and thus [save] sick people from having to go on the work parties'. On one of these occasions he claimed to have been bashed; on the other he escaped a bashing 'because it was not that party's turn to be beaten'.

In the early days the Japanese had offered incentives to the Australians to meet their work quotas. Owen Campbell remembered a guard rewarding prisoners with turtle eggs for a hard day's work: 'They used to kid to you a lot', he told Tim Bowden. 'A lot of blokes fell for it. They said if you do eight trucks today you go home early. So a lot of them raced and did their eight trucks. And next day they come back they had to do ten trucks. Or eleven trucks. And of course they spoilt it for everybody else. Everybody else had to do the same.'

As construction of the airfield fell further behind schedule, work quotas increased, and failure to meet the quotas often resulted in harsh group punishment. In his book *Return to a Dark Age* Bill Young wrote:

[The] quota was constantly being revised and supervised, by guards who were continually patrolling around the bank of the digging. If only one man was found slacking in a group, then the whole gang would be called out, for what we sarcastically called Flying Practice.

This mean lining up in the gruelling hot sun, arms raised, finger tips just touching those on either side. The guards would walk down the back of the line with pick handles at the ready. Any of us who failed to keep our arms raised got a stripe across the back.

The damage inflicted during flying practice was not just to muscle and bone. Nelson Short told Bowden that being forced to stare for hours into the sun had left him nearly blind: he had solar burns in both eyes and cataracts. His memory of the guards was very different from Sticpewich's; as he told Bowden, 'I don't know one good guard in Sandakan prison camp, not one.'

Dick Braithwaite told the war crimes commission that if men 'looked sideways while they were working, they were beaten'. Forced to stand to attention with a piece of heavy timber such as mangrove or teak above their heads, the prisoners were beaten again if they moved. Sometimes, rather than inflicting violence themselves, the guards ordered prisoners to bash each other. Men in charge of work parties were forced to 'line up their working parties and strike them'. If they were 'not striking hard enough' in the guard's opinion he would offer a demonstration, 'generally with disastrous results'. Braithwaite described being made to strike another man on his work party: 'He insisted on being struck by me. He said, "I would rather you hit me than have him hit me."'

Like Hoshijima's Formosan basher gang, the kitchi guards revelled in their licence to hand out random beatings. Their arrival coincided with a sharp deterioration in the rations, Sticpewich recalling that before April 1943 'we were getting fish and vegetables fairly regularly and had canteen supplies. We had sufficient food and tobacco. Up to this period the death rate was very low. In the first twelve months there were only 24 deaths . . . mainly from beriberi and general debility.'

Along with the kitchi guards came a new officer, Captain Nagai Hirawa, who became second in command to Hoshijima. Jackson recorded that Nagai immediately 'ordered extra working parties . . . and did not consider that the working parties should be depleted because of a rising sick toll'. According to Sticpewich, Nagai raised the working party figures from 300 to 800, and Sticpewich 'often heard' Nagai and Moritake ordering the guards to be 'more hard on us for breaches of the rules and that we had to be punished for these breaches'. Under Nagai arbitrary bashings increased. 'Although he would not take part . . . himself,' Botterill told the war crimes commission, 'he made all the other guards carry them out.'

On 16 October 1943 the last few Allied officers, bar eight who had been hand-picked by the Japanese, were sent to Kuching. Their depar- ture had been inevitable since Captain Steele and his seven companions had escaped from Berhala Island in June. As mortifying as the break- out had been for him, it had given Hoshijima the justification he needed to clear out all but a handful of officers.

Those chosen by Hoshijima to stay behind were expected to be capable but above all to be compliant. Braithwaite writes that the eight 'were pulled out of the departing group seemingly at the last minute'. Captain George Cook, the new camp commanding officer, had during the previous 12 months made himself invaluable to the commandant in his role as liaison officer, responsible for communicating Hoshijima's orders to the prisoners.

Having sailed to Singapore as a 'voyage only' officer (an officer given temporary promotion for the duration of the voyage), Cook had been sucked into the maelstrom of the Allied collapse—but he was an admin- istrator, not a fighting soldier. The departing officers viewed Cook's elevation to leader with what Silver described as 'a mixture of fury and disbelief'. The men left behind soon understood why.

When Dick Braithwaite got into trouble with a Japanese guard for accepting tobacco from a villager, he approached Captain Cook for help. Forty years later he recalled the conversation to Tim Bowden: '[Cook] said, "What do you want me to do about it?" And I said, "Well, I thought that you may put in a word for me, because I feel that I was innocent of any wrongdoing and I don't deserve what I might get". "Oh," he said, "you fellows get yourselves into these things, you get yourself out of it."'

The departing officers took with them not just authority but experience: a number would have served as NCOs during the First World War. Cook, with no experience of combat and little respect from the men he commanded, was unlikely to have any influence over the Japanese. The deteriorating camp rations had done no harm to what Silver called his 'cherubic features,' while his apparent willingness to do Hoshijima's bidding reinforced the view that Cook could not be counted on to stand up for the interests of his men.

Chapter 13

VERY GOOD FRIENDS

———>◦<———

The removal of nearly all the officers from Sandakan trimmed a prisoner population already reduced by death, transfer and escape. With the officers gone the number of Australian prisoners at 8 Mile Camp was around 1750. Until then Hoshijima had kept B and E Forces in separate quarters, but in October 1943 he ordered the latter out of the rudimentary and unsanitary No. 3 Camp and into the main No. 1 Camp. The sick were moved en masse into the newly vacated No. 3 Camp.

While nobody from E Force would have been sorry to move, No. 1 Camp was no longer the place it used to be. Once equipped with electric lighting and running water to each hut, the camp had been systematically ransacked by the Japanese and pipes and electric cables stripped out for use in the barracks. The supply of piped water and electricity to the Australian camp dwindled and then stopped altogether, and men were forced to rely on rainwater and polluted creek water collected in buckets.

Hygiene at the camp, difficult to maintain from the beginning, steadily deteriorated. The system of bucket latrines broke down when the Japanese refused to replace the worn-out buckets. With the influx of new prisoners the two pit latrines proved hopelessly inadequate, but permission to dig more was refused before finally being granted. Dick Braithwaite recalled having to bail out the overflowing pit latrines with shovels, the faeces being thrown into the swamp or, on Japanese orders, used to manure the gardens. Since most of the gardeners worked barefoot and the majority suffered from tropical ulcers, the number of skin infections and dysentery cases soared.

According to Nelson Short, the departure of the officers made 'no [difference] whatsoever' to life inside the camp, with competent NCOs taking over responsibilities that had previously belonged to the officers. But having Cook in charge changed the dynamics of the camp.

At his trial Hoshijima depicted a working relationship with Cook that was based on professionalism and mutual respect:

I consulted Captain Cook in a friendly manner in carrying out the administration of the camp. And in October 1942 [when Cook acted as liaison officer] both of us swore together and agreed that we would both do our best to carry out the administration of the camp in a rightful manner. And although I conversed with him in my broken English we understood each other and carried out the work.

Before Hoshijima left Sandakan in May 1945, he and Cook even exchanged home addresses and 'agreed to maintain our friendship in the future'.

Officers and men both noticed Cook's willingness to do whatever Hoshijima asked, and they viewed his kowtowing to Hoshijima as collaboration with a hated enemy. In a short memoir written immediately after the war, Major Rayson made a scathing assessment of Cook's leadership: 'Captain Cook began to show up in a very unfavourable light, being, apparently, definitely in favour with the IJA authorities and to keep this position he did not hesitate to sacrifice the interests of the PsOW.'

With Hoshijima under mounting pressure to finish the airfield, medical officers and even the sick were routinely ordered to work. Rayson recorded what happened on one occasion when the aerodrome quota was 'below IJA requirements':

> The whole parade was marched out including all MOs and most AMC orderlies, leaving some 300 sick in hospital unattended. Fortunately Lt. Kellaher had been missed and he organised some sort of a service for the patients . . . On yet another occasion, when hospital orderlies were reduced to 24, the remainder being sent out on working parties, I sent a written protest to Lt. Hoshijima giving a nominal roll of those men in possession of Red Cross identity cards, drawing attention to the provisions of the Geneva Convention. The protest was brushed aside and I was told that more and yet more men must go out on working parties irrespective of our medical classification.

Rayson correctly predicted that the commandant's policy of forcing sick men to work 'may be a source of trouble for Hoshijima at his subsequent trial'.

Captain Cook was either unwilling or unable to challenge these abuses. Perceptions of him as a 'white Jap' were fuelled by his habit of dining and socialising with Hoshijima and by his eagerness to outdo the Japanese in punishing men for breaking camp rules. A Formosan guard, Uemura Soichi, stated that 'Capt. Hoshijima and Capt. Cook were very good friends. Capt. Cook came to Capt. Hoshijima's house very often. Capt. Cook went . . . fishing with Capt. Hoshijima.'

As commanding officer, Cook took it upon himself to introduce a new code of conduct. Silver suggests that he 'believed that the way to counter a lack of respect and ill-discipline was more rigid punishment'. Until then minor offences had usually been handled by the men themselves. While most punishments were kept within the confines of the hut, those guilty of grave offences might have to suffer the public humiliation of being forced to cross the muddy pond inside the camp.

When money began disappearing from Dick Braithwaite's hut the men took the matter into their own hands. 'Hotheads reckoned they knew the culprit, and the occupants of the hut held a kangaroo court.' The alleged thief was found guilty and sent to Coventry—'very severe punishment in these circumstances. No one had anything further to do with him.' The accused man became morose. When it was discovered that a rat had stolen the notes and used them to build its nest the men apologised to him, but according to Braithwaite 'it was too late. He had changed and never really recovered.'

To compel obedience and counter the men's disrespect towards himself, Cook took the extraordinary step of asking Hoshijima to build another cage and actively urged him to put offenders in it. Keith Botterill, one of the early occupants, never forgave him for this. He stated that Cook 'requested' several Australian POWs be put in the cage 'for the duration'. Three men—Privates Annear and Anderson and Sergeant Bancroft— who had been accused of stealing food from the quartermaster's store to give to the sick, were 'sentenced to be imprisoned for the duration and these three died after about three months'.

At his trial, Hoshijima gave five reasons for putting men in the cage:

1. Breaking camp regulations.
2. Stealing food outside the camp.
3. Stealing food from the Japanese Q store.
4. Sneaking off from working parties and stealing food.
5. Breaking of tools deliberately.

Hoshijima confirmed that when a man was found to be 'continually breaking regulations and causing trouble', he and Captain Cook 'would have a talk and decide that it would be better to segregate the man from the others'.

Keith Botterill was in and out of trouble. Accused of stealing ducks from a pen in which they were being fattened up for the officers' table, Botterill denied the offence but admitted to an 'outraged' Cook that he had thought about doing it. The 'confession' was enough for Cook to convict him of having 'intent to steal' and sentence him to seven days in the cage.

Eventually there were three cages in operation at Sandakan. Botterill himself had three separate spells in the cage, the longest of which lasted for a biblical 40 days and 40 nights. There was no water for the first three days, after which he was forced to drink water until he was sick, and for the first seven days he got no food. After the seventh day he subsisted on half camp rations. His offence, as he described it, was to have taken part in a raid on the quartermaster's store to steal food for the sick. During the 40 days he was in the cage Botterill was not allowed to wash or shave and was bashed every morning in a PT session. He described this in his evidence to the Australian war crimes commission: 'Each morning those in the cage were taken out and given what the Japanese called "PT". This consisted of severe bashing. Men had to be carried back into the cage crying; some collapsed but a bucket of water was thrown over them to bring them to again.'

Had it not been for the English cooks who worked for the guards—Australians were not trusted anywhere near the cookhouse—Botterill and his fellow internees would probably have starved. At five o'clock each evening the cage door was opened for a latrine break and, as he told Tim Bowden:

The Englishmen knew that we got out at five o'clock, so they'd come down to feed the dogs at five o'clock with this swill, kitchen rubbish . . .

they'd pour it into this trough. And when we seen them coming, we'd position ourselves to beat the dogs to the trough, and we'd all hit together, dogs and all us. And we'd fight over this dog food, pig swill or whatever it was. Fight the dogs for it.

Even those like Sticpewich who spent little or no time inside the cage could see the psychological harm it inflicted. Being locked in the cage, Sticpewich told the judges at Hoshijima's trial, 'affected you physically and mostly mentally. After a period of more than three or four days you could notice the prisoner's condition falling away fast. It had a drastic mental effect.'

By the time he got out of the cage Botterill was in awful physical shape, wasted from hunger and infested with scabies. Mentally, though, he was undaunted, claiming afterwards to have gone under the wire 'the very next night' to forage for sweet potatoes.

Botterill's final spell in the cage came after he was caught sneaking out of the aerodrome to dig for tapioca root. After being thrashed by a guard he was sentenced to twelve days in the cage. Seventeen other prisoners were crammed in there with him. 'The cage was about nine feet by 18 feet and we could not all lay down together,' he told the war crimes commission. 'When we lay on our sides close together, four still had to sit up.'

Although Botterill had nothing good to say about him, there were occasions when Cook did intercede with Hoshijima on behalf of the prisoners. At his trial, Hoshijima admitted to regularly shutting down the camp canteen when prisoners escaped or 'did other things that were not good'. He largely stopped doing this, he told the court, 'after Capt Cook consulted me and asked me not to punish all the PW for the fault of one'.

Chapter 14

PYTHON

———⟶●⟵———

Evidence extracted under torture by the Kempei-Tai from members of the Sandakan underground left the Japanese in no doubt that Captain Matthews had been in contact with the guerrillas in Tawi-Tawi and that he was planning a prisoner uprising to coincide with a landing by American-led fighters. While the destruction of the Sandakan underground put paid to Matthews' revolt, planning continued in Australia for a campaign of sabotage and organised resistance against the Japanese in British North Borneo. Its cornerstone was an undercover operation codenamed 'Python', the failure of which had grim consequences for the prisoners at Sandakan.

Operation Python was the brainchild of Special Operations Australia (SOA), a secretive unit created in 1943 on the orders of Australia's commander-in-chief of military forces, General Blamey. Modelled on Britain's Special Operations Executive, SOA was known for security reasons as the Services Reconnaissance Department (SRD).

The initial object of Python, spelt out in a 'Most Secret' document dated 8 September 1943, was to establish an 'intelligence organisation' in North Borneo to provide detailed information on shipping movements, the strength and disposition of Japanese forces, the location of enemy defences and the location of beaches suitable for landings. This intelligence, essential if a rescue for the Sandakan POWs was ever to be attempted, was to be transmitted by wireless to Australia. The group would also make contact with Colonel Suarez in Tawi-Tawi and arrange for the delivery of arms and equipment to a group of Filipino guerrillas under the command of an American officer, Captain John Hamner.

On 24 September 1943, after a short training period in Brisbane, a six-man party led by Major Gort Chester left Garden Island in Western Australia on board the American submarine *Kingfish*. Arriving off the Borneo coast at dawn on 6 October, the men waited until dusk before paddling ashore in rubber boats, bringing with them a vast amount of equipment. The list of stores included six ounces (170 grams) of finely cut tobacco, twelve eiderdown sleeping bags and six bottles of citronella oil but no axes. Using only native-style machetes, the Australians began clearing trees and undergrowth to build a vertical aerial and wireless station in the jungle.

Just three days after the Python team landed, around a hundred Chinese guerrillas led by Albert Kwok attacked administration buildings, police stations and Japanese army facilities at Jesselton on the north-west coast of Borneo, slaughtering the 50-strong Japanese garrison. An old friend of Chester from the latter's pre-war days as a rubber planter near Jesselton, Kwok had visited Tawi-Tawi to plead with Suarez for guns and ammunition but the weapons had not arrived, so Kwok's rebels had attacked with machetes and spears. Five days after the uprising the Japanese struck back, bombing nearby villages and sending soldiers to retake the town.

The total number of Chinese guerrillas on the west coast was thought to be as high as 2000, and it took the Japanese more than two months to crush the revolt. During that time Chester stitched together an intelligence network extending from Tarakan in the south to Sandakan in the north. Supplementing its own observations with sightings from local agents, Python was able to send detailed reports of enemy shipping movements around the north-east coast, including those in and out of the oil terminals of Tarakan and Balikpapan.

In early December Chester visited Tawi-Tawi to meet Suarez, arriving just in time to see Japanese planes bombing and machine-gunning the village of Batu Batu. On his return he was contacted by one of Kwok's lieutenants, who echoed Kwok's plea for arms to support the uprising. Chester promised to supply guns, ammunition and medicine from Australia, but before the shipment could be delivered news arrived that Kwok had been captured and his fighters 'scattered to the four winds'. During a second raid on Jesselton Kwok's men were alleged to have pillaged local shops, antagonising the civilian population.

In a lengthy field report to his superiors Chester bemoaned Kwok's 'last act of foolishness', which had provoked further retaliation by Japanese troops and the Kempei-Tai and stymied his own plans to extend Python's area of operations west towards Jesselton:

> The local police have deserted and are living in the jungle and the whole area reported now to be policed by Jap soldiers, whilst reprisals have been made and villages from Kota Belud to Beaufort reported burned to the ground.
>
> The effect of this on the local natives will have been considerable, and it is doubtful whether through fear, they will be as helpful as I had hoped.

Cornered by Japanese troops, Kwok had surrendered in order to save the inhabitants of the valley in which he and his men were sheltering. After suffering terrible tortures, Kwok and four of his top lieutenants were beheaded. Altogether an estimated 4000 rebels and sympathisers were exterminated for their role in the Jesselton uprising.

On 21 January a follow-up Python party arrived on the American submarine *Tinosa*. Chester had asked for reinforcements in the hope of lending support to Kwok's guerrillas, but the capture of Kwok and his lieutenants put an end to that. More than 2 tonnes of stores were unloaded and brought ashore by boat in an operation that so impressed the submarine's captain that, according to Python's 'Paddy' O'Keefe, he 'invited our boat party on board for dinner'. Guns and ammunition that would in any case have been too late to save Kwok were inadvertently left behind at Fremantle, but a bigger disaster was about to befall Python: one that had dire repercussions for the Australians in 8 Mile Camp.

A signal from Chester dated 6 February revealed that one of the reinforcement party, Sergeant Bill Brandis, had gone missing. Less than 24 hours after his arrival Brandis had 'lost himself in the jungle':

> Within thirty minutes after he was lost the entire camp were searching for him. Search continued throughout the night and for the next ten days. He lost his way whilst walking back from beach to camp (about 150 yards in direct line) to warn me of a strange native boat entering the river.

Despite frantic efforts to find him, 'no trace or sound' of Brandis had been detected. Guessing that if Brandis had already been found by locals he would be taken to the police station at Tungku, Chester contacted his agents in the police (one of the 'native' constables, he wrote, was 'an old coolie of mine') and arranged for Brandis to be 'hidden until we can fetch him'. Meanwhile the search for him continued, 'especially river & swamps'.

In a field report also dated 6 February, Chester advised that there was 'a large airfield under construction' outside Sandakan at mile 8 'on the right hand side of the road', and that the Japanese were 'reported to be using POWs'. The POW camp was 'also at mile 8 close to aerodrome'. The drome, Chester reported, was 'NOT yet completed' but was in use, although he had no information about the number of planes using it.

An addendum to the main report dated 10 days later asserted that the aerodrome was 'now completed'. The airfield, running east-west, was '2 miles long and approx. 800 yards wide' and was being further widened. 'The whole surface is gravelled, and planes can land on any portion'. Chester's informant told him that Australian prisoners had been present at the opening ceremony.

While Chester could not provide any information about the condition of the Sandakan POWs there were three men who could: the Berhala Island escapees Ray Steele, Walter Wallace and Jim Kennedy, who had been safely evacuated to Australia by American submarine.

In a short 'note' attached to the bottom of his report, Chester raised for the first time the possibility of a rescue plan. He wrote:

Suggest [director of intelligence] interview Wallace (although very unreliable), who has details of this camp and its occupants, contacts etc and a plan to return. Although Wallace is NOT the man to return, his plan may be practicable. Most of the prisoners would need building up morally before <u>any</u> contact is made with them.

Chester's rejection of Wallace as a candidate to return to Sandakan reflected in part his fury at the disappearance and likely capture of Sergeant Brandis, whose jungle and survival skills he considered utterly inadequate. In a five-page administrative report marked 'Most Secret' and included with the field report, Chester wrote that he was 'extremely disappointed with the lack of care taken in the choosing of personnel'. Personal ability, although of 'great importance', was 'NOT everything', and future Python operatives needed to be 'chosen with special regard to being round pegs in round holes' capable of living in small groups without discord 'for many months in great discomfort and with NO little NERVE strain'. The 'last-minute selection of merely healthy bodies' was 'useless', Chester told his superiors, and the 'unfortunate loss of Sig. Sgt Brandis is another proof of the necessity for the greatest care in the selection of personnel'. He went on:

> The golden rules of the jungle must be told to each and every man, such as—
>
> (a) If lost stay until found.
> (b) Direction of coast from position.
> (c) Most water in rivers runs to sea, etc.
>
> These may appear childish, but are NOT, in view of the unfortunate loss of Brandis, who apparently did NOT know them.

Security was a constant worry, and the Python party knew all too well that if Brandis fell into Japanese hands all of their lives would be at risk. Few could resist the Kempei-Tai's tortures for long. As Major Bill Jinkins wrote in one of his operation reports, 'the Jap method in this area to make natives talk is MOST effective—also that used against white people . . . Therefore if any captures are made, knowledge of Python's whereabouts, activities and contacts will become known.'

Brandis was eventually spotted by a villager on a beach on Tambisan Island, a tiny islet just a few hundred metres off the mainland. Disoriented, starving and almost naked after wandering along the coast for nearly three weeks, he was given food, but when a Japanese spy discovered the presence of an Australian soldier the headman was forced to hand him over to save the village from reprisals.

It did not take the Kempei-Tai long to extract the information they needed from Brandis, and within days it was clear to Chester that the Japanese knew all about Python. On 16 February a group of about a hundred Japanese soldiers spent two hours looking around a spot a couple of kilometres from the Python camp near the mouth of the Nyamuk River. The next morning 60 Japanese came within a few hundred metres of the Python observation post, forcing the Australians to douse their camp fire and hurriedly shift several kilometres north.

A draft history of Python written as part of an official history of Special Operations Australia stated: 'It was obvious now that the Japanese were on their trail. From information received from agents, [Chester] learnt that the enemy was aware that there were white men on the island.' Chester decided to move Python west, but his efforts to make contact with the remnants of Kwok's group and arrange for a boat to collect the Python party came to nothing.

The net was closing around Python. After finding a rubber dinghy and some empty storage containers the Japanese narrowed their search. Enemy patrols discovered Python food dumps, and on 24 March they stumbled upon a just-abandoned wireless station. Two men, Lieutenant 'Jack' Rudwick and Sergeant Don McKenzie, vanished. A desperate signal reached Australia:

> Japs found radio site one hour after we left. Jack and Mac missing believed killed or captured. Have been on run last five days... Doubtful if we can keep [wireless] contact much longer. Also food position very serious so arrange immediate pick-up at Jinkins Beach and give dates at once . . . Position critical.

Rudwick and McKenzie had been ambushed by a Japanese patrol not far from the abandoned wireless station. Captured and taken to Kempei-Tai headquarters at Sandakan, the pair was put in a cell with Brandis to await interrogation and torture. The Japanese were determined to execute all three for espionage. Brandis had been found virtually without clothes, while McKenzie and Rudwick were wearing jungle greens with no insignia or badges of rank and were not carrying identification discs or other official documents such as pay-books. The Kempei-Tai refused to accept that they were soldiers on a military mission and therefore protected by international law against prosecution as spies.

The three men's fate was sealed by the discovery of McKenzie's notebook, which contained detailed information about ships observed by Python, some of which had been torpedoed by American submarines. Tried at Kuching, the trio was convicted of spying, sentenced to death and hanged.

Between 30 March and 8 June 1944 four separate attempts were made to evacuate Chester's party by submarine, the last of which was successful. According to the heavily rewritten draft history of the operation, canoes were dispatched from the submarine and paddled to within 100 metres of the mangroves, where the water was less than 6 inches (15 centimetres) deep. 'The mud was too thick to allow Python to walk out. They were compelled to crawl through the mud and water to reach the canoes.' A paragraph cut from the final draft evoked the scene:

> The return to the submarine commenced at about 0200 hours. The members of the shore party were covered in mud, were told to throw away their clothes to avoid both the bad smell and bringing the mud aboard the submarine. Major Chester and WO Chew did this, but the others were either too excited or too tired to comply.

The official report commended Python for its success in setting up an intelligence network on the east coast of British North Borneo and noted that 'approximately 500 Japanese troops and 20 launches' were tied up 'searching continually for three months' for Chester's party before they were evacuated.

Python achieved nothing for the Sandakan POWs; the operation sent back no useful intelligence about the condition of the prisoners at 8 Mile Camp. The interrogation of Brandis, Rudwick and McKenzie convinced the Kempei-Tai that Python had received local help and that a nexus had been established between Python, the Sandakan underground and the POWs. Like the Jesselton uprising, this triggered a punitive cut in the prisoners' rice rations.

Chapter 15

LIES

———>●<———

Rations at 8 Mile Camp had been decreasing steadily since September 1943. 'We could never get enough rice during the last two years spent at Sandakan,' Sticpewich wrote in his 'Notes on the interrogation of WATANABE Capt [Captain Watanabe Genzo]'. Suga visited the camp roughly every six months, and Sticpewich recalled that after each visit 'our food ration got worse and so did our treatment'.

In June 1944 General Yamawaki Masataka, commander of the Japanese 37th Army in Borneo, ordered the rice ration to be further reduced in anticipation of American submarine attacks choking off deliveries of rice by ship from Kuching. In place of the lost rice the prisoners were given tapioca. They were still getting vegetables, some of which they grew themselves. In a letter to his pre-trial interrogator Captain Brereton, Hoshijima claimed that when he realised food supplies were 'getting low' towards the end of 1943 he 'made necessary the farming of vegetables' to feed the prisoners. In addition, he told Brereton, '[W]e made possible as food to the P's.W. such as ducks, chickens and pigs until I was dismissed of my command . . . in May 1945.'

As usual Sticpewich was on hand to elaborate on, correct or if necessary contradict Hoshijima's evidence. In the notes he made on Hoshijima's letter, Sticpewich said that prisoners 'did work under slave conditions making vegetable gardens'. The gardeners were mostly sick men who 'were not fit to go to the drome to work'. Much of the garden produce went to the Japanese themselves, who, in Sticpewich's words, 'took the pick of this and plenty'.

As for ducks and fowls, Sticpewich said these were still obtainable through the prisoners' own canteen up until Christmas 1943, although they were mostly used to feed the sick in hospital. Pigs, too, could be bought through the canteen, although they had to be kept outside the camp, and the Japanese decided when the animals could be killed and took what they wanted for themselves. As Sticpewich put it, '[B]ig days for us [were] Jap festive days then we had the pleasure of eating our own pork, also at Christmas and New Year if they thought fit'.

In his letter Hoshijima also asserted that he initiated 'fishing activities' and that after October 1944, when control of the prisoners' food supplies was taken out of his hands and given to the Sandakan field supply depot, he was 'at times . . . able to receive the head, neck and legs of the ox that were killed . . . for food for various units'. He remembered the prisoners being 'happy when we gave them protein food such as meat'.

Sticpewich, an abattoir worker before the war, told war crimes investigators exactly how often cattle were killed—he recalled only 'five occasions' when cattle were butchered—and how the carcasses were distributed. In his notes on Hoshijima's letter he recalled how he had 'done the killing and dressing of cattle, slaughtered in farm and camp sites'. The prisoners received 'heads less tongues—lungs, spleens, stomachs and intestines, also the feet'. As per Japanese custom the killing party received the head of the first animal, which 'went into camp use'.

Refuting Hoshijima's assertion that on one occasion the Japanese had shot three goats, Sticpewich insisted that 'goats never came into our camp'. He was similarly dismissive of Hoshijima's claim that when food at the camp was scarce Suga 'tried every possible way to get food over to Sandakan'. Sticpewich commented 'Lies'.

As rations were cut and cut again the prisoners became sicker, although Richard Braithwaite notes that in the period directly after the 'Sandakan incident' mortality actually fell. 'By this stage,' he wrote, 'the prisoners were tough men indeed . . . Objectively, they must have been physically weaker, but mentally stronger'.

Work continued on extending and improving the runways at the aerodrome, but fewer and fewer prisoners were fit enough to do it.

Chapter 16

ALL DEAD

In June 1944 Captain Nagai, Hoshijima's second in command, was ordered to take a hundred British prisoners to build an airstrip on Labuan, the island off the west coast where Hoshijima would eventually be put on trial. The men's fate, Major Jackson wrote, was to be 'equally as tragic as that of their comrades who remained at Sandakan'.

Two months after their arrival the hundred British POWs assigned to the airstrip at Labuan were joined by 200 prisoners from Kuching, including five Australians, some of whom had been at Sandakan. Hard physical labour, inadequate rations and malaria took a heavy toll, and by the time Nagai was relieved of command nearly half of the 300 prisoners were dead.

The deaths continued under his successor, Sergeant Major Sugino. On 6 March 1945, 112 survivors were transferred to Brunei, a day's sailing away. Two months later only 81 were left to make the trip from Brunei to

Kuala Belait, where seven Indian soldiers, prisoners of the Kempei-Tai, were added to the party. Just 51 men survived to be transferred to Miri, in north-western Sarawak near the border of Brunei, on 27 May but most of these were in reasonable health on 8 June when Sugino received news that Allied warships were sailing towards the west coast.

At midnight on 9–10 June Allied ships began shelling Miri. According to his superior in Miri, Lieutenant Nishimura, Sugino received orders to take the surviving 44 prisoners into the mountains. On 10 June Sugino divided the party, sending back 15 of the fittest prisoners with four Formosan guards to fetch rice, salt, office stores and medicine from a supply compound south of Miri while the rest made camp near an abandoned house. While he was there Sugino took the opportunity to burn 'some old PW documents and letters'.

That evening Sugino ordered his guards to fire on POWs sitting outside the house. When others ran from the house they were shot or bayoneted to death. Leaving some of the guards to bury the bodies in a swamp, Sugino took the rest and went in search of the stores-carrying party, whom they found resting beside the road near some huts. Once again Sugino ordered his men to open fire; survivors were finished off with bayonets. Of the original 300 prisoners sent to Labuan Island between June and August 1944, not a single man was left alive twelve months later.

In December 1945 Sergeant Major Sugino became one of the first Japanese to be tried for war crimes against Allied prisoners of war. He faced two charges:

Massacre of approx. 36 prisoners at or near 5 mile Riam Rd near Miri in Sarawak on or about 10 Jun 45.
Massacre of approx. 15 prisoners at or near 5 mile Riam Rd near Miri in Sarawak on or about 10 Jun 45.

He pleaded not guilty to both charges.

In a statement dated 11 October 1945 Sugino gave a detailed account of the day's events, claiming that while he was burning the documents on the afternoon before the massacre he noticed one of the POW officers 'going into the house acting in what I thought was a suspicious manner as he was looking to all sides as he walked'. Since this officer would be in the stores-carrying party, Sugino warned one of the Formosan guards that 'he would probably try to escape in which case he was to be killed'.

At 7 pm 'five or six' POWs led by Sergeant Acland 'jumped up from where they were sitting outside the house and started to run away'. Sugino immediately ordered his guards to shoot the 'escaping PWs'. In the 'confusion' some of the bullets struck the house, causing the prisoners inside to 'come out'. As they emerged from the house these men were 'shot and bayonetted by the guards', and sick prisoners who 'tried to crawl away' were dealt with in the same way. According to Sugino, he 'did not give any orders to cease fire in order to save the sick because I was so excited that I did not know what was happening'. Those who were not killed outright were 'put out of their agony by shooting or bayonetting'.

When this was over Sugino counted 32 bodies. He had no sooner ordered 'three or four guards' to bury them than he heard a burst of firing coming from about a kilometre back along Riam Road. Sugino then 'called about six guards and ran in the direction of the firing', and upon arrival found all the prisoners dead. 'Several men were digging two graves that were about one foot deep . . . When the graves were dug the PWs were buried and the whole work was completed by about 2030 hours'.

Only then did Sugino ask one of the Formosan guards what had happened. The Formosan, Naga, told him that the prisoners had been shot trying to escape. Sugino 'did not ask any further questions because I understood that the PWs had not been trying to escape when they were killed. Although I gave orders before they left to kill the PWs if they attempted to escape I knew myself that they would be killed in any case'.

After these prisoners had been buried Sugino returned to 'supervise the burial of the others, which finished at midnight'.

Matsumoto Hideo, a Formosan guard who took part in the killings, gave a different account. At Dahan, a satellite labour camp near Kuching, Matsumoto had been notorious for beating prisoners. Asked by his interrogator 'Did you boast about being the worst basher in the camp at Dahan?' he replied 'Yes.' Matsumoto was then questioned about the Riam Road killings:

Q: Why were [the prisoners] killed?

A: S/M Sugino ordered us to kill them.

Q: Why?

A: He told us to kill them.

Q: Did any try to escape?

A: No. After they were shot some of the wounded tried to crawl away and S/M Sugino ordered us to kill them with our bayonets.

Q: How many did you kill yourself?

A: 2 or 3 of the British and about 4 Indians.

Q: Why?

A: S/M Sugino ordered it.

A fortnight after signing his statement Sugino admitted that his account of the second massacre was 'not completely true'. On 25 October he made another statement in which he vowed to tell 'the complete truth':

After the killing of the 32 PWs, I together with six or seven Formosan guards, immediately went to the 5 mile [post] and waited until the arrival of Nango and three other Formosan guards escorting 15 PW, who rested on a small track leading off the road . . . Shortly afterwards, L/Cpl Kaneko and eight members of the Nishimura Tai [Unit] also arrived from the 5½ mile.

I thought at the time that as food was getting short, some of the PWs might try to escape and I decided that it would be better that we kill them. After the PW had been resting about ten minutes, one of the European PW tried to escape by running into the grass. I then gave the order to shoot the whole 15 PW. All the Nishimura Tai and five or six Formosan guards took part in the shooting.

After the shooting, some of the PW were not dead, so I ordered that they be shot and bayonetted as they lay on the ground. The man who had previously run into the grass was also shot. We then buried the bodies in two graves and I sent the members of the Nishimura Tai straight back to 7 mile and together with my own men, I returned to 5½ mile to complete the burial of the PW killed there. I later went to 7 mile, where I spent the night.

Sugino's trial took place six weeks later at Labuan. The prosecutor, Captain Russell Brereton, who had previously interrogated Hoshijima, accused Sugino of having committed 'deliberate, calculated, cold-blooded murder'.

A Chinese gardener, Chin Kai, had been hunting wild pigs when he saw prisoners of war being led down the road. He saw Japanese soldiers digging graves and witnessed them shooting the prisoners. 'Some were dead when they were put in the grave and some not,' he told the court. He identified Sugino as the one who ordered the shooting. Other civilian witnesses also testified to the shooting and to the fact that some of the prisoners wore Australian-style slouch hats.

Although he had no first-hand knowledge of what had happened to the Labuan prisoners, Sticpewich testified in court that hats of the kind described by civilian witnesses were worn by Australian prisoners of war—a significant point, given the direction from Allied Land Forces headquarters that Australian military courts should only try cases in which Australians were among the victims.

The court rejected Sugino's defence that the killings were not 'premeditated' and that executing the prisoners was lawful in any case because
they were attempting to escape. Nor was it moved by the defence's assertion that Sergeant Major Sugino, 'a painter by profession', was 'faithful and
loyal and a model type of Japanese soldier who understands humanity . . .
neither a mad man nor a bloodsucker . . . [and] not the kind of man who
indulges in beastly pleasure of cold blooded cruelty'.

Sugino was found guilty and sentenced to death by shooting. In his
petition to the court, dated nine days after he was sentenced, he did not
deny ordering the killing of the prisoners but maintained that his unit
was only obeying orders from Nishimura to 'dispose of all prisoners
of war in their custody immediately and proceed further to interior
carrying salt as much as possible and other provisions'. Nishimura
denied giving any such order.

Sugino had already admitted to lying in his statement of 11 October,
so it was perhaps not surprising that the court dismissed his claims to
have been acting on Nishimura's orders. Nor was it likely to heed Sugino's
protestation about his family depending on his military salary for their
'hand-to-mouth sort of living'. A month after submitting his petition
Sugino wrote a further 'imploration' for leniency on behalf of himself
and his 'old parents . . . and sister of sixteen', who were 'eagerly longing'
for his return and whose livelihood he imagined becoming 'miserable'
without his help:

It was in 1936 when I was conscripted in the active service of the
army at the age of 21. In July of the same year Chino-Japanese war
broke out. At that time Japanese militarism ruled all over our country
and our military education became severer than before.
    I spent nearly four years in North China mainly engaged in war
theatre during which time I actually had no time to satisfy my intellectual desires . . . [the] military education I was taught was one of the

most strict ... Among other things, to obey order of any kind was the most important point of Japanese army discipline. To obey absolutely to superior's orders regardless of its nature was the motto of the military life, as the result ... it was imbued deepest in my mind.

I, nothing but a minor soldier, was directed to know nothing about the general condition of war but to obey and carry out what my superior ordered. I must jump without hesitation even into fire if my superior orders to do so.

... I am now beginning to doubt about the military education of Japan since I came to Labuan and observed the real conditions of Australian army personally. I now realise that the traditional meaning of order of Japanese army that an order of superior must be obeyed absolutely was wrong.

Sugino's imploration did not save him from the firing squad. His sentence was confirmed by Lieutenant General Sturdee, acting commander-in-chief of the Australian military forces, on 26 February 1946. Sugino was shot at 7.30 am on 6 March at Morotai. Sticpewich, who had played a small but useful part in convicting him, would have a far more significant role in the trials to come.

Chapter 17

HOME FOR XMAS!

Sickness and inadequate rations continued to reduce Hoshijima's work-force, but by the end of September 1944 the aerodrome's east–west runway was finished. All his efforts then went into extending the north–south runway so that it, too, could be used by bombers. But Sandakan was now within range of Allied aircraft. Dick Braithwaite said of the first Allied air raid on Sandakan that it 'bucked our fellows up considerably although some were killed and wounded'. He remembered some of his mates jubilantly calling out, 'Home for Xmas!'

The first raids on the aerodrome were by American P-38 Lightning fighter-bombers; attacks by much heavier B-24 Liberator bombers came later. Hoshijima, worried that 8 Mile Camp might be bombed, ordered a total night-time blackout and put the ever-obliging Sticpewich to work constructing a huge sign with the letters 'POW' painted in white on a black cloth. Hoshijima remembered it as being 'about 36 feet long and

36 feet wide'. The sign, which was placed in sunken ground, did not prevent a strafing attack by three Lightnings that killed three prisoners. Sticpewich thought the strafing was an accident, as 'one plane took a sharp bank and had a good look at the sign'.

The Lightnings flew so fast that pilots sometimes started firing before the POW sign came into view. Richard Braithwaite recorded several stories told to him by his father about American air raids on Sandakan in which prisoners were inadvertently killed or wounded.

After a raid on 30 October Hoshijima tried to make the sign more visible from the air by having it shifted to higher ground. At the same time he moved his lodgings to a nearby house to take advantage of the protection afforded by the POW sign.

Sticpewich gave evidence that the camp 'was not interfered with' while the POW sign was exhibited. However, the destruction of the aerodrome had immediate repercussions for the prisoners: supplies of quinine and drugs to treat dysentery were abruptly cut off.

For a while the prisoners were kept busy filling in craters and removing unexploded bombs. 'It was amazing the number of unexploded bombs that landed on that drome,' Dick Braithwaite told Bowden. 'We had to go and dig them out, and the Japs used to . . . get behind protection while we dug them out. [We] had a . . . rough tripod and [had to] loosen the soil round them and dig them out, up to 500 pounders, and then carry them on sticks . . . we used to sort of stagger a bit towards where the Japs were hiding and they'd let out a yell and tell us where to take it.'

The Australians had always done their best to turn Christmas dinner into a festive occasion with delicacies such as ducks, chickens and pork procured from the prisoners' canteen, but the canteen had been closed since September and trading with the locals had been forbidden. Keith Botterill recalled that Christmas dinner 1944 consisted of 'half an M&V [meat and vegetable] tin of corn and rice with dried fish mixed with it and pork soup'. The usual fare at this time was 'boiled tapioca, a small tin of rice and about three-quarters of an M&V tin of stew made out of greens'.

Christmas Day 1944 also brought something else. In Jackson's words, 'The PW received a great Christmas box on Xmas day 1944 in the form of a heavy bombing raid by Liberators. The raid, which took place at about 1100 hrs, put the aerodrome out of action and thus put an end to Japanese air activities in the Sandakan area.'

The Christmas Day raid exposed some of the many acts of sabotage that had helped sustain the morale of prisoners working on the aerodrome over the past two and a half years. Newly made bomb craters revealed 'Japanese shovels, chunkels, picks, metal bars, trucks and many other useful appliances' that had been buried by the POWs while they were engaged in the task of filling in and levelling off ground for the runways.

While Hoshijima sent prisoners out the day after the Liberator raid to fill in the craters, the frequency of the Allied bombing raids made attempts to repair the runways futile. Sticpewich gave evidence that raids on the aerodrome 'stopped Jap air activities completely Xmas Day 44'. This fact impinged directly on the fate of the prisoners at Sandakan, since their only value to the Japanese was as a labour force to build and maintain the airfield. Keeping the prisoners fit, and even keeping them alive, no longer served any practical purpose once the aerodrome was out of action. After October 1944, when the air raids began, the death rate of the Australians at Sandakan began to rise steeply. Sticpewich was able to supply the necessary details. Men who got malaria in the early stages, he told the judges at Hoshijima's trial:

had sufficient resistance and with a minimum of treatment survived. Men who got malaria at the end of 1944 and early 1945, they got beriberi and subsequently died. Their spleen would swell up and cause great pain, they would linger unconscious up to 8 or 9 days before they died. About 15 per cent died of dysentery. More than half died of beriberi and ulcers, and starvation. There were beatings of PW . . . A man was subjected to beatings in such a low state that he could not stand it . . . he would not appear for work for days and others never worked again. Besides affecting them physically it broke them up completely.

Until then the dead had been buried in coffins made by Sticpewich's technical party, a practice that stopped in December 1944 after more than 50 Australian and British prisoners died from malarial meningitis. Sticpewich testified that the 'coffin-making ceased because it became too big a job and the materials were not in sufficient quantities to keep up with demand'. On Hoshijima's orders the dead were to be stripped and put straight in the ground. Dick Braithwaite recalled bodies being wrapped in banana leaves and buried by the only men with 'strength enough to dig the graves'.

By the start of 1945 it was clear to everyone inside the camp that the war had turned decisively in the Allies' favour. Suga, now promoted to colonel, had assured the prisoners that the bombing raids on Sandakan were just the 'overflow' of what was happening in the Philippines and that Japanese forces would soon drive the Americans back, but nobody believed it. The war, it seemed, could only end in defeat for Japan, but the prisoners at Sandakan could still be made to suffer. In his statement to Captain Ruse, Sticpewich described an encounter that reflected this bitter new reality:

I remember one incident connected with Ramona [a kitchi guard] which took place about Christmas 1944. He was on guard outside the fence about half past six in the morning and called one of our chaps, who was smoking at an authorised time, to come over to the fence . . . The prisoner took no notice of him and later answered

him back, 'Go and get fucked'. The man who . . . answered him back
was wearing a bandage and could not be identified in the light except
for the bandage on his leg. When Ramona came off guard at about
0800 hours the work parties were assembled and everyone with
a bandage on his leg was pulled out and put in a separate squad and a
few other guards stood around while Ramona with a stick went
through this separate party bashing them with a stick and he concentrated his thrashings on their wounds which were bandaged.

With no more work to do at the aerodrome, other tasks had to be
found for the prisoners. Garden parties marched miles to dig potatoes
and pull up tapioca root, which they shared with the Japanese on a
'percentage basis', with the Japanese units always taking the bigger share.
Wood-fetching parties had to haul timber from as far as the 12-mile peg,
suffering the usual bashings and kickings as they walked.

On 10 January 1945 Hoshijima ended the allocation of rice from the
Japanese Q store. From then on, according to Sticpewich, the prisoners
had to make do with what they had managed to stockpile for an emergency. Some of this, around a hundred bags, was kept in the prisoners'
own Q store and the remaining 70 bags were held on credit by the
Japanese. In place of the rice, the prisoners now depended on vegetables brought in by the garden parties. 'Sometimes,' Major Jackson wrote,
'the PW would come in for a grand treat when they would be given fly
blown meat condemned by the Japs, or sun dried fish which had gone
bad. The PW cooked them without oil and ate them ravenously. Their
drinking water came from a buffalo wallow, now being used as a dam.'

Chapter 18

TWENTY-ONE DAYS TO RANAU

—⟫●⟪—

Three days after Hoshijima stopped the rice ration Captain Yamamoto Shoichi, who had spent the previous three months supervising fortifications around Sandakan township and the then-idle aerodrome, was given orders by 37th Army HQ to move 360 infantry and a company of machine-gunners 400 kilometres west to Tuaran, roughly midway between Jesselton and Kota Belud. With American troops firmly in control of the Philippines, a move against Japanese forces along the west coast of Borneo looked increasingly likely. Allied submarine activity made the transfer of Yamamoto's men by ship impossible, so walking was the only option.

As well as his own troops, Yamamoto was told to take with him 500 prisoners of war. He would take them as far as Ranau, a distance of about 260 kilometres, where they would be handed to the odious

Captain Nagai. According to Yamamoto, his orders from the 37th Army Corps chief of staff were that 'PsW must be those who would endure the march'.

The arrangement undoubtedly suited Hoshijima: having prisoners taken off his hands saved him from having to deal with them himself. Once their labour was no longer needed the whole tendency of Japanese policy towards POWs, not just at Sandakan but in Siam and Burma as well, was to let them die.

Sticpewich testified that before the first march the 'condition of most of the Australians was very poor. Rations had been cut down to two meals a day, only one of which was rice'. The rice issue per man per day was approximately 120 grams, with the rest made up of tapioca and sweet potatoes. By now there were 'very little greens' to be had. Hoshijima could have been in no doubt about the pitiful state of the prisoners, as he was having them regularly weighed.

The Japanese kept nearly all the medical supplies for their own use. Sticpewich personally witnessed the Japanese looting medical parcels meant for the prisoners, taking whatever they needed or wanted for themselves and leaving only 'bits and pieces'—mainly bandages—for the Australians. Owen Campbell recalled the delivery of American Red Cross parcels in January 1945. Prisoners tasked with sorting and storing the parcels counted enough to provide 'one for practically every prisoner', but when Hoshijima gave permission for them to be issued there was only one parcel for every ten prisoners, 'the Jap camp staff apparently having appropriated the remaining parcels'.

Recent changes to the route made the march from Sandakan to Ranau even more punishing. A reasonably well-trodden route that made use of rivers and walking tracks already existed between the east and west coasts of British North Borneo, but this was not the route Yamamoto took. He was told to use a new, more southerly track hacked out of the jungle the previous year by Javanese and local labourers along a route chosen by two local officials who—unbeknown to the Japanese—were fiercely hostile to Japan.

Believing the new track was to be used by Japanese troops, the two officials set out to make it as torturous as possible. Silver, an expert on the route of the death marches, describes the course of the track:

> Leaving the Beluran bridle path at the 42-mile peg, the track passed first through low-lying swampy ground which soon gave way to rain forest, so thick and dense that no sunlight penetrated its lush canopy. Cutting the path at frequent intervals were a number of rivers . . . Near the Telupid [River] the real mountains began and the going became very difficult with the headwaters of the Kuanan cutting through precipitous, jungle clad terrain of the Maitland Range.

Beyond that an old track no more than a metre wide in places snaked up to Paginatan before climbing yet again to the Ranau plain at peg 164.

It was Yamamoto, not Hoshijima, who worried about the difficulty of the march, although his concern was for his own troops rather than for the prisoners. Army HQ rebuffed his efforts to buy time to put extra food dumps along the route and to allow the marchers to avoid the wet season: the march was to go ahead as planned. Ten parties of 50 POWs, each party accompanied by an equivalent number of Japanese soldiers, would depart from Sandakan at one-day intervals and arrive at Ranau 21 days later.

According to Captain Iino Shigeru, who accompanied Yamamoto in the first party, the latter gave orders that prisoners who could not keep up were to be left behind at 'rest houses' along the route. The men who fell out were to be 'taken care [of] as much as possible'. Yamamoto, however, gave evidence that the orders he received from Lieutenant General Baba stipulated that 'no PW was to be allowed to fall out of the line along the way'. His instructions to his own men, therefore, were that 'under no circumstances should any PW be left behind at a rest house. No matter how sick a PW was he had to be brought on.'

What about prisoners who could not be 'brought on'? Captain Abe Kazuo, the officer in command of the machine gun company, was assigned to lead the ninth and last group of prisoners. Abe claimed to have 'received orders from Captain Yamamoto that if there was no other course available PWs that were too ill to travel were to be killed'. This order, Abe said, had been 'given to me personally by Capt Yamamoto . . . because I was in charge of the last party'. No other officers were present when the order was given.

At Yamamoto's trial Abe said that this order applied equally to the Japanese soldiers on the march: 'If food and medical attention were not available and nothing further could be done, both Japanese and POW were to be disposed of.'

On 26 January 1945, a fortnight after Yamamoto received his instructions from 37th Army HQ, Hoshijima informed the Sandakan POWs that 500 of the fittest men were to be moved. He did not tell them where they were going but said it was to a place where they would get plenty to eat.

In a statement he made at Yamamoto's trial, Sticpewich noted that in January 1945 the average POW was 20 kilograms lighter than his normal weight. 'Of course,' he wrote, 'cooks and those working in the cookhouse very much spoilt the average as they were in good condition and there were about 40 or 50 of those.' As the camp's designated butcher, Sticpewich might have added, he was in excellent shape himself.

Sticpewich said that prisoners 'volunteered' to undertake the first march from the facts given to them by the Japanese. 'Where they were going there was more food than at Sandakan and at least the day before they went they got a feed of pork and some extra rations. That was the enticement.'

Hoshijima knew there was hardly one man in the camp well enough to complete a forced march to Ranau, let alone 500. Captain Cook drew up a list of names, including those of Keith Botterill (a serial nuisance to both him and Hoshijima) and Bill Moxham. Hoshijima claimed to have tried to prevent 100 men from going, but 'Army HQ . . . said they must go'. Even so, he could only muster 455 of the required 500 prisoners, keeping back 45 who were 'too sick' to attempt the journey. Optimists among the group, encouraged by the promise of more food, might have convinced themselves that with Allied victory now inevitable the Japanese had decided to hand over at least some healthy prisoners.

To commemorate their departure, Hoshijima graciously allowed the prisoners to eat the horse on which in better days he used to ride around the camp barking orders. Refuting the charge that he had wilfully starved the prisoners, Hoshijima often referred to the gift of his horse, but by January 1945 the animal was nearly as emaciated as they were. Sticpewich said it could no longer wander around eating grass due to the frequency of Allied air attacks and was 'losing weight and . . . would have died owing to the condition it was in'. Since the Japanese were not fond of horseflesh, the prisoners had it to themselves.

Before they left, Hoshijima bestowed 'rubber plates' on the shoeless prisoners that 'kept the feet off the ground'. The men did not think much of them; Hoshijima noticed that some 'carried the shoes on their shoulders'. He sent them off with a gift of tapioca and dried fish.

Yamamoto's troops were waiting for the first group of prisoners at the 9-mile peg. In his pre-trial interrogation Yamamoto said: 'I did not have enough shoes to supply the prisoners. I knew they could not march without shoes. I knew it was wrong to make them march.'

Chapter 19

A VISITOR

———≫•≪———

In the days before the first group of prisoners set out for Ranau, Owen Campbell had a strange encounter. While gathering wood near the Sibuga River he asked permission from a guard to defecate. As was the custom, he moved as far as possible from the group while remaining in view of the guard. He was squatting over the hole he had dug when he heard a voice, the speaker telling him not to look around or do anything that might alert the Japanese. Campbell told Don Wall what happened next:

> He said, 'Are you in Sandakan camp?'
> I said, 'Yes.'
> He said, 'How many others in there?'
> I said, 'Oh, about two thousand.'
> [He said] 'And what's their health like?'
> I said, 'Pretty miserable . . . A lot die.'

He said, 'How many Japs are there?'

I said, 'About 50 or 60 Japs around the camp.'

He said, 'And what do they intend to do with you?'

'Well,' I said, 'they've been working us on the aerodrome till they bombed it . . . and now I don't know what they'll do with us.'

And he said, 'How many fit men would there be in the camp?'

I said, 'You'll find three or four hundred who'd take up arms if they had 'em.'

Campbell described the stranger to Wall as 'a bloke about my build, about five foot six . . . I'd say he weighed 12 stone. Solid . . . dressed in camouflage greens.' He wore a beret, not a slouch hat, and carried what Campbell called a 'peculiar-looking machine gun'—a weapon he had never seen before. When Campbell asked where the soldier was from the answer he received was that he was not 'from the Yanks'. Nor would he tell Campbell why he wanted information about the POW camp. He did, however, tell Campbell to 'go back and find out the full strength of the Japs . . . tell one of your officers but don't tell too many . . . 'cause somebody's likely to talk and the Japs might overhear it.' After being told that the wood-gathering party came to the same place every day, the stranger promised Campbell he would be back 'tomorrow or the next day'.

Campbell did as he was told and mentioned the encounter to only a single officer, who suggested asking the stranger to come into the camp at night. Campbell made a point of going to the same place each day until the guards became suspicious about his need to always defecate in the same spot, but the visitor never returned.

Who was the mysterious soldier in camouflage greens and beret? Campbell suspected him of being an undercover agent who had been delivered by submarine and then come inland by river. Silver asserts that 'who this visitor was, or where he came from, is still not known'. However, she points out that the Netherlands covert intelligence organisation

NEFIS sent a party into Borneo around this time to gather information ahead of the Allied landing at Tarakan.

Japanese activity forced the party to abort the Tarakan mission, but the Dutch agents continued to collect intelligence from British North Borneo until their evacuation in February 1945. It is not impossible that the revised operation took the party close to Sandakan. NEFIS issued its undercover agents with a new automatic weapon, the British-designed Sten sub-machine gun, which had only recently been brought into service and would not have been familiar to Campbell. Perhaps the soldier Campbell saw on his wood-gathering expedition was a Dutch agent. Whoever he was, the unidentified visitor in camouflage greens was not the last to offer false hope of rescue for the Australians at Sandakan.

Chapter 20

FOR THE DURATION

⸺⧓⸺

During the three years he was a prisoner at Sandakan, Bill Sticpewich insinuated himself into every aspect of the camp's economy. In his eight-page statement 'War crimes and events' he described his 'technical party' as the 'source of all news and the channel through which inward supplies and contraband were obtained from outside sources, such as extra food for the dangerously ill patients in hospital and medical supplies'.

As well as making himself useful to the Japanese as a carpenter and handyman, Sticpewich did bookkeeping and administration for Captain Cook. The Japanese appreciated his handiwork and rewarded him and his technical party with extra food and quinine. Thanks to his superior rations, he was able to stay healthy throughout his captivity apart from having a 'bad ulcer' that allegedly stopped him working sometime in early 1943. But Sticpewich had also played a role in the smuggling of contraband into the camp and was a member of what he called a 'secret committee' of prisoners that met to discuss grievances. His practical and organisational skills made him more or less indispensable not just to the Japanese and to his own superiors but to his fellow prisoners as well.

Hardly anything happened at 8 Mile Camp without Sticpewich getting to hear of it. With his personal licence to roam around the camp he was able to see how much food there was, where it went and who ate it. After the war he gave meticulous evidence about the relentless cut in the prisoners' rice ration: 17 ounces (482 grams) per man per day until March 1943; between 11 and 13 ounces (312–386 grams) until June 1944; 8 ounces (227 grams) until September 1944; and finally 6 ounces (170 grams) per man per day until January 1945, when the rice issue was stopped altogether. 'I was in a position to see practically everything that was going on by both sides and I was in a position to know if any rice was issued,' he told the judges at Hoshijima's trial.

Sticpewich watched the Japanese plundering greens from the prisoners' garden: 'They took considerably greater [than the POWs],' he told the court. 'More than three times per head from the garden.' Sticpewich was like a ghost—he went everywhere and saw everything. 'I worked outside No 1 compound and my work took me over the whole area,' he said. He watched Japanese guards eating their meals and was close enough to see the food on their plates:

> In 1945 the Japanese guards were eating large quantities of rice, they also had fish or meat daily, soya beans and large quantities of vegetables, mainly potatoes and very little tapioca . . . they often had food left over. This also included rice left over which was more than four or five men could eat. All the Japanese looked healthy and well fed.

The prisoners' canteen stopped functioning after September 1944 because, according to the Japanese, it was no longer possible to buy food from local vendors. Sticpewich described this as 'passive resistance' by local villagers. 'There was plenty of food in the area,' he said. 'It only wanted organising.'

Sticpewich tried to do the organising himself. In late 1944 he devised a system to supply food to the prisoners, mainly protein and fruit, on a 'credit basis', with payment to be made by the Australian Government when the war ended 'irrespective of who won'. Captain Cook was 'instructed' twice by the prisoners' committee to put this scheme to Hoshijima or alternatively to ask for all prisoners to be released 'and we would find our own food'. Cook took the request to Hoshijima, whose only response was 'we will look into it'. According to Sticpewich, the arrangement 'was never approved of by Hoshijima at any stage', but the prisoners were watched more closely after his 'contact with the natives'.

By his own account, Sticpewich played a central role in the smuggling of medical supplies into the camp. Small quantities of medicines were 'brought in through my store. I was one of the chain it passed through.' The medicines, which included quinine, came from Sandakan hospital and from Dr Taylor's 'secret dump'. To begin with the drugs were smuggled in by Chinese civilians; later they were brought in by Japanese guards who stole them from Sandakan while they were on leave. In exchange for the medicines the prisoners handed over 'jewellery, diamonds, rings, watches and clothing' but 'none of these secret supplies [of medicine] were anywhere near sufficient'.

To supplement the camp's dwindling supply of meat, Hoshijima allowed some prisoners to fish in Sandakan Bay. Inevitably, Sticpewich was involved. At first the fishing party went out in what he called a ship's lifeboat: 'It was very heavy and five of us had to pull this and there were always two guards.' They took the lifeboat out three times, but Sticpewich found it a frustrating experience. As soon as the boat came close to Berhala Island the Japanese guards would see the coconut grove and demand to be put ashore, where they would 'get coconuts, drink the juice and lie down'.

As the fishing party was not allowed to set out before daylight and had to be back before dark there was very little time for fishing once they had ferried the guards ashore at Berhala Island. After complaining to Hoshijima about the size of the boat and how heavy it was, the prisoners were allowed to use a *prahu*, or traditional sailing boat, but the guards still insisted on going to the island to snooze and drink coconut milk. 'Actually every difficulty was put in the way [of] making the fishing trip a success,' Sticpewich said at Hoshijima's trial. 'We naturally caught very little fish. We were not trusted and to be successful you had to fish with the tide.'

Vigilance and cunning together with an aptitude for ingratiating himself with individual guards largely kept Sticpewich out of trouble. He witnessed but was seldom the target of violence, although violence at Sandakan was arbitrary and ubiquitous.*

After three men—Privates Gordon Barber and Arthur Clement and Signalman Fred Weeks—were caught outside the wire in the prisoners' garden, Hoshijima called a parade during which he announced that the trio would be put in the cage. Accusing the camp masters, including Captain Cook, of being unable to control their men, Hoshijima gave them a public belting. Sticpewich—along with the respected RAAF Sergeant Major John Kinder—got off scot free. As he put it,

---

* Paul Ham, perhaps a little disingenuously, writes that Sticpewich had 'an *odd gift* [my italics] for getting away with things that others would get a bashing for'. It is unlikely that any of his fellow survivors would have described it that way. In keeping with his exuberant description of Sticpewich as 'one of the most vibrant figures in the camp . . . [a] raffish fixer and consummate wheeler-dealer', Ham often refers to him as 'Wild Bill' Sticpewich, although there is no evidence that he was known by this nickname at Sandakan. In recorded interviews with Don Wall and Tim Bowden, Sticpewich was nearly always referred to by other survivors as 'Stippy'. Asked whether she had ever heard anyone use the nickname 'Wild Bill' for Sticpewich, Lynette Silver told this author 'Never'.

'Two of the camp masters who were omitted from this bashing were WO Kinder and myself.' He offered no reason for his good fortune.

Prisoners sentenced to a spell in the cage were beaten by guards using 'sticks or anything [the guards] could lay their hands on'. A favourite weapon was the broom from the guard house. 'They would break it over a PW and I would have to repair it,' Sticpewich said.* The average stay in the cage was 'around 20 days', but some prisoners such as Botterill were sentenced to double that. During his three years at Sandakan Sticpewich spent only a brief spell in the cage, but as always he took careful notice of everything and filed it away for future use:

At one time I was in the cage and I measured it. The walls consisted of 2x2 [inch] bars about 2½ inches apart. These bars were of wood. This cage was always out in the open. When it rained it used to blow in and

---

*   In the statutory declaration he made at Labuan in January 1946 Sticpewich gave more details of his repair work: 'Kiyoshima [nicknamed "Panther tooth" because he "used to sneak on unsuspecting PW at night time"] did not like guard duties, and as a result, when he was on guard, he indulged in excessive beatings of PW . . . [He] was very severe on PW confined in the cage . . . On one occasion, in front of the Guard-house, I saw him break a broom-handle while bashing a PW, and on two other occasions I have had to re-fit the head of the broom into new handles, the head having been broken off during a bashing.' Sensing, perhaps, that his apparent willingness to repair weapons used for bashing his fellow POWs might not go down well with Australian war crimes investigators, Sticpewich went on to describe a bashing he had received from Kiyoshima over a 'protest for more food'. Kiyoshima, he said, 'came from behind me . . . and punched me several times behind the ears, kicked me on the shins, and smacked me on the face with his open hand, at the same time making me stand strictly to attention. He continued this for . . . 5 to 10 minutes until he was stopped by S/M Murozumi.' Ham avoids the awkward implications of Sticpewich's apparent co-operation in the beating of fellow prisoners by writing that 'Sticpewich witnessed [Kiyoshima] break two handles, refit new ones, and resume a bashing'—a statement that is at odds with Sticpewich's own account.

made things very uncomfortable. To get into the cage we had to crawl
in through a small door. A larger cage was built later on.

Anything longer than a few days in the cage could leave men permanently marked. 'A lot of men were reasonably fit . . . when they went
into the cage but came out walking skeletons, mentally sick,' Sticpewich
told the judges at Hoshijima's trial.

Thirty-seven-year-old Gordon Barber had been a mate of his.
Sticpewich said he 'knew Private Barber very well'. After about five days
in the small cage Barber was taken out and put in the second cage near
the English camp. There were scales around the camp and the prisoners were weighed 'very frequently'. Before he went into the cage Barber
had weighed 'around about 12 stone [76 kilograms] . . . He did not have
any disease when he went in. When he arrived back from the small cage
on the hill he was considerably lighter and showed signs of being badly
treated . . . I saw his body after Pte Barber died and I would estimate his
weight to be around about 5½ or 6 stone [35–38 kilograms].'

Barber, Clement and Weeks were all severely bashed during their
time in the cage. In Sticpewich's opinion Barber '[d]efinitely . . . died
from the treatment in the cage': in a handwritten list of dead prisoners
he gave to the Australian interrogators at Morotai he wrote the words
'result of torture' next to Barber's name. Weeks was eventually released
suffering from 'paralysis and internal injuries'. Within a week he, too,
was dead. Sticpewich was convinced that 'the cage treatment caused
his death'.

Cook was 'instructed by the committee to see Hoshijima' to protest
about the treatment of the three prisoners in the cage but there is no
evidence to suggest he did as he was told. In fact, very soon another eight
Australians were put in the cage for stealing food from the Japanese
quartermaster to give to seriously ill prisoners in the camp hospital. As
soon as he found out that prisoners under his command were eating

stolen food Cook had informed his 'good friend' and fishing companion Hoshijima.

In his evidence to the war crimes commission Keith Botterill stated: 'Capt Cook requested that these men . . . be imprisoned for the duration'. He recalled that during 1944 two of the eight—Privates Annear and Anderson—'served more time in the cage than out of it, they were in for 20 days, during which time I was in with them, then they were in for 44 days and subsequently they were again in for about six weeks. They had scarcely come out than they were put back in for the duration'.

Even Hoshijima must have realised that being caged for the rest of the war was a punishment no prisoner at Sandakan could possibly survive. Sticpewich noted '[t]hey would be in for a while and then get sick, be returned to camp and then put in again' once they had recovered.

A possible reason for Cook's failure to protest about the treatment of Barber, Clement and Weeks is the fact that he had asked Hoshijima to impose even harsher punishment on Annear, Anderson and the rest. Keith Botterill told Silver he was 'stunned' by Cook's behaviour towards his own men. According to Botterill three of the eight, including Annear and Anderson, died after 'about three months' in the cage. Sticpewich, perhaps diplomatically given his close working relationship with Cook and the fact that Cook had been killed at Ranau, professed not to know the sentence Cook had insisted on for Annear's group but told the judges 'it was a long one'. Sticpewich gave his opinion that seven of the eight men sentenced 'for the duration' died as a direct result of their time in the cage.

Chapter 21

A SOLDIER'S WAY

Sticpewich was not among the 455 British and Australian prisoners who began marching out of 8 Mile Camp on 29 January 1945 as his name had not been included on Cook's list, perhaps due to his usefulness around the camp. Staying behind made him a crucial witness to what happened during the final months of Hoshijima's command.

The marchers were divided into nine groups of approximately 50 men. In the evidence he gave at Yamamoto's trial Botterill said prisoners were given '3 pounds [1.4 kilograms] of rice, ¼ pound [115 grams] of dried fish and an ounce [28 grams] of salt and there was about 1 pound [450 grams] of sugar given to the officer in charge of the party'.

Botterill was in the third group to leave and Bill Moxham in the seventh. Guarding Botterill's group were Lieutenant Toyohara Kihaku, a sergeant major, corporal and lance corporal and about fifteen privates. Botterill and his companions 'moved out of the gate and down to the road and we were given about 120 pounds [54 kilograms] of rice'. As well as having to carry a portion of the rice, each prisoner 'on average . . . carried 40 to 60 pounds [18–27 kilograms], whatever he was assigned to carry'. The loads consisted of ammunition, Japanese officers' gear and rice, the latter sewn up in hessian bags and the ammunition carried in a bag slung on the chest. Before leaving the camp Botterill was issued with 'a pair of 2nd hand shorts and a shirt or a giggle jacket and we were issued with rubber shoes which were no good as they slipped straight off our feet'. About 'six or seven' men in the group had boots they had managed to keep with them since Singapore.

For the first few days of the march it rained constantly. By the end of the first day most of the prisoners in Botterill's group were marching through the mud in bare feet, having given up on Hoshijima's 'rubber plates'. On the second day, after wading for hours along a flooded track on the edge of a lagoon, Botterill's group reached a wooden boardwalk mounted on poles above a mangrove swamp. The prisoners were warned by Toyohara that any man who broke a leg by slipping off the boardwalk would be shot. Botterill told Tim Bowden that he and others, including some of the guards, decided it was safer to get off the boardwalk and walk through the mud. The bog, he said, was 'above our knees a lot of the way'.

Toyohara's soldiers, unlike those accompanying some other groups, were well disciplined and did not bash the POWs, but the journey was brutal. A few days out from Sandakan and with the worst of the wet country behind them, an Australian NCO could no longer keep up. Botterill told the war crimes commission:

He seemed to go off his head and was grabbing Sgt-Maj Warrington and begging him to shoot him. [Toyohara] tried to save as many men as he could but as the sergeant was suffering from beriberi and was too weak to go any further he asked the Australian sergeant-major to give him permission to shoot him. Warrington wrote out an authority and then the Japanese handed him his revolver and told him to shoot the sergeant. This Warrington did . . . The sergeant was fighting all the time and went completely mad; he was paralysed from the waist down. He would not be carried and fought against those who were trying to help him.

The plan had been for each group to replenish their supplies from food dumps sited at strategic points along the route, but the deeper they went into the interior the less they could rely on the dumps. The Japanese carried emergency rations of dried fish and soya bean powder, but the prisoners knew better than to expect any of it to be shared. Botterill gave evidence that at a dump near Boto his group found six cucumbers and a minuscule quantity of rice; he said it had to last 40 men for three days.

Sergeant Major Gotanda was ordered to walk a day ahead of the main group to ensure there was food waiting when the column arrived. He claimed that after finding nothing at one food dump he marched 50 kilometres and then travelled further by boat during the night in order to bring back 30 kilograms of rice.

As one of the fitter members of the group Botterill did his best to help the stragglers keep up, but some were beyond his or anyone else's help. Leeches were a perpetual torment. Each prisoner had been given 2 ounces (57 grams) of tobacco before leaving Sandakan and Botterill remembered having a lighted cigarette in his mouth the whole time in order to burn the leeches off his body.

A few kilometres short of Tampias the prisoners had to get up and down a mountain; one man died, and another who could go no further was shot by the guards. In his written statement before Yamamoto's trial Botterill said he saw four men from his party shot by 'the sergeant-major' (Gotanda) after they had fallen out. Confusingly, he later changed his evidence and said that 'a Japanese corporal shot two of them'.

Each day the stragglers fell further behind. Nearly every prisoner was suffering from malaria, beriberi or dysentery and some from all three. The men at the front could be hours ahead of those at the rear:

> As we were going along men would fall out as they became too weak to carry on. We would go on and then shortly after hear shots and men squealing out; when this occurred there were always Japanese behind us, and it was they who did the shooting. Although I did not see the bodies of any men who had been shot in the parties that had gone before us, often I could smell them.

Asked how he had managed to survive the march, Botterill told Tim Bowden he had 'no idea . . . I just kept plodding along . . . I was heart-broken, and I thought there was safety in numbers. I just kept going.'

Paginatan was a further day's climb from Tampias. As per his orders Gotanda had gone on ahead. Coming back he found the prisoners struggling under the weight of the soldiers' mosquito nets, which they had been ordered by the corporal to carry. Gotanda told them to leave the mosquito nets behind as they would never be able to get over the hill with them and to carry only what they had. Then, Botterill said, Gotanda asked whether they were all there. The prisoners told him there were 'two men about three miles back, and one was very sick and the other was helping him along'. Gotanda left and returned with only one prisoner, Private Richard Murray. When they asked Murray what had happened to the other man he replied, '[T]he Sergeant had to shoot him, he could not come any further.'

The food dump at Paginatan was well stocked and the prisoners were able to stay in the guesthouse. Gotanda said he traded two shirts for a 'not very big' pig and that later Lieutenant Toyohara 'gave the native a piece of blanket which the POW had'. Botterill agreed that the pig was shared equally between the POWs and the Japanese. Toyohara allowed three prisoners with bad malaria to stay behind at Paginatan until they were well enough to continue, an act of compassion that was almost invariably denied to sick marchers in other groups.

Seventeen days after leaving Sandakan Botterill's group reached Ranau, a picturesque village on a river flat nearly 800 metres above sea level. Looming over the scene was the spectacular, razor-edged peak of Borneo's highest mountain, Mount Kinabalu. A Japanese airstrip lay a kilometre to the east of the village.

Of the 50 prisoners who set out from Sandakan in Botterill's group, only 37 reached Ranau. The Japanese, already in what Botterill described as 'very good physical condition', benefited from having more rations than the prisoners. Botterill saw two soldiers with malaria who had been left behind at one of the rest stops come through about six weeks later. Gotanda later claimed to have been told by his commander that '5 Japanese and 10 PsW had died on the way from malaria, dysentery and beriberi' and that he did not know 'where and by what causes' prisoners in the third group had died.

The Liwagu River at Ranau was 'swift-flowing' and 'sprinkled with large, smooth, grey boulders', Harry Jackson wrote in his official report. 'At night the fireflies cast their phosphorescent glow above its course and in the morning its noise is the first thing that greets your ears.' While there was no snow on the summit of Kinabalu, '[A]fter a shower of rain the rocks . . . glisten white as if lightly covered with snow . . . and huge waterfalls show up like strands of cotton as the water . . . makes its way to the lower slopes.'

Of more significance to Keith Botterill and the emaciated survivors of the third group was the POW camp perched on a slope above the south-west corner of the airstrip. Ranau's No. 1 Camp consisted of a large, open-sided atap hut in a bamboo stockade. Two rows of bamboo decking, filthy with vermin ran along either side of a central aisle. Prisoners slept on the decking. No. 1 Camp had no hospital, so sick and dying men lay at one end of the hut while a Japanese stood guard at the other end, and the rest jostled for space in between.

Two groups of marchers had already moved into the camp when the third group arrived. Botterill found conditions already 'fairly well crowded'. After groups four and five reached Ranau there was no more room in No. 1 Camp, so groups six to nine had to stop at Paginatan.

Bill Moxham, who arrived at Paginatan with group seven on 23 February, testified that when they set off from Sandakan 'the members of my party were all in very weak condition'. They were about three days out of camp when they were told by Lieutenant Sugimura Shunichi that the rations they were carrying would have to last them not for four days but for eight. At Boto they were able to trade clothes for rice and tapioca, but these were confiscated by the Kempei-Tai. The food dumps were nevertheless all well stocked.

Despite the number of sick men in the party the mortality rate in Moxham's group, at 14 per cent, was lower than in any other group. Moxham reckoned his party was the 'most fortunate in the carrying of gear'. In group six half a dozen prisoners were needed just to haul the baggage of 48-year-old Lieutenant Tanaka Shojiro, but the soldiers in group seven carried all their own equipment. Moxham said, 'We did not have to carry any Japanese gear but just a little rice and salt.'

When they were only a couple of days out of Sandakan Lieutenant Sugimura allowed a prisoner who was sick with malaria to return with two soldiers, but there were killings later on. At one place Moxham and Sergeant Major Kinder attempted to go back to help a prisoner who had been unable to reach the resting camp. On the way they met 'two Japanese soldiers, one a corporal and one a private, and they said that they had shot the POW and thrown him over the side of an embankment'.

Moxham recalled seeing 'approximately ten bodies', either at resting camps or beside the path. On one occasion he saw 'a man from number six party who was sprawled right across the track with a shovel in his hand and he had not been dead very long'. Another man from group six had been bashed and thrown down a gully. Moxham's party heard 'moaning and groaning from one side of the road about a mile from the camp', so he and another prisoner went to investigate. The man 'was not dead but he was in great agony and he was paralysed'. The guards would not let them approach, and 'hunted us straight on our journey'. The men in the later groups were never allowed to examine bodies they saw beside the track.

Around 140 men from groups six to nine reached Paginatan, where they were forced to wait until more huts could be built at Ranau. By the end of March, when the survivors were ordered to move to Ranau, only 50 to 60 men were still alive. More died attempting to walk the 42 kilometres to Ranau.

Botterill and Moxham agreed that 'number six party was the worst party of the lot'. Moxham spoke to men from groups one to five and came to the conclusion that 'we were in the best party that came through' on the grounds that 'our party was the only one out of the lot that did not have to carry Japanese ammunition and guns'.

While the later groups waited at Paginatan, dysentery swept through the camp at Ranau, killing a dozen prisoners in little more than a week. Yamamoto had taken his regular soldiers with him to Tuaran, leaving the prisoners once again in the hands of the Formosan guards who had terrorised them at Sandakan. Among them were Hayashi, nicknamed 'Ming the Merciless', and the 6'2" (188 centimetre) Suzuki Saburō, remembered by Nelson Short as the most brutal guard he ever encountered.

The exhausted marchers were given little time to recover from their journey before being put back to work. Botterill volunteered to join a party carrying 20-kilogram sacks of rice to the Japanese soldiers and POWs waiting at Paginatan. By the time the rice-carrying party returned there was a new officer in charge at Ranau: Captain Nagai, newly arrived from Labuan with more Formosans, and another officer,

Lieutenant Suzuki. Seeing the hated Nagai was enough to make Botterill volunteer for a second trip: three days to Paginatan hauling rice and two back again to Ranau. He eventually made six trips and in his own words became 'one of the fittest men in the camp', thanks in part to the tapioca he, Richard Murray and Corporal Ron Sullivan used to filch from the gardens at night and then 'cook up and make a decent meal of'.

The prisoners on the rice-carrying parties used bamboo straws to siphon rice from the sacks they were carrying into their empty water bottles. Since the sacks were then lighter, the prisoners took care to dunk them in the river before they reached Paginatan to conceal the discrepancy. Along the way they ate anything they could catch: frogs, slugs or a snake if they were lucky.

Despite the opportunties for extra food, most did not survive the arduous journey. 'We used to help those who were weak and practically carried many of them back to camp', Botterill told the war crimes commission. Those who were beyond helping were shot or bayoneted. One of these was Gunner Albert Sheard. Exhausted by the trip, Sheard was lying on the ground with his hands up crying 'Don't shoot me' when a guard killed him. He was left where he lay.

As Sticpewich put it, '[T]hese PWs who fell by the wayside, too ill or exhausted to carry on, were not allowed to rest, but were disposed of, as the Japs term it, (otherwise killed)'. Any man too exhausted to make the punishing climb back to Ranau 'would be substituted by one who had rested or recovered somewhat, but [very] few ever returned'.

The rice-party survivors returned each time to the news that more prisoners had died at Ranau. During Botterill's second trip to Paginatan, Gunners Wally Crease and Albert Cleary escaped. Betrayed by villagers eager for a reward from the Japanese, both men were beaten and subjected to log torture. After returning from Paginatan Botterill saw Cleary being given the log treatment. Moxham didn't witness the torture, as he was still at Paginatan with the remnants of groups six to nine. He told the war crimes commission that he 'did not see this occur . . . but it definitely did happen', and went on to describe how the two men were 'stripped and tied at the guardhouse to a post, without food; the weather was very cold, much colder than at Sandakan'.

Crease escaped again and was shot in the jungle, but Cleary was kept tied to a tree with a rope around his neck and wearing nothing but a loincloth. 'They kept Cleary there until he was practically dead,' Moxham stated. Wracked with dysentery, Cleary was near death when Botterill returned to Ranau on 18 March from another rice-carrying trip. By the next day the smell was so bad that Cleary was untied and made to lie in a ditch some distance from the guardhouse. Botterill told the war crimes commission about the log torture but did not say Cleary had been bashed to death. Cleary, he said, was 'just about dead when the Japanese sergeant told us to take him into the hut, where he died about ten minutes later . . . He was out in the open for two weeks with very little food.'

Including Cleary, more than 60 prisoners had died since arriving in Ranau. The old cemetery was full and the Australians had to start burying their comrades in a new graveyard 100 metres up the hill.

Each death eased the cramped conditions in the atap hut where the prisoners slept. 'You'd wake up of a morning and you'd look to your right to see if the chap next to you was still alive,' Botterill told Tim Bowden.

If he was dead you'd just roll him over a little bit and see if he had any belongings that would suit you, that were worth anything to you; if not you would just leave him there and wouldn't bother with him. And you'd turn to the other side, check your next neighbour and do the same for him, see if he was dead or alive. There was a burial party every morning at approximately nine o'clock. And we used to bury them on this hill, it was called Boot Hill.

There was no dignity for the living and none for the dead. The prisoners had no padre, and the soil was too hard and the tools too inadequate for the burial party to dig deeper than 15 centimetres. The dead were put in the ground naked. 'We'd lay the body in,' Botterill told Bowden, 'and the only mark of respect they got . . . we'd spit on the body and then cover them.' It was, he said, 'a soldier's way'.

Nagai found their helplessness amusing. 'Sometimes we would be carrying the dead up . . . [the] hill and when some of the men fell and rolled down, Nagai would stand at the bottom laughing and then put the guards on to us.'

The sixth and last rice-carrying trip was the hardest, as chronic illness and malnutrition sapped the prisoners' last reserves of strength. At first Botterill and Murray refused to go, having barely struggled back from the fifth trip, but when Nagai threatened to march them all the way back to Sandakan they changed their minds. Those who faltered were killed. Five prisoners—a quarter of the party—died making the return trip to Paginatan, the last two bayoneted as they lay unconscious on the ground.

On the outward journey the rice carriers met a party of prisoners coming the other way: they were the surviving members of groups six to nine, dragging themselves the 42 kilometres from Paginatan to Ranau. Among them was Bill Moxham. The party could only manage 10 or 11 kilometres a day. Leaving at 7 am, they would be 'knocked up completely' by 10 am only to be sent off to scrounge for the Japanese, who bartered the prisoners' clothing and boots for food. In return the prisoners received 'a few small sweet potatoes' and, once, the skin of a pig.

Sergeant Major Kinder, who often walked at the rear, told Moxham he had seen 'wicked things [happen]. The Japs used to make him stay behind while a man was shot to death, or kicked to death. They made Kinder watch it.'

Of the 452 Australian and British POWs who had marched out of Sandakan between 29 January and 6 February 1945, more than 300 were dead by the time the survivors from groups six to nine reached Ranau on 31 March. The rest, including Botterill and Moxham, were scarcely alive. Their only medical officer, Captain Rod Jeffrey, had given up looking after his own men and was treating the Japanese in return for extra rations for himself. Dysentery was rife and dying men took up most of the space in the atap hut, which was now in such a disgusting state that the guards had been moved to a small barracks next door.

Botterill told Lynette Silver that at the time, ballooned with beriberi, he lost his own will to live: 'no toilet paper, no comb, no soap, no tooth-brush, no clothes, no food, no medicine. But plenty of lice, plenty of bugs, plenty of crabs, plenty of mites, plenty of flies, but above all, no hope.' Others felt the same as Botterill; Bill Moxham told Justice Mansfield, 'If they had lined us up and shot us, it would have been all right. But they did not do that—they marched us and slowly starved the men to death.'

Appalled by what he had seen and heard during his 1946 trip to Borneo, Major Harry Jackson came to think that the horrors of the march and the conditions at Ranau had reduced the prisoners to something less than human:

> Whereas the PW invariably shared what they had or obtained prior to the movement from Sandakan, when they arrived at Ranau most of them developed the habit of keeping all they could get for themselves, jealousy and suspicion was rife, and maltreatment and starvation had affected some of their minds to such a state that they acted like primi-tive people and animals in the same manner as they do when they are quarrelling over food etc.

Fewer than 60 prisoners were still alive at Ranau when, on 25 April, American Lightning fighter-bombers dived out of a tranquil sky and began attacking the airstrip and adjacent guardhouse. Moxham thought the Japanese must have got wind of what was coming: two days earlier, the guards had started digging 'funkholes' for their own protection in the event of an air raid.

A barbed-wire fence surrounded the atap hut where the POWs slept. When the Lightnings began strafing the camp, men ran out of the hut to see guards pointing their rifles and preparing to shoot any prisoner attempting to get beyond the wire.

With the pilots circling overhead oblivious to the presence of the POWs, Sergeant Major Kinder got off his sick bed and confronted Lieutenant Suzuki. 'Kinder called out, "We'll have to get these men out!"' Moxham told Justice Mansfield. 'Kinder called "Right-oh" to us; we ran out and just got into holes before the planes came down a second time. They flew over several more times and flattened the place . . . one man, an Englishman, was killed.'

According to Moxham, by the next morning Captain Nagai had gone, leaving Lieutenant Suzuki in charge of the camp. Staying at No. 1 Camp—what was left of it—was no longer an option. Although Captain Jeffrey remained the senior officer, he had effectively ceded his authority to Sergeant Major Kinder, whose refusal to be kowtowed by the Japanese had won him the men's respect. It was Kinder who told Suzuki that they would have to abandon the camp and find somewhere safe from bombing attacks.

'When we were bombed and burned out of Ranau by the Americans, they moved us a mile or two into the hills, into this small native hut,' Botterill told Bowden. 'And each day they'd let us go down the gully to avoid being strafed. We told them that we would not escape. And each night we returned to the hut, and they let us cook a meal. And that went on for six weeks or so.'

All bar a handful of prisoners were too weak even to contemplate escape. Captain Jeffrey, no longer capable of doing his duty as doctor or senior officer, died in the first week of May. Ten more prisoners were buried the following week. When a rumour began to circulate that the remaining prisoners would be forced to march to Jesselton, Botterill and his brother-in-arms Richie Murray began plotting their escape. Finding food was, as always, the main priority.

While on a wood-gathering expedition Botterill had learned of the existence of a secret Japanese food store. One night he, Murray and two others raided the store, stealing a 20-kilogram bag of rice and a box of biscuits. After burying the rice, they took a bag of biscuits back to camp and distributed some among the sick and others to mates who had acted as lookouts. Botterill and two others hid their biscuits in the jungle, but Murray stashed his in the crawl space beneath the hut.

Five days passed before the theft was discovered when a guard happened to peer beneath the hut and noticed an empty calico bag. A search of the secret food store revealed that a bag of rice was missing. The theft of rice was a capital offence. Suzuki ordered a muster of the 30 POWs still alive from the march and demanded to know the culprit. Ignoring Botterill's whispered advice to say nothing, Murray stepped forward and confessed to stealing the rice. The others watched while he was taken away at bayonet point and tied to a tree.

An hour later Botterill saw his friend being marched down a track by Suzuki and three guards, one of whom was the Formosan Kawakami Kiyoshi (the 'Gold-toothed shin-kicking bastard'). After twenty minutes the guards returned without Murray. According to Silver, Kawakami 'swaggered down to the Formosan hut and made a great show of wiping his bayonet on the grass, boasting to his fellow guards that he had "blooded his blade" on the prisoner'. Convinced that he was as guilty as Murray, Kawakami forced Botterill to his knees and had to be stopped by another Formosan guard from beheading the Australian with Suzuki's sword.

By 10 June only 21 prisoners were left alive at Ranau, eleven of them very near death. That morning their number was reduced by one when

John Kinder succumbed to dysentery and malaria. The same day the survivors were informed that fit prisoners would be moving to another camp, to be known as Jungle Camp No. 2, and told to be ready at 3 am to avoid strafing by American planes.

Botterill knew the place—he had been on a working party carrying atap to the new site about 8 kilometres south of Ranau—and decided not to go. 'I thought, now I'll stop here, with the sick men,' he told Tim Bowden. In the meantime the nine fit men, including Moxham, lined up outside. As the prisoners were counted off one of the Japanese asked, 'Where is the wood soldier?' This was the name given by the guards to Botterill because he was often sent to cut wood. Told that the wood soldier was staying behind with the sick men, the guard went to the hut and told Botterill to get on his feet and join the others. 'So that morning, there was ten fit men, including me, ready to go to the new camp,' Botterill told Bowden. 'We left the ten sick behind, and they shot them.'

Two more prisoners died before the last eight were massacred. 'Everyone fired at least one shot and most of us two,' said Formosan Ishii Fujio. 'I personally did as my first shot entered below the breast-bone and did not kill the man. At the time the PWs were killed they were lying on the ground too sick to move and so did not have their hands tied behind their backs. They had no chance to escape and did not make any effort to do so.'

Chapter 22

WE'VE GOT NOTHING

———⟶◆⟵———

At Sandakan the POWs who had stayed behind were subsisting on rice drawn entirely from their own reserves. According to a written statement by Sticpewich, the prisoners' Q store held 105 bags that had been saved over the previous two and a half years, enough to supply everyone with 130 grams a day for two months. 'Our QM cut the ration to 70 grams,' he wrote. 'If this had not been done we would probably have been killed off much sooner.'

Hoshijima claimed that between January and May the camp received 'three truck loads of fresh fish and one turtle and about three cases of dried fish' as well as ducks and pigs 'from our own farm'. In reality the Sandakan POWs were reduced to eating snakes and swamp rats. Some died from the latter, while others died from eating inadequately prepared tapioca root. Short told Tim Bowden that he ate slugs: 'We used to lay out leaves all over the place and the slugs would get underneath the leaves and then you'd thread them on a bit of wire and toast them over the fire. Well, they was clean, I mean to say, they only eat greens, and when the slime was off it just tastes like pork, and they . . . was all right. And [we ate] frogs. Anything you could see that moved.'

At his trial Hoshijima conceded Captain Cook had verbally complained to him that the prisoners' food was 'not satisfactory' but maintained that Cook 'did not say anything about a shortage of food'. Hoshijima also claimed to be providing 'very sick' prisoners with bottles of milk from a locally owned dairy farm a kilometre from the camp, and to be cultivating potatoes at the aerodrome. Realising that his malnourished prisoners were becoming too weak to do gardening work, he sent 'native coolies . . . [to] gather coconuts which were given to the PW'.

Twice a week Hoshijima let the POWs go fishing—not in the sparkling waters of Sandakan Bay, but in drainage channels around the camp. In his 'notes' on Hoshijima's letter, Sticpewich stated that prisoners 'supplied their own fishing tackle, for example pieces of string or cotton and . . . pins for hooks':

The fishing was done in drains just outside of camp—fresh water drains—10 to 20 PsW in party at a time—Wednesday evenings when guards were made available, also Sundays. Wednesday was for cripples and no-duty PsW and Sundays were for work parties personnel who did not go on Wednesday. The quantity of the catch would sometimes give about 6 hospital patients a taste of fish—size ranged from 1 inch [2.5 centimetres] to big ones 5 inches [12 centimetres] which were rare, 40 small fish were a good catch for the party.

Sticpewich was usually scrupulous about placing himself at the centre of events in which he was personally involved, so perhaps he did not consider fishing in drains worth his time.

The prisoners were so weak by now that Hoshijima countermanded an order from 37th Army HQ to put 50 men to work repairing the airstrip. Conscripted local workers did the gardening work the prisoners could no longer manage by themselves.

The number of deaths in the Australian camp doubled from 57 in January 1945 to 119 in February and climbed again to more than 200 in March. In the same month nearly a hundred British prisoners died. With starving prisoners still prepared to risk a spell in the cage by scrounging for food beyond the wire, Hoshijima announced that the next prisoner found outside the camp would be shot.

On 4 March at around 8 pm a rifle shot rang out in the darkness. Sticpewich later claimed to have heard the guards outside the hut saying words to the effect of 'He is dead.' He then heard Hoshijima say, 'Remove the body.' Hut masters were ordered to check the numbers to ensure that everyone was accounted for. According to Sticpewich, Captain Cook was assured by hut masters that 'all is correct' but this was contradicted by Lieutenant Moritake, who said, 'I think you are wrong; make another check.' The second check revealed that Private John Orr was missing. Nothing more was said that night, but the next morning Cook was summoned by the Japanese to identify the body. He told Sticpewich that he had seen 'a wound in the back which had entered the back and come out through his chest'.

Later that morning Sticpewich examined the bloodstains on the ground: it was clear to him that Private Orr's body had been moved to disguise the fact that Orr had been shot in the back at close range.

In April, after a visit by a colonel from 37th Army HQ, Hoshijima was ordered by telegram to remove the POW sign outside the wire that had largely protected the camp from attack by American bombers. He was then relieved of his role as commandant and replaced by Captain Takakuwa Takuo, a man described by Silver as a 'notorious womaniser whose extra-curricular activities had left him with a hefty dose of syphilis'.

Hoshijima attributed his removal as commandant to his having put up the unauthorised POW sign. Like the prisoners themselves, however, Hoshijima had effectively been made redundant by the destruction of the aerodrome. Once the airfield had been put out of action there was no further use for his engineering skills or for the prisoners' labour.

Before leaving, Hoshijima organised a fishing competition that was won by Sergeant Major Ichikawa Takehora, the quartermaster, with second prize going to Lieutenant Good and third to an 'English officer'. The presentation of prizes, Hoshijima told the military court, was 'enjoyed in a thoroughly friendly atmosphere'. The fishing competition was followed by a farewell dinner attended by Captains Cook and Mills, who gave 'memorable table speeches expressing their highest gratitude for my daily efforts in procuring food and for kind treatment'. At the dinner Cook and Hoshijima 'agreed to maintain our friendship in future' and Cook told Hoshijima the Australians had nicknamed him 'Trump', not in reference to card games but because 'I was good and a man of righteousness'.

Meanwhile 37th Army HQ, worried by increasing Allied activity in Borneo, decided that the remaining prisoners at Sandakan should be moved, initially to a temporary site on the Labuk River and then on to Ranau. A build-up of Allied aircraft on Morotai that had been interpreted as evidence of a coming assault on Sandakan made the situation more urgent, and on 20 May—three days after Hoshijima's departure—Captain Takakuwa received orders that all POWs were to be marched directly to Ranau.

Hoshijima estimated that between 900 and 1000 prisoners were still alive when he left Sandakan on 17 May, around half of them in the hospital. 'About four or five' prisoners were dying each day. Hoshijima denied Athol Moffitt's suggestion that 'it looked as though a lot would die within a month or six weeks'.

Takakuwa did not share Hoshijima's optimism, advising 37th Army HQ that 'at least 400' POWs would have to be carried on stretchers and most of the rest 'would probably break down after two or three days marching'. Convinced that if he carried out his orders and marched the prisoners to Ranau 'many of them would die', Takakuwa sent a message to HQ 'giving them the facts' and asking for 'further advice'.

The difficulties of the Sandakan to Ranau track were by now well known to army headquarters. A succession of troop movements by Japanese infantry battalions in both directions along the track between Sandakan and Jesselton had cost the lives of thousands of Japanese soldiers. Takakuwa, however, got no reply to his request for advice.

Time had run out for the POWs at 8 Mile Camp. With Hoshijima's POW sign gone and erroneous reports reaching Australia that all prisoners had been moved from Sandakan, the camp was a target for Allied bombers for the first time since October 1944. Air raids on 23 and 24 May killed several prisoners and were followed on 27 May by a joint naval and air bombardment during which PT boats destroyed the harbour with torpedoes while aircraft bombed and strafed the town.

Anticipating an imminent landing by Allied troops, the garrison unit under Colonel Otsuka fell back to the 11 mile post, leaving 8 Mile Camp ahead of the Japanese front line. Takakuwa then decided, as he put it, 'that it was best to withdraw back for the safety of the PW'. It was clearer than ever to Takakuwa that it was impossible for him to carry out the order from army HQ to march all the Sandakan prisoners to Ranau, so after conferring with Cook he made the decision to 'leave the sick PW behind' and send 500 of the 'best conditioned' prisoners forward. Even then, as Takakuwa told the military court, 'I did not think that many of these 500 would survive the trip to Ranau.'

On the morning of 29 May, as nearby munition dumps exploded, prisoners were told they were going to be moved to a place where there was more food. Sticpewich testified that guards led by Lieutenant Moritake and Sergeant Major Murozumi went through the hospital getting 'as many on their feet as possible by tipping them off beds; others were on crutches and walking sticks; all were forced out the gate to participate in the march to Ranau'. According to Silver, three prisoners on stretchers died before they even reached the gate and had to be hastily buried in a slit trench.

Takakuwa wanted to march at night to avoid being seen by enemy aircraft. Beyond the promise of more food, the prisoners were not told where they would be going. Some thought the war was virtually over and the Japanese were making preparations to send them home.

Sticpewich said they asked for the POW sign to be replaced, both for their own safety and for the protection of the Japanese. The Australians knew how the war was going, he said, and did not want to leave the area. 'We knew of [the] Tarakan invasion and the west drive [and] also the . . . increased air activities. We knew help was very near and thought that Sandakan was next to be invaded so who would want to run out knowing this?'

As the so-called 'fit' prisoners gathered for the march, Dick Braithwaite saw a Catalina flying boat pass over the camp. The Catalina was flying so low that Braithwaite could see the face of an American crewman standing in the doorway. 'I felt like, if I could jump a bit higher he could grab me by the hand and take me with him! They . . . didn't do anything, they just flew over [and] had a look.'

Some didn't believe what they had been told about moving to a place with more food, but Dick Braithwaite and many others did. They were sure of one thing: wherever they were being taken it could not be to a place worse than Sandakan.

Despite having beriberi and feet ulcers, Nelson Short joined the marchers. He told Bowden:

Any man that could get on his feet and march got on his feet. The ones that couldn't, were sick, they stopped behind. I had ulcers on both feet, I had one big ulcer . . . near the big toe on my right foot and . . .

I was swollen right up . . . [both] legs, with beriberi . . . And one of the chaps that was stopping behind . . . he said, 'Don't you go on that march', he said, 'they'll send buses down or whatever it is or trucks or something and pick the sick up and take us down to the water'. They all thought they were going home . . . [they] thought that the war was over. And I said, 'Oh no, I think I'll go.'

Takakuwa gave orders for pigs to be killed and cooked, but there was scarcely time for the prisoners to eat their minuscule portions. An Allied invasion was expected the following morning and Takakuwa was impatient to get started, so every man capable of walking was to be ready to move within the hour. Short told Bowden that Captain Cook 'gave the order, he said every man's got to be out of the camp, sick and all . . . they've got one hour to be outside.'

The seriously ill and dying were carried outside the gates and laid in what the locals called a *padang* and Short called a 'paddock'. The 23 bags of rice that remained out of the 105 bags in the prisoners' QM store were left to feed those who were not going on the march. The prisoners who could walk were told to assemble in groups of 50, each group to be led by an officer or NCO. Takakuwa had given orders for the camp to be incinerated; the huts in No. 2 and No. 3 camps were already alight.

The marchers were too weak to carry more than a few personal possessions so most of their belongings had to be left behind. Braithwaite took a haversack with a blanket, a pair of shorts and a shirt that he had been saving and an old hat. He lost a chess set he had carved out of ebony and bulloak, while others left guitars they had hacked out of solid timber. For some of the Australians, watching the huts burn made them feel as if they were losing a home. 'We always talked about how glad we'd be to see the last of the place,' Braithwaite told Tim Bowden, 'and yet when we stood there and saw the place going up in flame we thought, well, we've got nothing'.

According to Sticpewich, between 530 and 536 men (Takakuwa gave a figure of 540) lined up on the road outside the camp. An interrogation report compiled in September 1945 by Captain Thomas Mort, OC of the prisoner contact and enquiry team, stated that 'the final speech by the Japs . . . before leaving Sandakan was as follows: "Don't be afraid. The troops you are leaving will be well looked after."'

Only around a hundred of the marchers could have been classified as being fit. They included Sticpewich, members of his technical party and Captain Cook as well as the camp cooks, who had all benefited, by various means, from better rations than the rest. The whole camp—huts, hospital, administrative buildings, barracks—was now ablaze, together with all the prisoners' records.

Before leaving Sandakan, Takakuwa called his officers and NCOs together and issued his orders. The march would be difficult, he told them, and prisoners 'would probably die of illness on the way and fall out because of weariness'. When this happened the soldiers were to do 'everything they could to help them along, but as the enemy would be landing and advancing quickly those PW who could not go on anymore and were likely to die would hamper the Japanese army and could be put out of their misery by being shot'.

At 8 pm the marchers, organised into eleven groups, moved off, leaving the camp engulfed in flames and 288 sick and dying mates lying out in the open. Sticpewich was in charge of group two. The road from 8 Mile Camp led to the main bitumen road. At the junction they could either turn left towards Sandakan town or right. Turning left could only mean one thing: they were going home. 'When we got there we turned right,' Short told Bowden. 'So we went to the 8 Mile peg and then come straight into the jungle, because that is as far as that bitumen road went. And that was the end, it was straight into the jungle and it was [another] 165 miles [265 kilometres to Ranau].'

Chapter 23

NOW OR NEVER

The prisoners marched until the early hours of the morning, when Takakuwa allowed them a short break. During those few hours of marching six men from Sticpewich's group dropped out. Around noon, while resting in a clearing, the group came under attack by Allied planes and was forced to take cover until it was dark. The next day the marchers managed only a few kilometres through swampy jungle in pouring rain, and by the following morning when Sticpewich took the roll call he found his group was twelve men short: another six had fallen out. When this was reported through Captain Cook the Japanese—in Sticpewich's words—'did not appear to be concerned at all', although they warned Cook that 'no officer was to drop out—they all must complete the march'.

Setting off each morning between 6.30 and 7.30, the groups were to leapfrog each other along the track so there was a different party leading each day. No one was in any doubt about the fate of the men who could not keep up; Sticpewich said he never saw again the men who dropped out of his party. Stragglers were either shot or bludgeoned to death with rifle butts by two Formosan guards under the command of Lieutenant (later Captain) Watanabe Genzo. The same fate befell men who stopped for a rest and could not get up. As Nelson Short recalled:

After about four hours or three hours' rest, men couldn't get on their feet. They became paralysed in the legs and . . . the ones that couldn't get up, they was all put together, and we went on for a distance and all you heard was the rattle . . . of a tommy gun . . . And that's every resting place, the blokes that fell over and couldn't go on, they just machine-gunned them.

Camp sites, Sticpewich wrote, 'were just anywhere in the jungle, at the side of the track':

The contour of the ground did not worry the Japs, often the camp would be on mud on the side of a hill. PWs had to crawl in where the area for each party was lined out. Some made shelters from their blankets and ground sheet; most suffered the long nights in the open air, and perished sooner than those who had improvised shelters. Rain fell on most nights throughout the march, and it was bitterly cold, which accounted for those who, finally cramped with rheuma-tism from exposure, were left behind in camps and killed off by the Japs daily.

Short, who was walking barefoot, was one of very few prisoners on the second march who did not suffer from malaria. After two days his tropical ulcers had begun to heal and his body had miraculously shaken off the symptoms of beriberi. 'I don't know why . . . but after two days, the ulcers that I had [on my feet] . . . had cleared up in the mud . . . And all the beriberi had left me. But the others, they blew up like balloons . . . it either starts from your head down, the beriberi, or your feet up. And then it hits your heart, that was the end of you. So many got worse and . . . couldn't go on, they just dropped.'

On the fourth day each group leader was issued about 700 grams of salt and 1 kilo of sugar by the prisoners' quartermaster, Lieutenant Good. With his usual shrewdness Sticpewich immediately distributed the issue among his group; parties that kept their issue in bulk soon had it taken from them by the Japanese. When guards demanded that Sticpewich produce his sugar and salt he told them his men had eaten it.

Dick Braithwaite was struggling up a slippery slope somewhere beyond the 55-mile peg when a guard clubbed him from behind with the butt of his rifle. While he floundered in the mud the guard hit him again on the side of the head. He turned just in time to avoid another blow that would have smashed his cheekbone but instead glanced off his mouth, bloodying his lips without knocking any teeth out. 'Fortunately he did not do that again,' Braithwaite told the war crimes commission. 'He was quite satisfied with rubbing his rifle butt in the dirt and gouging my eyes with it . . . I could not lift a finger. My mind was quite active and I knew what was going on. He searched me and then marched off and left me.' Luckily for Braithwaite he had set out that morning at the head of the column; by the time the end of the column came through he was able to continue. He recalled Bob Sykes, a warrant officer in his unit, standing over him saying, 'Come on, son, you can make it.' Those encouraging words were enough to get Braithwaite back on his feet.

Every morning after they had travelled 2 or 3 kilometres from their overnight camp the marchers would hear rifle and machine-gun fire from the direction of the camp. Friendly guards warned Sticpewich always to keep moving 'because if you stopped you would be "marti" meaning dead'.

While Sticpewich did not claim to have seen any prisoner being shot, he said he saw Warrant Officer Dixon 'bashed into insensibility' by Matsuda, a guard the Australians called 'Top Hat'. According to Sticpewich, Top Hat had wanted Dixon's gold ring and the prisoner refused to give it up. At the time Dixon was far ahead of his own party, having leapfrogged into another group. The bashing left Dixon collapsed at the side of the road alongside another Australian prisoner, Jimmy Barlow, who had dropped out. Top Hat was standing over the pair when they both regained consciousness and refused to allow the Australians to rejoin the march. 'Dixon and Barlow never joined camp when we stopped that night and I never saw either of them again', Sticpewich told Captain Ruse. 'Later during the march I saw Top Hat wearing Dixon's gold ring.'

Other guards said they never saw Matsuda wearing a gold ring and claimed that he would have been punished by his superiors if he had been caught wearing one. Sticpewich gave inconsistent accounts of the incident but Matsuda was sentenced to twenty years for Dixon's murder, largely on the basis of Sticpewich's evidence. The prosecution successfully argued that Matsuda was equally guilty whether he inflicted the fatal blow himself or left Dixon to be murdered by the killing squad he knew to be following.

Rations were inadequate from the start. Braithwaite recalled being fed on 'half a pint of rice a day'. The stronger prisoners sometimes 'dived into . . . ditches and dragged out a shell or a snail that lived in these creeks. They would get a handful of them, crack the shells and eat them.' Others ate bracken tips. Sticpewich reported:

[We] caught fish in the evening when reaching camp, in creeks etc. and ate frogs, snails, lizards, snakes, a monkey and a very sick thin pig which was too sick to travel fast enough to get out of our way. When killed, it was found that it had intestinal and generalised tuberculosis; we ate it just the same, or at least we only got the forequarters, head and intestines, which were most acceptable. We also ate grasshoppers and large white wood grubs, these two being delicacies.

A handful of Australians managed to slip away from the march unde-
tected, but nothing more was ever heard of them.

The further the marchers went the clearer it became that many of their
comrades had died on the first march. 'Gruesome relics of the previous
death march became more evident, bleached skeletons and decom-
posed bodies were often seen, and many spots on the track exuded the
stench of death,' Major Jackson wrote in his report. As well as skeletons,
the marchers noticed equipment and personal items belonging to their
mates: pieces of footwear, tins used for cooking rice, rotted webbing
belts, paybooks and 'photographs with image removed by the elements'.
Sticpewich told Justice Mansfield that he also saw 'havasacks and packs'
on the side of the track. The Japanese 'did not take the Australian havasacks because they said they were too heavy'.

Owen Campbell had always seen the march as an opportunity for
escape—perhaps the only opportunity he would get. Warned by a guard
that when the walk was finished they would all be killed, Campbell realised
it was now or never. On 7 June the column came under attack from three
Allied aircraft whose pilots had mistaken the marchers for retreating
Japanese soldiers. As prisoners and guards ran for cover, Campbell and
four other prisoners made their break. At a bend in the track out of sight
of the guards posted behind and in front of the group they slid around
60 metres down a muddy bank. Guards often forced prisoners to carry
their packs, and before disappearing into the jungle Campbell and his
mates were able to load up with dried fish and a slab of soya bean powder
along with six tins of salmon and 3 kilograms of rice. Their own equipment included fishing lines and a compass. Knowing that 'the Yanks were
out there somewhere, and the guerrillas were out there somewhere', they
headed for the coast.

Other prisoners, fearing that it could soon be their turn to drop out,
were also thinking of escape as their only hope of survival. Nelson Short
discussed it with a few mates but most of the men, including him, knew

they were in such poor condition they would never make it. Sticpewich was in much better shape than most but was not yet ready to try his luck in the jungle. The day after Campbell's escape an incident occurred that demonstrated Sticpewich's personal courage.

Numerous rivers and creeks lay between Sandakan and Ranau, some of which could only be crossed by means of a single log. At one of these crossings a prisoner slipped on the log, lost his nerve and was unable to move. With the column at a standstill and nobody able to pass, a Japanese civilian from a camp on the opposite bank took a pistol and was preparing to shoot the man when Sticpewich, who had already got across, went back and fetched both the man and his gear. No sooner had he carried the man to the bank than the Japanese civilian 'took his gear and blankets and left him with nothing except what he stood up in'. The frightened man eventually reached Ranau, where he died.*

Although hardly able to walk, Dick Braithwaite was the next to go, two days after Campbell's group. Braithwaite had sold his watch for 30 quinine tablets but the tablets were finished and he was wracked with malaria; a couple of mates had to hold him during the roll call. Among the Japanese who were struggling to continue the march was Hoshijima's elderly interpreter Osawa. Braithwaite noticed him 'walking round in circles' as the rest of the group moved off. Half a dozen prisoners remained behind, unable to go on. Braithwaite had not gone very far when he heard shots, so he knew that if he did not make his move soon it would be too late.

---

* There are other documented examples of Sticpewich's courage, one of which Kevin Smith cites in his book, *Borneo*. After a fellow prisoner accidentally dropped a bucket down a well Sticpewich climbed down 6 metres to retrieve it. According to Smith, 'Loss of the bucket could well have led to punishment for that prisoner.' The source of the anecdote was Lieutenant Hugh Waring, who was later transferred with other officers from Sandakan to Kuching. Like the log incident, it is hard to think of this as other than a courageous act on behalf of a fellow prisoner.

A little further on the track passed through a gully blocked by fallen trees. While making a detour around the trees the column began to string out, putting some men out of sight of the guards. Braithwaite seized his chance and took off, but he did not get far as another huge fallen tree blocked his path. Too weak to get over or around it, he lay down in front of the tree and tried not to make a sound as giant ants almost 4 centimetres long crawled over his body.

Braithwaite's malarial cough eventually attracted the attention of a guard, who looked at him and unslung his rifle but moved on without giving him away. Hours later, as he came round a bend, Braithwaite came face to face with another Japanese soldier. 'He must have been pretty sick too,' Braithwaite told Bowden, 'because he was just hobbling, getting along, he didn't have a rifle or a bayonet or anything and . . . we more or less ran into each other on the track.' Braithwaite was the first to react, grabbing a branch and beating the Japanese repeatedly over the head until he was dead, then dragging his body off the track and covering it with leaf litter.

This was not quite the story Braithwaite had told the war crimes commission four decades earlier. Suddenly remembering an incident he 'had not mentioned before', Braithwaite told the commission that he had 'struck a Jap' while retracing his steps after escaping from the march. 'I wanted a rifle and some food. I stalked him and killed him with the branch of a tree.'

In *Six from Borneo*, an ABC radio documentary produced two years after the war ended, Braithwaite recalled the rage he felt as he battered the sick Japanese soldier: 'I don't think he ever knew what hit him . . . I seemed to go berserk then. I hit him and hit him and smashed him as he lay dead. I was crying, and saying as I did it, "That's for Cec! That's for Reg! That's for murdering my mates!" . . . I dragged him into the jungle. I searched his pack for food, but he had none.'

More and more prisoners died as the rest of the column struggled over the mountains beyond Boto, and those who could not keep up were ordered by the Japanese to fall out. 'In the morning,' Short told Justice Mansfield, 'when the men were too weak to stand, we used to shake hands with them and say goodbye as they more or less knew what was going to happen.' When a prisoner dropped out the guards took the rice he was carrying, so when the Australian men woke up to this they gave the rice to their mates.

Padre Thompson, who was suffering from a big ulcer under his foot, was, as Sticpewich put it, 'fairly well done-up and in poor shape' when a guard picked him out of the line and told him he could not go any further. Sticpewich never saw the padre again.

When the column reached Ranau on 26 June only 142 Australians and 41 English prisoners were left of the nearly 540 men who had set out from 8 Mile Camp on the evening of 29 May. The great majority were in terrible condition, but not all: most of the officers and the members of Sticpewich's technical party—especially their leader—had come through in reasonable shape. Keith Botterill, lean as a whippet after his rice-carrying trips to Paginatan, described Captain Cook to Silver as being 'as fat as a pig'.

Cook was informed that five Australians and one British prisoner would be added to their number. These six, including Botterill, were survivors from the group of ten that had moved from Jungle Camp No. 1 two weeks earlier. That evening as Sticpewich was cooking he spotted the six prisoners Cook had been told about. Sticpewich recognised them as having been on the first march that set off from Sandakan at the end of January.

The Japanese prevented any contact between the six prisoners and the new arrivals, and it was a day or two before Sticpewich found the opportunity to speak to two of them: Sapper Bird and Sergeant Stacy. They told him that 350 men had survived the march from Sandakan to Ranau but that 'all the others had died from malnutrition and from exhaustion brought on by the rice-carrying from Ranau to Paginatan'.

Chapter 24

SHOOT ON SIGHT

———◦———

Jungle Camp No. 2 consisted of three huts the Japanese had built for themselves in the creek bed under cover of the jungle. Sticpewich concluded they were hiding in anticipation of an invasion by Allied forces. As he told Captain Ruse:

> We were camped in a valley up above the Jap quarters in an area about 50 yards square. The . . . prisoners were all kept in this square and no buildings or tents were available for us and there was no provision for cooking. The only protection we had was to crawl under the scrub. There were no sanitary arrangements made. We were in this square for three days, during which the sickness rate increased and there were about 19 died in this three days. There were no medical supplies given to us and no medical treatment afforded to us at all . . . Our food ration consisted of about 70 to 75 grams of rice per man per day.

The prisoners were kept in this area under guard for three weeks. 'No one can imagine the filth and the death rate that occurred during the 21 days spent in this cess pool,' Sticpewich wrote in his 'War crimes and events' statement. 'Mud was ankle deep, sick men were lying about unable to move, in their own filth.'

Soon after reaching Ranau Sticpewich received a message from a Formosan guard named Takahara, who had been transferred from 8 Mile Camp in June 1944 'under suspicion of being too easy' with prisoners. 'This Jap guard while at Sandakan had been friendly towards us and treated us very decently,' Sticpewich told Ruse. 'He supplied us with medical stores which he had stolen for us, also food and he carried notes and communications for us to the native contacts we had. He was a Christian.'

In his message to Sticpewich, Takahara warned his friend not to try to communicate with him as it was 'dangerous'. Takahara continued, however, to do what he could for the prisoners, slipping bottles of quinine or Atebrin into Sticpewich's hand as they passed or gesturing to where he had hidden some bananas.

The new arrivals were soon put to work fetching wood, water and vegetables and cutting bamboo to build more huts. Sticpewich, a capable carpenter among his many other accomplishments, was immediately put in charge of hut construction.

Water had to be collected in a bucket from a creek in which the Japanese bathed and washed their clothes and urinated upstream. 'They had to carry water from the creek a distance of about a quarter of a mile up a steep incline on which you could scarcely stand,' Sticpewich told Ruse.

The average was about 130 buckets of water a day for the Jap officers . . . One man had to do this on his own. The other five men were on the Jap guards' kitchen chopping wood, peeling vegetables and carrying water and all had to do washing of the Japs' clothes too. As the men carrying the water to the Jap officers got too sick to work they were fallen out and another man took his place. Every man who was on the job of carrying water to the officers' mess, with the exception of one, died within about three to four days after knocking off the job. About 18 or 19 passed through that job and all but one died.

Short recalled being sent to fetch water by Lieutenant Suzuki: 'When I got back the bucket had about a couple of inches of water in it as I was that weak, I couldn't carry it. And he rushed at me with the butt of a rifle, and he . . . opened it up right across the eye . . . He didn't do any more, if he would have hit me . . . he would have killed me stone dead. But it was just a glancing blow.'

Cook was the fittest of the five surviving officers. As Jackson diplomatically put it, 'the camp master was endeavouring to conserve his strength as he wanted to keep himself alive for the purpose of retaining the camp records that he had painstakingly kept' since his arrival at Sandakan in June 1942. In order to 'conserve his strength', Cook had relinquished everyday command to Sticpewich, an arrangement that once again enabled Sticpewich to avoid the heaviest work. As Sticpewich wrote:

All were worn out except a few, who were as follows: the two Doctors who had a full time job with the sick; others who lay down and pretended, and W.O. Sticpewich who was very much worn but carried out grave digging and administration of PWs affairs for Capt Cook who was one of the ones in reserve and avoiding the Jap. W.O. Sticpewich carried out duty of OC from the 11th July.

As well as overseeing construction of the hut, Sticpewich controlled the distribution of food. Jackson reported him to be 'probably the fittest PW in the camp throughout his internment' and quoted Sticpewich's own description of himself as 'really never starving'. On the three occasions when the POWs were given meat at Ranau it was Sticpewich who organised the slaughtering, although the only parts of the cattle given to the prisoners were the stomach and intestines and sometimes 'a portion of the lung'.

Sticpewich's ability to ingratiate himself with the Japanese brought the same life-saving benefits at Ranau as it had at Sandakan: information, better rations and less physical labour. While escorting the cattle-killing party a Formosan guard grumbled to Sticpewich about being bashed by Takakuwa and Suzuki for having a dirty rifle. Sticpewich told him that such a thing would never happen in the Australian army and that even Japanese POWs were well treated in Australia. The guard said he knew that already from having read the letters of a friend whose father was a POW in Australia.

In his 'War crimes and events' statement Sticpewich wrote that the guard 'was sorry for what he had done as he wanted to be our friend; that the Japs over him were no good and they would kill us all eventually'. The guard then said that when the Allies won the war the Japanese could not be taken prisoner 'as it was a disgrace', so he would kill himself. He also claimed to have seen Takakuwa's orders that all prisoners were to be shot. Sensing an opportunity, Sticpewich told the guard that 'if we were in the same position and were going to die or be killed, we would shoot the one we disliked'. Before the cattle-killing party returned to Ranau the guard told Sticpewich 'Tomorrow I die', and vowed to kill Takakuwa and all the other officers 'as they had treated him badly and also killed Australians'.

The following evening, 2 July 1945, the guard walked into the officers' hut and shot Suzuki dead, also injuring Takakuwa and Sergeant Fujita. Captain Cook was slightly wounded. The guard then shot himself through the head. '[He] would have killed many more Japanese if he had remembered to pull the pin out of the grenade that he threw into their quarters', Jackson wrote scornfully.

Berated by their superiors over the incident, the Formosan guards responded in familiar fashion by attacking the POWs. Prisoners were bashed for leaving the camp to get water or defecate or for being too slow to bury their dead. They were so weak that even carrying the corpses was an impossibility, so a piece of rattan was tied around the arms of the man who had died and it took five prisoners to drag the corpse to a shallow grave that had taken four men as much as four hours to dig. Sticpewich claimed to have seen as many as eight bodies put in a single hole. 'The Jap guards would stand over the grave-digging party and persistently harass and beat them,' he wrote.

Five days after the killing of Lieutenant Suzuki, Botterill and Moxham made their break. 'We wanted to get away before we became too weak,' Botterill told the war crimes commission. 'We did not discuss our escape with Capt. Cook because we were afraid he may report us, but we asked a lot of men to come with us. However, they were either too weak or too frightened to come after seeing the treatment that had been meted out to Crease and Cleary.'

Eventually they found two men to go with them: Nelson Short and Gunner Andy Anderson. Before leaving they shook hands and said goodbye to the two doctors, Captains Picone and Oakeshott, and Moxham helped himself to Oakeshott's boots. After all the horrors they had witnessed, an act of bestiality on the eve of their escape convinced Botterill and Moxham that the Japanese were determined to kill every last one of them.

The victim was Sapper Arthur Bird, who was suffering from terrible tropical ulcers. When Bird was assigned to the hut-building team Sticpewich immediately protested to Fukushima, the Formosan guard known to the Australians as the 'Black Bastard'. In his own words Sticpewich 'wanted another man but I didn't want Bird and he couldn't do the job as it was no use having him climbing around the building as he was not fit to work'. Sticpewich claimed to have been 'smacked over the ear' for his insolence. Bird was then assigned to another party, although Sticpewich considered him to be 'very sick [and] . . . very cramped up due to exposure and he had ulcers on his leg . . . [he] could hardly walk'. When Bird sat down to rest, the Black Bastard flew into a rage and started bashing and kicking him. All the working parties were then sent off.

Sticpewich saw Bird that evening with blood in his ear and 'marked considerably about the face'. Doctor Picone apparently decided there was nothing he could do for him. At the next day's 6.30 am roll call and sick parade, Bird was listed among the dead.

The Black Bastard's attack on Sapper Bird convinced Botterill and Moxham that their time at Ranau was up. It was 'die in the camp or die in the jungle', Botterill told Tim Bowden. With Short and Anderson, they slipped away that night.

'We went about nine o'clock . . . we had [someone] watching the guard, and he said, "He hasn't moved". They used to do a four-hour shift. [He said,] "He hasn't moved, he's sitting under that tree and he hasn't moved for an hour." So we just walked straight past him, up onto the track and then headed off.'

Sticpewich, not yet ready to go, decided to bide his time.

In fury over the escape of four prisoners the Japanese cancelled the vegetable ration, leaving the remaining POWs to survive on nothing but their daily 70 grams of rice, and even that was reduced on 15 July. Despite this men were still sent out on work parties but few were capable of any kind of physical labour. Sticpewich, however, continued with the construction of the prisoners' hut, which was finally completed on 18 July.

The new hut, which comprised a floor with an atap roof, needed to accommodate only 72 prisoners, the rest having died during the three weeks it had taken to build it. Just five officers remained alive. The men with dysentery—nearly half the total—slept under the floor in an effort to protect those who did not have the disease.

By 28 July 119 Australians and 14 English prisoners had died at

Ranau, a fact Sticpewich attributed after the war to 'sheer exhaustion from the conditions of the working parties, malnutrition, exposure, starvation on ridiculously small rations and also the filthy conditions under which we had to live'. The Japanese made sure that each death was attributed to natural causes.

The guards were now, in Jackson's words, 'vy[ing] with each other for the privilege of ransacking the gear of the sick PW'. When 48-year-old Sergeant Robert Horder, an ambulanceman, caught Suzuki Saburō and another guard trying to steal his watch and ring he loudly denounced them as 'thieves and mongrels'. Horder was 'immediately belted down by the two of them and kicked into insensibility while he was on the ground and finished up unconscious', Sticpewich wrote. The pair bashed him 'solidly for about ten minutes. Up till then S/Sgt Horder had been in fair condition . . . he never regained consciousness and he died during the night'.

In the days leading up to Sticpewich's escape, a Japanese medical orderly told him he had instructions to 'obtain from me or the doctors a hypodermic syringe (nothing smaller than 10cc)'. Sticpewich put him off with the lie that he had no syringes. 'I had heard of syringes being used by the Japanese previously to inject petrol into the PWs to cause immediate death,' he told his interrogators at Morotai. 'I heard some Japanese guards and a medical orderly talking about gasoline and syringes.'

The same medical orderly told Sticpewich that he had seen an order from Captain Takakuwa 'to the effect that we were all to be killed'. At Sandakan he had been told the same thing by a guard named Yoshikoa: 'He made a joke of it and said it would be good.' Finally, at around 9 pm on the night of 27 July, Sticpewich's faithful friend Takahara told him to 'leave camp immediately and go to the jungle . . . as everyone "was going to be dead"'.

Sticpewich made up his mind to go but believed his chances would be better with a companion. He hoped to persuade Captain Picone to escape with him but Picone was determined to stay with the men. Oakeshott, who had a large ulcer on his foot and (thanks to Moxham) no boots, also turned him down, insisting that he would be 'too much of an encumbrance'. Cook, Sticpewich concluded, was 'too sick to make the attempt'. Of the remaining men, Driver Herman 'Algie' Reither 'was sick but was willing to have a shot'. The other personnel, he wrote, were 'all too sick or incompetent'.

The next day there was no one apart from Sticpewich fit enough to bury the dead, but he feigned sickness all day so he could rest up for his escape. At night he cooked and served the meal as usual and at about half past nine he and Reither sneaked out of the camp. The guard had been doubled since the move to the new hut, which had no sides and thus enabled those in the guardhouse to keep an eye on the prisoners, but Sticpewich and Reither got away without being seen.

Knowing that the Japanese would immediately start searching the nearby country, Sticpewich decided that he and Reither would be safer staying close to the camp. From their hiding place in the jungle, just up the track and within sight of the guardhouse, the two Australians were able to observe the confusion inside the camp and watch the guards being slapped and king hit as punishment for their escape. They saw a search party set out in the morning and return at about five o'clock in the evening. At dusk Sticpewich and Reither emerged from their refuge and started walking along the road to Ranau.

On the night the pair escaped there were 32 men still alive at Jungle Camp No. 2. Sticpewich knew 'for certain' that at least eight very sick prisoners would die that night—six of the eight were already unconscious.

At Morotai Sticpewich supplied a list of the remaining 24 Australian prisoners, including Captains Cook, Picone and Oakeshott, whose chances of surviving from 28 July 1945 to 'the present time' (8–12 October) he rated as 'nil'. He based this opinion not just on their 'extremely low' medical condition but also on his absolute conviction that the Japanese intended to kill all surviving POWs.

Sticpewich was not present to see his grim prophecy come true, so the evidence about what happened to the remaining prisoners had to come from the Japanese. At Labuan the officers and guards were interrogated about the murder of the last prisoners at Ranau. Their signed statements, annotated by Sticpewich, described massacres that allegedly took place near Ranau on 1 August 1945.

At 8 am Captain Takakuwa summoned his officers and NCOs and told them, in the words of Sergeant Major Beppu, that 'owing to certain regrettable incidents of PW escaping during the last fortnight . . . it was necessary for the rest of them to be disposed of'. After considering the 'problem' of their disposal, Takakuwa announced his solution: the 32 remaining prisoners were to be executed in three groups: those too sick to walk, the five officers and the rest. Of these, the sick were to be got rid of at once. Takakuwa then handed each NCO a list of names.

Three hours later Sergeant Okada took nine Formosan guards to the POWs' hut and picked out the 17 prisoners on his list. As Okada said in his statement:

> One or two of the 17 PWs walked up to the cemetery. The remainder were carried up on stretchers. The Formosans . . . carried the PWs on the stretchers. As I had no interpreter with me the PWs were not told what was going to happen to them, but they probably realised their fate when they got to the cemetery. The PWs were put on the ground, the guards lined up and I ordered them to open fire. The Formosans did not want to shoot and neither did I, but I had my orders and so had to fire first to set an example to them. We then kept firing until they were all dead. After the death of the prisoners Yoshikawa . . . brought up spades and shovels for us to dig the graves.

Sergeant Major Beppu went with eight guards to fetch the five Allied officers and told the prisoners they were being taken for questioning by the Kempei-Tai at Ranau. At his trial Beppu claimed to have felt 'feverish' and to have 'rested in the shade of a tree' while the guards led the prisoners to a spot chosen by Takakuwa on the right-hand side of the road to Ranau, near the 111-mile peg. After he had 'rested about 20 or 30 minutes', Beppu heard shooting. He went to the killing site and found all five officers dead. Their hands, he said, were not bound nor were they blindfolded, and he had not heard any screams. Two guards, Suzuki and Nakayama, arrived about 25 minutes later carrying shovels to dig the graves. 'We thought it strange to have to take shovels but asked no questions,' Nakayama said. After returning to camp after the killings, Beppu felt so ill that he 'went straight to bed and did not speak to the others'.

Sergeant Major Tsuji led the final killing party. The prisoners in his group were taken 'about half a mile along the Tambunan Road' and given tobacco and tea before Tsuji announced they were all to be killed. Matsuba Shokichi remembered them 'just sitting about in a rough circle. None made any attempt to escape.' Some of the guards claimed not to have shot any prisoners. Matsuba said he 'refused [to shoot] and was scolded by Tsuji so I then fired but missed. Tsuji took the rifle and killed the PW himself. They then dug a hole and buried the lot.'

Before shooting the eighth prisoner Takeuchi Yoshimitsu asked whether he had anything to say. 'He said "yes, shoot me in the forehead" and this I did.' Others admitted killing under duress. Takata Kunio told interrogators that any guards who refused to carry out the order to kill the POWs 'were threatened that their families and themselves would be killed if they refused to obey'. Nishikawa Moriji said:

We took the PW along the Tambunan Road about 400 yds [365 metres]. There Tsuji ordered us to kill the PW but I said I did not want to do so. He said we are sons of the Emperor and must do so. I then took one PW to Tsuji who had gone about 30 to 35 yds [27–32 metres] away; I was again ordered to shoot. I could do nothing about it so fired and killed the PW . . . I was the first to kill a PW and Goto . . . was coming up with the next PW when I was going back. On return to camp the whole party was lined up and reprimanded by Takakuwa for not carrying out our orders smoothly.

Like some other guards involved in murdering POWs at Ranau and Sandakan, Nishikawa had previously tried to behave decently towards the prisoners. A comment by Sticpewich at the bottom of Nishikawa's interrogation statement described him as 'Very easy going type; dodged as much of the bashing as he could; was an ordinary guard; did not ill treat unless forced to'.

The officers and guards accused of having taken part in the killings all asserted that the prisoners were shot on 1 August 1945, three days after Sticpewich's escape. Ishii Fujio, who was part of a search party sent by Takakuwa to hunt him down, named four other guards who were away from the camp searching for Sticpewich when the last 32 prisoners were murdered. 'Sgt Iwabe was with us the whole time and did not return to camp,' Ishii said in his statement. 'He could not have been present at the killings. When I returned to camp about 2 August all the PWs were dead.'*

---

* While the court accepted 1 August as the date on which the last prisoners at Ranau were massacred, local sources suggest this date is false. Sticpewich told Captain Ruse that on 2 August 'after a lot of adventures I had contacted a campong chief . . . and at my instigation [he] sent a coolie with vegetables into the Jap camp to find out how many [prisoners] were still there. The coolie came back and reported that there were still 20 to 21 alive in the hut'. During August there were several sightings by villagers of POWs dressed in rags and slouch hats. Edmuno Jaimi, from Ranau, claimed to have seen ten prisoners, thin and dressed in rags, near the 112-mile peg on 27 August, nearly two weeks after Emperor Hirohito announced Japan's capitulation and five days after surrender

Iwabe's group was not the only one sent to hunt for Sticpewich: Sergeant Major Beppu led a second search party. Beppu was interrogated by Australian war crimes investigators on 25 November and a week later gave another statement in which he admitted that 'portions' of the original statement were 'not correct' and promised to tell the 'true story': 'When S/M Sticpewich escaped I was sent out with a party to look for him and after spending six days in fruitless search returned to No. 2 jungle camp on the night of the 31st July 1945. The following day, 1st August, 1945, I was suffering with a bad attack of malaria and wished to spend the day in bed.'

At about 0800 hours, according to Beppu's revised statement, Takakuwa instructed all NCOs and officers to assemble in his quarters. Although ill, Beppu was 'forced to attend' the meeting, at which Takakuwa allegedly gave orders for all the remaining POWs at Ranau to be killed that day.*

-----

leaflets had been dropped in the area. There were no sightings after 27 August. A Formosan guard, Toyonaga Shigemori, told interrogators, 'I remember the time WO Sticpewich escaped from No. 2 Camp. It was about 10 days after this that the balance of these PWs were killed'. This suggests the last prisoners were killed around 7 August. It is hard to agree with Michele Cunningham's contention that 'there is little reason to doubt the Japanese testimony that they killed the men on 1 August'. The Japanese must have known that Australian outrage over the massacre of POWs would be even greater if it became known that the prisoners were executed after the war had ended. Court transcripts show that the guards lied about many things, and they had good reason to lie about the date of the Ranau killings.

* Beppu's contradictory evidence illustrates the unreliability of Japanese witness statements about the Ranau massacres. His revised statement described how a party under his command murdered the five remaining officers while he slept under a tree due to feeling 'ill and feverish'. His dates, however, rule out 1 August as the date of the massacres. If Beppu spent 'six days in fruitless search' for Sticpewich he could not have returned to camp earlier than 3 August and could not have been party to any massacre of POWs on 1 August. By numerous Japanese accounts, however, including his own, Beppu was present at the murders even if, as he told his interrogators, he 'did not kill any'.

The Japanese, only too aware of how much Sticpewich knew about their terrible crimes, had spared no effort to find him. 'When S/M Sticpewich escaped,' Captain Watanabe told his interrogators, 'the orders were to recapture him and find out the plans made by others to escape.' Ishii Fujio gave a different account: 'Our orders,' he said, 'were to shoot S/M Sticpewich on sight.'

Chapter 25

WITH TEARS I SHOT

———⟫•⟪———

Three days after the 'fit' prisoners left Sandakan on the second death march on 29 May 1945, Takakuwa sent orders that the remaining 275 prisoners—the sick and dying who were left without shelter when the camp was burnt—were either to be sent to Ranau or otherwise disposed of. Moritake picked out 75 prisoners to walk to Ranau, escorted by two Formosan guards and 55 soldiers also in a poor state. Only four of the marchers got as far as the 40-mile peg; none reached Ranau. According to Major Jackson, the sole survivor of the march, a Formosan guard, was alive when the war ended but died before he could be interrogated.

Of those too sick to attempt the third march, Jackson estimated that only 53 were alive by the middle of July. Lieutenant Moritake was seriously ill with malaria and Sergeant Major Murozumi was giving most of the orders—the same Murozumi who, according to Sticpewich, used to ride around on a pushbike flogging prisoners who were not working hard enough, and the same Murozumi who, when Hoshijima was commandant, used to delight in removing prisoners from the cage in order to give them a special beating, which he then ordered the guards to continue, and who thrashed Sticpewich himself on two occasions, 'once with his hands and once with a stick'. If the last few survivors at Sandakan hoped for any mercy they would not get it from a man like Murozumi.

On the morning of 13 July Moritake and Murozumi went together to the aerodrome to select a suitable killing site. That afternoon Murozumi returned to the site with twelve guards and 23 prisoners. The prisoners were separated into two groups and ordered to stand at either end of a 10-metre fortification trench that had been dug as protection against Allied air raids. One of the guards, Goto Yoshitaro, described what happened next: 'The firing party kept firing till there were no more signs of life. Then we dragged the bodies into a nearby air-raid shelter and filled it in.'

Another guard, Nagata Shinichi, claimed that 'the PWs that were killed were treated nicely and when they were killed wreaths were placed on their graves . . . it was impossible to put individual crosses up so we put one cross up for the whole.' Yanagawa Hideo told his interrogators that 'when I had to shoot the PWs I prayed to God to forgive me for killing a PW and with tears I shot; I prayed for the peace of their souls'. Murozumi did not kill any prisoners himself but stood 'three paces in our rear' with his pistol drawn, giving orders to shoot. He made sure the paperwork showed that all 23 died of natural causes.

Lieutenant Moritake died four days later. 'He was worn out on his return from Malarang,' said a Formosan guard. 'He was a sick man when he gave the orders. Murozumi was quite well.'

Fewer than 20 prisoners were still left alive. 'They were very sick,' Yanagawa recalled, 'and did not have much appetite.' They were not taken and shot, Murozumi said, 'because we knew they would die in any case, in the near future'. Another guard said Murozumi hastened their deaths by giving away all the prisoners' rice and salt 'to his Chinese and Malay molls'. Goto stated that

> all the PWs who were left were too sick to care for themselves. For food we gave these PWs some kane kong [water spinach], tapioca, coconut oil . . . We did not cook for the PWs at this stage; those who were able to crawl about were caring for the others. These PWs eventually died from lack of care and starvation, being too weak to eat . . . From 13 July to 13 August 30-odd PWs died from malnutrition and lack of medical attention.

Murozumi admitted that the prisoners he had not bothered to shoot 'were given practically nothing to eat. As they died, their bodies were thrown into slit trenches by Javanese coolies and buried. The largest number buried by the Javanese coolies in any one day was seven or eight, but over the whole period they would have buried about 150 PWs. Myself and the Formosans assisted the Javanese coolies to bury the bodies.'

On the morning of 15 August 1945 a solitary prisoner was left alive of the nearly 2500 who had been sent to Sandakan: the Australian Private John Skinner from Tenterfield in New South Wales. According to a statement made in 1947 by Wong Hiong, a young Chinese man who worked at the Japanese barracks, Skinner was dragged to the edge of a slit trench, blindfolded and then decapitated by Murozumi with a single stroke of his sword. At noon on the same day Japanese radio broadcast the voice of Emperor Hirohito proclaiming his country's surrender.

Murozumi was never charged with killing John Skinner but he and ten guards were tried at Labuan in January 1946 for murdering the 23 prisoners on 13 July 1945. Murozumi was convicted and sentenced to life imprisonment. Three guards were found not guilty, while the others were sentenced to between twelve and fifteen years.

Toyoda Kokichi admitted shooting the prisoners and was sentenced to twelve years. In his comments on Toyoda's interrogation statement Sticpewich described him as being 'always good to the PW giving them food etc. He was easy to get on with and was spoken well of by all PW.' Botterill thought the same, and after seeing him in the Japanese prisoners' compound at Rabaul in May 1946 he asked for Toyoda's sentence to be reviewed. After Botterill spoke up for him, Toyoda's sentence for taking part in the Sandakan killings was commuted to two years.

Chapter 26

IT'S AN AUSSIE

—————

Dick Braithwaite was the first of the escaped Sandakan POWs to reach safety. After killing the Japanese soldier he made his way along the bank of the river, surviving on raw shellfish but too weak to travel more than a couple of kilometres a day. At one point he almost ran into a six-man Japanese patrol, spotting it just in time to hide. 'I could have reached out and touched them,' he told Bowden. Having 'no experience . . . at all' of surviving in the jungle, he did not know what was safe to eat. Some dark berries—'a bit like Brazilian cherries'—upset his guts so much that he was convinced he had blackwater fever.

After walking for days Braithwaite stumbled into a swamp, the vegetation of which was so dense that he lost all sense of direction. 'I just sat down on a log . . . thinking, well, this is where it happens, mate, you're finished,' he told Tim Bowden. 'And then after about half an hour just sitting, thinking about things, all of a sudden I thought no, you're not finished, you're not going to die in a place like this, and I became really angry and I just put my head down like a bull and charged that jungle and . . . it just seemed to part.'

Braithwaite found his way back to the river but was too frail to build himself a raft. He saw an elderly man paddling upstream in a canoe and called to him in Malay. Eventually the old man paddled over, then he took Braithwaite back to his village where his family fed and looked after him, keeping him hidden behind a false wall that concealed their store of rice. It was a dangerous place, however, with a Japanese camp just a few kilometres away.

While he was there news reached the village that the Americans were near Sandakan. It was not only Braithwaite who was eager to make contact with the Americans; the village had been strafed by US fighter aircraft and the village elders wanted this to stop. Using two boats—one a decoy in case they ran into a Japanese patrol—eight Malay men paddled all night and the next day to the mouth of the river before heading out the following morning to Libaran Island, just off the coast. Braithwaite said:

> They put me in . . . the headman's bed, he had a beautiful innerspring mattress. I had dysentery pretty badly and a touch of malaria and I think the sandflies were the worst I've ever struck in my life . . . the next day we saw this PT boat come through, and we hopped out into the small boat and paddled out with a white flag and we get up along-side . . . they thought that I was a Jap that the natives had captured, and we get up alongside, we see this giant hanging over the side, he said, 'Good Christ, it's an Aussie.'

Braithwaite was the first Allied prisoner to be recovered since the rescue of American POWs in the Philippines. The second to be recovered was Owen Campbell, who had escaped with four companions on 7 June 1945, two days before Braithwaite.

Soon after making his break Campbell had fallen ill with malaria, forcing the group to rest until the attack passed. The jungle was heavy going; there were places where they could barely crawl through the vegetation on hands and knees. After Private Ted Skinner, John's older brother, came down with dysentery the four decided to split up. 'I said I'd stay with [Skinner] and the others said they'd go on,' Campbell recalled later. 'And they'd leave marks [on] the way . . . so I'd know where they'd gone. [Skinner] had berri berri and dysentery. Very religious chap he was. He had a bible and he used to read it all the time. And that's when he sent me down the river and he did the deed on himself while I was away . . . He cut his throat. When I come back I found him dead so all I could do was bury him and move on.'

Two days later Campbell caught up with the others, but one was ill with dysentery and malaria so they decided to seek help from the first Malay they met. Two of the group, Privates Sid Webber and Ted Emmett, called out to a passing boat and were immediately shot dead by a Japanese soldier with a machine gun who had been hiding beneath an awning. Campbell was out of sight and the boat passed by without stopping. The sick man died a few days later, leaving Campbell to press on alone. 'The only thing I was frightened of was crocs,' he told Tim Bowden, 'because those rivers were lousy with them. Crocs and hippos.' While swimming across a river he was fired upon by a Japanese soldier, escaping with a wounded arm.

On the eleventh day, exhausted and often delirious from malaria, Campbell stumbled across some Malays checking their fish traps. They took him away in their boat and kept him hidden from the Japanese. After the Kempei-Tai searched the village Campbell had to move, and finally his rescuers delivered him by canoe to an SRD intelligence party camped near the Bongaya River. 'Oh they were cunning,' he said of the villagers who paddled him down the river. 'They had an Australian flag on a pole and they had a Japanese flag. So if an Australian or American airplane came over they put up the Australian flag. If a Jap plane came over they'd put up the Jap flag.' A few days later Campbell, delirious and bloated with beriberi, was evacuated by sea plane to a US naval ship anchored off Tawi-Tawi.

Keith Botterill, Bill Moxham and Nelson Short were still at large as Campbell slowly regained his health. Along with Gunner Andy Anderson they had escaped from Ranau on 7 July 1945, ten days before Sticpewich finished building his hut. They had only a week's worth of rice, stolen from an unlocked Japanese rice dump they had discovered outside the camp. A guard had forced Moxham to hand over a thick jacket with a map stitched into the lining, but they still carried a few items that improved their chances of success: a billy can, a jackknife, some donated articles of clothing and a spectacle lens that would work as a magnifying glass.

After creeping out of the camp at about 9 pm, the four walked all night, halting only when it became light. They spent the next six days hiding in a cave before striking out on the 100-kilometre trek to Jesselton. While scrambling up a mountain Short, who was in charge of the billy can, slipped off the track and tumbled down the mountainside into a gully. A small sleeping mat that had been strapped to his back, his only possession other than a pair of shorts sewn together out of an old kitbag, broke his fall. Short recalled his three worried companions staring down at him and asking, 'How's the billy can?'

Twice they ran into lone Japanese soldiers. The first time they managed to flee from a soldier who approached and asked for a match. They were sheltering in a hut around 8 kilometres from Ranau when a second Japanese soldier came scrounging for food. 'When he came down to the hut and saw us, his eyes nearly popped out of his head,' Moxham told Justice Mansfield. 'We wanted to get him away before he made any noise.'

Told by the unarmed soldier that four prisoners had escaped from Ranau, Short feigned surprise and replied that he and his friends were sick with malaria and that their guard had gone to fetch some medicine.

Moxham, the whites of his eyes yellow from jaundice, and Anderson, hollowed out by dysentery, both looked desperately ill. As a last resort Moxham was ready to use the jackknife while Short and Botterill kept the soldier talking, but before that became necessary the Japanese heard aircraft approaching and took off into the jungle. 'He said he would come back at 6 o'clock with quinine for us. However, we carried Anderson and scrambled off into the scrub.'

The owner of the hut, a village headman named Baragah, had been bringing them food but it was barely enough to keep them alive. 'Although [Baragah] was feeding us, he was only feeding us on tapioca root, sweet potatoes and bananas, which was really killing us with beri-beri,' Botterill told Tim Bowden. 'We'd get an occasional egg off him and a small portion of meat, but it was not enough to . . . sustain us.'

After their narrow escape from the second Japanese soldier Baragah built the fugitives a new hut in a clearing deep in the jungle in which they would be safe 'until the English came'. The Kempei-Tai were now on their trail and were offering bags of rice and salt to anyone who would hand them over. 'We were in a pretty bad way then, all of us,' Moxham recalled, 'and decided to trust this native—whether he proved trustworthy or not had to take care of itself.'

Rescue came too late for Anderson, who died on 29 July; the remaining three were very weak. 'We were sick, we were filthy, we were almost down to the level of animals, and we hated the sight of each other,' Keith Botterill told the makers of the documentary *Six from Borneo*. 'But if we got an egg we'd cut it into three even parts. We'd watch each other like cats all the time to see that we got equal shares of everything. I spent my twenty-first birthday living like that.'

For nearly three weeks they stayed where they were, and by the middle of August an SRD party was not far away. 'One day [Baragah] said some English were about 30 miles away,' Moxham said. 'We could not believe that. However, we wrote a note and I put down our names and numbers etc, and the native set off with the note. He came back the next night with some medical supplies and food, and a note from an Australian, F/Lieut Ripley. The "English" were Australians, of course.'

The process had not been as straightforward as Moxham implied in the account he gave Justice Mansfield. Heavy rain prevented Baragah from delivering the first note and 24 hours later Moxham was asked to write another, which Short and Botterill both signed. The note finished: 'Three of us are camped here in the jungle, we escaped from camp as would only have died there on one meal a day. Baragah picked us up a few days out and has looked after us ever since. Could give you a lot of information but will wait until I hear from you. We are in a very weak condition but OK.'

In truth they were far from okay. 'We were all swollen up with beriberi,' Moxham told Justice Mansfield. 'Botterill was pretty badly swollen—you couldn't put his testicles in a hat.'

Baragah was away for two days, Short told Tim Bowden 40 years later, and when he came back 'he had a little note, he had a packet of Life Savers, and he had a bottle of vitamin pills, vitamin B, and on the note it said . . . The war is over. If you are well enough, make your way towards us; if you are not, stop where you are and we will come and get you.'

It was not until 24 August that the three Australians, guided and helped along nearly invisible jungle tracks by more than two dozen locals, finally made contact with members of the SRD party. Looking up, Short saw 'big Lofty [Private John Hodges], about six foot seven tall, boy oh boy . . . I said, it's really you. I cried, and they, they all cried . . . We all sat down and had a cup of tea together. And I couldn't eat . . . biscuits or anything like that, the stomach, it was shrunk, you know, and we couldn't eat much at all.'

The SRD men had brought stretchers 'and they said, "Righto, drop on the stretchers, you know, and we'll take you up to the camp". So they put Moxham on the stretcher and . . . Botterill and I said, "No, I'm all right . . . I'll walk the rest of the way with you if you'll just put your arm around me, I don't want to get on a stretcher."'

One of the rescuers, Private Norm Wallace, said later: 'Botterill, Moxham and Short were in a terrible physical condition . . . They were a shocking sight, the memory has remained with me all these years. It did not seem possible that human beings could be in such a condition and remain conscious and mentally alert.'

Botterill was so sick he was not expected to survive the night; he was certainly in no state to understand there was a fourth escaped prisoner in the camp: Warrant Officer Bill Sticpewich.

It was Sticpewich who had told Flight Lieutenant Ripley that Moxham's group had escaped on 7 July and might be at large in the jungle. On 10 August two locals had delivered Sticpewich, who was weak but still well enough to ride a horse, to the SRD camp. His companion, Private Reither, had died two days earlier, apparently of dysentery, although since escaping from Ranau he had sustained unexplained wounds to his stomach, legs and back.

According to Lynette Silver, when Moxham found out that Sticpewich had survived he 'flew into a terrible rage . . . He told rescuer John "Lofty" Hodges—"that bastard's still alive? I'm going to kill him with my bare hands". Hodges, disturbed by the vehemence of this threat, made sure that Moxham was kept well away from Sticpewich.'

The remaining survivors were not any happier to know that Sticpewich was alive. Don Wall told Botterill during one of their taped conversations that when he asked Campbell what Sticpewich's position would have been with the other Australians if the war had ended before the first death march, Campbell said they 'would have killed him'.

Sticpewich was gaunt but not emaciated when he was brought in. Although in much better health than the others, he was far from healthy. Seventeen-year-old Laniam binte Baranting helped build signal fires to guide in Allied planes to evacuate the four Australians. She told Kevin Smith in 1997, 'We called [Sticpewich] "Aligaric" because of the wobbly way he walked, because of being so thin and weak. His stomach was swollen because of malnutrition. When he came back to Ranau at a later time he looked much healthier.'

On 14 August 1945, four days after Sticpewich had made contact with Australian forces, his father received a telegram from the Minister for the Army that read:

I AM PLEASED TO INFORM YOU THAT QX9538 WARRANT OFFICER WILLIAM HECTOR STICPEWICH PREVIOUSLY REPORTED PRISONER OF WAR IS NOW REPORTED RECOVERED AND SAFE IN AUSTRALIAN HANDS STOP PRESENT REPORT STATES CONDITION WEAK BUT SATISFACTORY STOP PLEASE TREAT AS CONFIDENTIAL AND NOT DIVULGE INFORMATION OUTSIDE YOUR OWN HOUSEHOLD STOP LETTER FOLLOWS

A letter that followed the telegram, signed by the officer in charge of Queensland Echelon and Records, repeated the few facts contained in the telegram and again stressed the need for confidentiality 'as publicity at this stage would probably result in overwhelming enquiries being made regarding other Australian prisoners of war in Japanese hands'.

Sticpewich's mother Nellie wrote back, thanking the officer in charge for 'confirming release of my son Warrant Officer William H. Sticpewich from POW camp' and telling him she was 'worried to know how he is progressing and where he is also when I will expect him home as all the family are the same. I have not received any letter from him.'

Sticpewich's service and casualty form states that when he was transferred in late September to the Australian military hospital at

Labuan he was still suffering from 'dysentery, worm infestation and malnutrition'. It would be another three months before he arrived back in Australia. During that time Sticpewich would, as usual, find ways to make himself useful.

Chapter 27

STUPID QUESTIONS

———❖———

Before they were allowed to return home the Sandakan survivors had to face gruelling interrogations by Australian military intelligence, which was anxious to learn as much as it could about conditions in the camps and the fate of the other Australian prisoners.

Dick Braithwaite was flown to Morotai on 21 June after a preliminary bout of interrogation on Tawi-Tawi. A confidential report, dated 14 July 1945, stated that Braithwaite was 'recovering well, but at present can be interrogated for not more than 2 hrs daily. On some days he is not sufficiently well to be interrogated at all. Completion of his interrogation will take some time—probably a fortnight. His memory of events is remarkably good, and he is able to give much valuable information regarding other Aust. PWs.'

In the end Braithwaite was kept at Morotai for four weeks, during which time, according to another official report, he was 'interrogated as much as possible. The process was at times a considerable mental strain and he was finally evacuated upon medical advice.'

According to Richard Braithwaite, a colonel from the Second Echelon, the unit responsible for army records, presented his father with the entire roll of 18,000 names from 8th Division, wanting to know exactly what he remembered about each man. 'On each occasion, he asked for eye colour and next of kin. Understandably, Dick quickly became annoyed with this and . . . insisted to this man, who was a barrister in civilian life, that he either told it his way or the man could shut his book and that would be the end of it.' It was only when Braithwaite fell ill with pneumonia that the questioning stopped. The colonel described Braithwaite as 'uncooperative'.

Attached to his interrogation statements were two lists: schedule A contained the names of those 'known or believed by Bdr Braithwaite to be dead' while schedule B, which was incomplete, listed the men 'last seen alive'. The second list was already hopelessly out of date.

On the day Dick Braithwaite was evacuated by hospital ship to Australia, Owen Campbell arrived by American seaplane to be put through the same process. Campbell, although still 'in poor health' and 'suffering from beriberi and malaria', was considered by US doctors to have 'improved remarkably' during the few days he had been under their care. A preliminary interrogation report stamped 'SECRET' and written a week before he was transferred to Morotai commented that he had a 'very active and clear brain' and had 'recounted his story in the greatest detail'. Campbell's reinterrogation on Morotai was a much more gruelling process. He told Tim Bowden:

When I arrived in Morotai I was picked up by this military police off the plane, bundled into the jeep and away we went. Through all of the Australian camp and way up to this big marquee . . . 60 feet long. Great big thing with a bed in the centre. And that's where they put me . . . It was as though I was still a prisoner amongst my own people. They said it was for interrogation purposes.

The interrogators went on and on, insisting Campbell prove that he was who he said he was. 'I said to the bloke . . . "Who do you think I am, a spy or something?" And he said, "You could be." Eventually the colonel in charge of the hospital took pity on him. 'The old colonel said, "You just point your finger at me when you've had enough", and he was waiting outside and when I'd had enough I used to just go, "Hmp hmp", and he used to come in and stop them . . . It was hard to believe. The questions, the stupid questions that they asked.'

Moxham, Botterill and Short only endured brief stays at Morotai before being repatriated to Australia, but in Botterill's case it was long enough for the interrogators to conclude that he was an 'unreliable' informant. A report on Sticpewich's interrogation noted that on the day before Botterill was evacuated to Australia he 'visited the tent' in which Sticpewich was being questioned and 'was induced to take part in the interrogation'.

Whatever 'induced' Botterill to take part, he soon lost interest. According to the same report he 'showed a disinclination to give information' and 'tactful persuasion is necessary to induce him to fulfil his duty in this regard. The possibility of his making hasty and possibly exaggerated statements to shorten his interrogation should not be overlooked. He is a type who is both uncooperative and devoid of a sense of responsibility.'

Sticpewich, however, was considered by war crimes investigators to be 'a most reliable informant' who 'displayed an earnest desire to assist in the clarification of the fate of missing members, and applied himself to the task in an intelligent manner. There was a complete absence of any attempt at exaggeration or supposition on his part, and where he was uncertain of a casualty he refrained from expressing an opinion.'

Lieutenant McGinley reported that it was due to Sticpewich's 'untiring efforts throughout long periods of interrogation' that it had been possible to determine the fate of many Australian POWs. McGinley's superior, Lieutenant-Colonel Selden, later confirmed that he had been 'extremely co-operative'. Sticpewich's 'one aim', Selden wrote, 'was to give all possible information that might throw some light on the other PW in his area and he went to no end of trouble despite his medical condition, to ensure that he had not overlooked any possible avenue.'

Chapter 28

A DAY-OLD MULLET

Athol Moffitt enlisted in the Australian army with four friends, all members of the Killara Golf Club on Sydney's north shore. A young barrister with a double first in Mathematics and Law from the University of Sydney, Moffitt chose not to start as an officer but joined as a private in the artillery. Before long he was moving up the ranks, rising from gunner to sergeant and then, by early 1942, to lieutenant.

Moffitt's request to serve overseas was turned down, saving him from becoming one of the 15,000 Australian soldiers who became prisoners of war after the fall of Singapore and saving him, as well, from Sandakan. With the coastal defences along Australia's east coast effectively the front line against Japanese attack, Moffitt found himself acting as 'plotting officer' at Fort Cape Banks, near the north head of Botany Bay, collating and coordinating targeting information for the battery's 9.2-inch guns.

On the night of 31 May 1942 three Japanese midget submarines that had been launched from a group of bigger submarines loitering off Sydney Heads penetrated Sydney Harbour. All three of the midget submarines were sunk.

A few days after the midget submarine raid Moffitt was duty commander at Cape Banks when a shape emerged from the sea fog. 'Out of the fog, at about 7,000 yards, came a warship travelling north towards Sydney at speed, with a large bow wave,' Moffitt wrote in his unpublished memoir. 'There was no ETA or other warning. My orders were to shoot on sight.'

Fortunately, Moffitt recognised the ship's outline as belonging to one of the navy's Tribal Class destroyers; in fact it was Australia's newest warship, HMAS *Warramunga*. Despite the lack of a warning signal, Moffitt disobeyed his orders and did not order the guns to fire. At a distance of 7000 yards (6400 metres)—effectively point-blank range—the *Warramunga* would have been blown out of the water by the battery's armour-piercing high-explosive shells.

Moffitt's war after 1942 was uneventful. There was no repeat of the midget submarine raid on Sydney Harbour or of the shelling of Sydney's eastern suburbs a week later by a Japanese submarine. Moffitt, now a captain, was already making plans for a legal career in Sydney when he was chosen to go to North Borneo as part of the post-war military government.

Japan had capitulated on 15 August 1945 but Moffitt arrived at the Labuan headquarters of the 9th Australian Division to discover that the fighting in Borneo had not stopped: pockets of Japanese soldiers were defying the order to surrender. In Brunei, the harbour was strewn with sunk or destroyed Japanese ships, and Allied bombers had reduced much of the city to rubble.

While the six death march survivors slowly regained their health,

A Japanese midget submarine is recovered from Sydney Harbour. News of the raid in May 1942 prompted taunts from the guards at Sandakan. *State Library Victoria*

The dead Japanese submariners were given a full military funeral. When he heard that their ashes were being returned to Japan, Hoshijima gave the POWs a dugong. *State Library Victoria*

After raids by American P-38 Lightning fighter-bombers, Hoshijima ordered
Sticpewich to put up a sign with the letters 'POW' painted in white on a black cloth.
State Library of Queensland

A periscope photograph of a Japanese ship torpedoed by a US submarine.
Hoshijima blamed attacks on Japanese shipping for the POWs' dwindling rations.
US National Archives

Australian troops landed on Labuan on 10 June 1945. Here Australian soldiers protect themselves from Japanese snipers by crouching behind vehicles. *State Library Victoria*

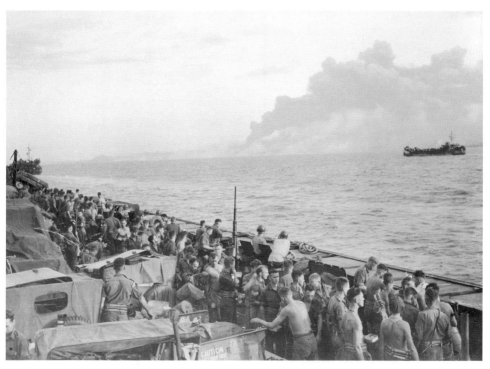

Australian troops on landing ships prepare to attack Balikpapan. Smoke from a naval bombardment can be seen rising from the shore. *State Library Victoria*

Members of the 2nd Pioneer Battalion building cages at Balikpapan to hold Japanese POWs. *State Library Victoria*

Emaciated POWs released from captivity at the hands of the Japanese. *State Library Victoria*

On arriving in Australia, POWs from Japanese camps were given stringent health checks. Most had suffered from malnutrition, dysentery and malaria. *State Library Victoria*

Australian POWs returning from Europe receive a raucous welcome in Sydney.
State Library Victoria

Captain Hoshijima Susumu (*centre*), commandant of the Japanese POW camp at Sandakan, talking to his defence counsel during his trial for war crimes. *Australian War Memorial*

Captain Athol Moffitt, who prosecuted Hoshijima and other Japanese war criminals. Moffitt later became a NSW Supreme Court judge. *Australian War Memorial*

From left Private Keith Botterill, Warrant Officer Bill Sticpewich and Private Nelson Short. Soon after these three escaped from Ranau, the remaining POWs were massacred. *State Library Victoria*

Sticpewich received valuable help from local police and Dyaks while searching for POW remains with 31 Australian War Graves Unit. *Australian War Memorial*

Sergeant Major Sugino (*second from left*) was the first Japanese to be tried at Labuan for war crimes against Australian POWs. Sticpewich's evidence helped convict him. Sugino was shot on Morotai on 6 March 1946. *Australian War Memorial*

The burnt ruins of Sandakan POW camp. In the background is the Big Tree, said to have been a hiding place for weapons and valuables. *Australian War Memorial*

A cross near the 16-mile peg marks the grave of a POW who was shot on one of the Sandakan–Ranau death marches. This prisoner was buried by a native gardener. His cross was erected by a Chinese. *Australian War Memorial*

Sticpewich stands by the grave of Captain Lionel Matthews, who was shot by the Japanese at Kuching for his part in the so-called 'Sandakan Incident'. *Australian War Memorial*

Moffitt got to work reviewing case files and investigating and prosecuting civil crimes committed during the Japanese occupation. Some investigations threw up evidence of war crimes, which at the time were outside his jurisdiction.

Moffitt was deeply unimpressed by the sultan of Brunei: 'The Sultan apparently was pretty friendly with the Japs,' he wrote in his diary, 'and it is said he prepared a reception for them. We have a photograph of him sitting in the middle of the Jap officer leaders in the area—a self-satisfied smile on his face—may be useful one day. This spineless creature is apparently a complete parasite on whoever is in power. Maybe I shall find more about him in future.'

Not long after writing these remarks Moffitt was invited to tea at the sultan's palace:

We all sat down to little tables interspersed with the upper class Malay gentlemen whom I must confess I find most boring. About their dress there was a poor cross between the East and the West. Running around amongst the people was the Sultan's 17 year old daughter, a big loose type of a girl with a skirt about 2" above the knees and colour on her lips, a thing unknown amongst the Malays except the Malay prostitutes.

After a while 'Royalty appeared in the shape of 5' nothing, an English morning dress complete with tails . . . it had a long mustache waxed and curled in almost a complete circle and it laughed like a schoolgirl'. Welcoming each of his guests in turn, the sultan extended a hand 'which was more like a day-old mullet—it did not grip or move': 'This Sultan is 32 and looks and is everything that is degenerate. He has V.D. and has a sickly purplish colour on his lips and it is said he has had so many women that he is now rather weak mentally. Here is the descendant of the famous and feared Sultans of Brunei.'

Encouraged, perhaps, by the prejudices of the Killara Golf Club and the pre-war Sydney Bar, Moffitt was quick to judge on appearances, and the months ahead would give him plenty of opportunity to indulge his preconceptions.

Chapter 29

FAT AND SADISTIC

—————»•«—————

During the final months of the war, SRD parties sent from Australia by
aircraft or submarine organised the indigenous people into armed guerrilla groups to fight the Japanese. The Dyaks were not always discouraged
by the Allies from their traditional practice of taking heads, and on a visit
to a Dyak longhouse Moffitt was shown a collection of Japanese skulls.

> In the 4 kampongs we visited having a population of 300 (there would
> not be more than 90 men amongst them) were 40 Jap skulls all claimed
> to have been killed by these people—for the loss of 2 Dyaks . . . the
> skulls were blackened and obviously Jap, the skin and hair still being
> on—they all showed signs of violence i.e. bullet holes or knife cuts.

In November 1945 Moffitt was in Lawas, a small town in Sarawak on
the Lawas River, when a message written on toilet paper was delivered

by an indigenous Murut runner from Australian SRD officer Rex Blow. The message said that Blow, who had been promoted to major since his escape from Berhala Island, was bringing in 317 Japanese soldiers and that the prisoners would need food and medical attention.

'All the Japs looked very worn out but most looked quite fat and healthy,' Moffitt wrote in his diary:

> The Japs were loaded straight onto 3 barges . . . However first the war criminals were separated out—there was a long list of wanted men and of these 10 were located. I had a close look at them and as a group they looked fat and sadistic . . . The head of the Kempei-Tai was there too—a big fat Jap with a ferocious black beard growing from under his face. I would hate to be in his power.

By December Moffitt was starting to tire of prosecuting local cases. Worried that as he had less than twelve months tropical service he might be assigned to garrison duty ('which will end God knows where'), he applied to help with the trials of accused war criminals. These were to be organised and run by the Australian Army. At the end of the month his appointment was confirmed: Moffitt was to go to 9th Division to work on the Australian war crimes trials.

The clamour for Japanese accused of war crimes against Australian soldiers to be brought to trial had caught the army unprepared. Difficult decisions had to be made about which trial to hold first and whether the accused should be prosecuted jointly or individually. On 18 November 1945 an Australian colonel wrote urgently to 37th Japanese Army HQ:

1. Trials of war criminals will commence here shortly.
2. According to British rules of justice, accused persons are permitted to have an officer in court to defend them.

3. Are you able to select a Japanese officer, preferably one who can speak English, qualified to appear before Japanese courts, and willing to perform this duty? If so please notify this HQ of his name and particulars without delay.

4. If an officer at present at Jesselton or Kuching is selected, arrangements will be made to bring him to Labuan.

5. The officer selected will be given an opportunity to acquaint himself with British legal procedure and to see such witnesses as are considered necessary.

The trial of 21 Japanese accused of the massacre of Australian POWs at Miri was scheduled to begin at Labuan on 23 November, but the army was short of prosecutors, interpreters and stenographers. Colonel Dunn, deputy head of legal services at army HQ on Morotai, received an urgent telegram: 'Permanent court incl. prosecutor desirable but cannot provide owing to very acute shortage suitable [officers] (.) no shorthand writer available here . . . cannot provide interpreter up to required standard (.) can landops assist (.) if NOT trial will proceed with best available (.)'

By the time Moffitt arrived at Labuan most of the logistical problems had been sorted out, although complaints from the Japanese about the quality of interpreters would cause ongoing trouble for Allied prosecutors. A courtroom had been established on the beach. A memo from 9th Division HQ dated 1 December advised that the trials would be 'open to the public but owing to the limited space available in the court the number of spectators attending must be strictly limited'. Entry would be by official admission cards. In the event, it was Australian soldiers rather than the public who attended the trials.

Moffitt's first job was to prosecute Hoshijima, the 'foul commander of the Sandakan death camp'. He anticipated that it would be a difficult case to prove; 'an alternate charge, however, will probably be sufficient to fix him'. The 'star witness' was to be 'W.O. Sticpewich', who was going to be flown from Australia for the case.

Sticpewich's importance to the prosecution case is indicated by a cipher message marked 'immediate' that was sent from 9th Division to HQ in Sydney: 'Please arrange for WO Sticpewich 8 Div AASC [Australian Army Service Corps] marched out from here to Sydney for discharge as repatriated PW to return here to give evidence in war crimes trials . . . Request passair highest possible priority.'

Sticpewich had already given evidence to the war crimes commission at Morotai and supplied war crimes investigators with lengthy written statements recounting in fastidious detail his time as a prisoner at Changi, Sandakan and Ranau. Campbell and Braithwaite had also been exhaustively interrogated at Morotai over a period of nearly six weeks before being allowed to fly home to Australia. Moxham, Botterill and Short had given evidence about events at Sandakan and Ranau to the war crimes commission in Sydney. In early November Sticpewich was taken to Labuan, where suspected Japanese war criminals were being held, and formally identified two of the prisoners as Captain Hoshijima and Captain Nagai.

Moffitt spent the next few days preparing the case against Hoshijima. 'It is easy to prove cruelty,' he wrote, 'but 1100 died during Hoshijima's time and 1250 within 2 months after his time and I want to lay direct responsibility at his foul door for the 1100 and indirect responsibility for the other 1250.' There were four charges: cruelty ('flogging and brutality meted out to the prisoners over three years'); cruelty by confinement and punishment in a cage resulting in several prisoner deaths; starvation and denial of medical attention (causing deaths); and forcing sick men to work.

On the 'vital' charge of starvation and denial of medical attention, Moffitt predicted that Hoshijima would blame the sinking of Japanese shipping for the lack of food and medicines and claim that the decision to cut the rice ration was made not by him but by 37th Army HQ. Although 'sure' this was not the truth, Moffitt was concerned that the 'evidence we have that H was a party to this starvation is not yet watertight'. Hoping that Japanese quartermasters would 'give a lead to H's part', he vowed to 'ferret them out and see what I can get'.

The next day, after obtaining 'vital evidence' from one of the Sandakan quartermasters, Moffitt was euphoric. 'His evidence is so important that I had it read over to him 3 times and had him say it was quite correct. The Japs I feel will try to get him to change it.'

Chapter 30

BEAST OF BORNEO

The trial of Captain Hoshijima Susumu began at Labuan on Tuesday, 7 January 1946. Asked how he pleaded to the four charges, Hoshijima ('with a fierce arrogance', Moffitt noted in his diary) replied 'Not guilty' to each.

In his opening address Moffitt set out the four charges and introduced his principal witness, Sticpewich, whose membership of the 'secret committee . . . of five which received reports from prisoners and made complaints through Captain Cook to Hoshijima' would enable him to give 'valuable hearsay' as well as 'weighty evidence on many other points'.

Primed by Sticpewich, Moffitt told the court about Hoshijima's systematic withholding of rice and meat rations, his refusal to supply the prisoners with quinine and other drugs, his failure to pass on Red Cross medical parcels, his violent assaults on individual prisoners and the cruel punishments inflicted on his orders and his forcing of sick men to work.

He cited the bashing of Private Jimmy Darlington as a 'typical' example of Japanese brutality: 'Hoshijima admits he was present, saw it and did nothing to release him until the next day.'

Moffitt concluded his address by comparing Hoshijima with the Nazis: 'There have been many prisoner of war camps in this war with grim records,' he told the judges, 'but the name of Sandakan PW camp and the tragedy it represents will live long as a blot on the barbaric Japanese army. The man responsible stands before the court. This sadist, though his method of slaughter was more subtle, ranks with the "Beast of Belsen".'

Sticpewich was the first witness to take the stand. Most of the Australian officers transferred from Sandakan to Kuching had returned to Australia and given evidence to the war crimes commission but none testified at Hoshijima's trial. In their absence the prosecution was allowed to present written statements, the truth of which Moffitt accepted unconditionally. The court's acceptance of these statements, the authors of which could not be cross-examined, put the defence at a significant disadvantage.

'The first witness was W.O. Sticpewich,' Moffitt wrote in his diary. 'He was brought from Australia at the request of the defence as they didn't like his witness statement. It was the greatest mistake they ever made for his verbal evidence was more convincing, fuller and easier to follow than his statement. He gave his evidence very well.'

Moffitt liked to scoff at his Japanese adversaries but army records on this issue are ambiguous to say the least. An unclassified telegram from 9th Division advises Colonel Dunn that 'Japs wish to call STICPEWICH as witness if not put in witness box by prosecution in case against HOSHIJIMA commandant SANDAKAN camp (.) have accordingly signalled MILBASE SYDNEY to arrange his return (.).'

Did the defence wish to call Sticpewich as a witness because, as Moffitt asserts, 'they didn't like his witness statement', or did Hoshijima's legal team have other reasons for thinking that putting Sticpewich on the stand might help Hoshijima? Did they hope to discredit Sticpewich's evidence against Hoshijima by exposing inconsistencies between his written statement and his testimony in court? Did they think Sticpewich might alter his evidence to avoid awkward revelations about his cosy relationship with the Japanese? Despite Moffitt's claim that Sticpewich was 'brought from Australia at the request of the defence', the court transcripts clearly identify him as the 'first witness for the prosecution'.*

Sticpewich's cross-examination began the following day, when he resisted every attempt by the defence to cast a more benign light on Hoshijima's conduct. Asked for instance whether 'between December 1944 and May 1945 Captain Hoshijima allowed prisoners to go fishing', Sticpewich replied, 'Yes. It was just a form of recreation. The fish caught was negligible. The whole catch would not be sufficient for the dangerously ill patients in the hospital.' Moffitt found the spectacle of Sticpewich swatting away questions by Hoshijima's lawyers 'rather pathetic ... an unequal contest'.

---

*   Ham is keen to play up the drama of Sticpewich's courtroom appearance, but
     unfortunately at the expense of the evidence: 'The smile [on Hoshijima's face]
     disappears when Sticpewich enters the courtroom,' Ham writes, 'and Hoshijima
     visibly pales. Here all of a sudden is the living antidote to the commandant's
     poison; here is a man who saw everything. Hoshijima and his henchmen had
     presumed the prisoners were all dead—especially this one, who has witnessed
     their atrocities first-hand and knows, literally, where the bodies are hidden.'
     The truth, as shown above, is that the defence was well aware Sticpewich had
     survived—it had even considered calling him as a witness. On 3 November 1945
     Sticpewich had visited the Labuan prisoners' compound with Captain Brereton
     and formally identified Hoshijima, Nagai, Watanabe Genzō and Watanabe
     Katsumi. (Moxham also visited the compound to point out guards guilty of
     mistreating POWs.) Sticpewich's appearance on the witness stand two months
     later would have been anything but a surprise.

Hoshijima began his evidence on Thursday and was still talking on Monday, delivering a 'revolting set of lies' and 'combing over the slightest thing he did good in the three years'. The evidence he gave in court often contradicted the answers he had given in September to war crimes investigator Captain Russell Brereton. In answer to Brereton's question 'Did you punish any of the prisoners of war?', Hoshijima had then replied 'Plenty'. Asked whether he ever beat the prisoners, Hoshijima told Brereton, 'In the early part of 1943 I was in charge of the Camp and also of the aerodrome construction. I was very irritable and I beat the prisoners to make them work harder.'

Hoshijima was not the only one giving evidence to war crimes investigators in September 1945. Owen Campbell provided the war crimes commission with a detailed account of a bashing he had witnessed by Hoshijima:

A party of about 250 POW were working on drome at Sandakan. Two Aust cooks were burning rice on a shovel over a fire for the purpose [of] using the rice to brown the stew. Hoshijima lined up the party and through an interpreter informed the prisoners that using the shovel to burn rice would 'send the shovel bad'. He called out the two POW responsible, stood them to attention and king hit them three times each, knocking them down on each occasion. After each assault he ordered them to stand at attention and repeated the assault. He then gave each of the two prisoners seven days in the 'bird cage', three days of which were without food. Hoshijima was a big powerful man about six feet tall and well built. I heard from other POW lots of cases of bashings by this officer.

During his four months in custody Hoshijima had time to rue the incriminating answers he had given Captain Brereton. The story he eventually told the judges was very different: he admitted slapping prisoners for lying or disobedience but 'only with an open palm and . . . only once'. At his trial he categorically denied the existence of a 'basher squad'. There was, he said, a 'labour party' that the prisoners called a basher squad:

> They were not to beat any prisoners because the prisoners were of a different nationality and had different customs, but if they did not obey orders they were to be reprimanded but if they still continued disobeying orders they could be beaten. These beatings were only as a warning so that they would not disobey orders again. Even then they were not to strike PW indiscriminately but to think about it first and then not beat them too hard.

Asked by his defence counsel whether he had ever punished a soldier for mistreating a prisoner, Hoshijima said he had not because he had 'never seen or heard of an incident in which the treatment was severe enough to justify my punishing a guard'.

While admitting that one prisoner had died in the cage, Hoshijima insisted that the cause of death was a 'sudden attack of malaria'. As to Sticpewich's allegation that prisoners in the cage were dragged out every day and beaten and kicked by the guards, Hoshijima had 'never heard or seen such things', although he had seen prisoners in the cage being taken out for 'exercises'.* Asked why he had never put a British

---

*   Hayashi (Ming the Merciless) was the most zealous exponent of these 'exercises': 'Practically every day PW confined in the cage were taken out, ostensibly for PT exercises but in reality the PT exercises turned out to be a most severe form of punishment', Sticpewich wrote in his statutory declaration. 'During such so-called PT exercises HAYASHI excelled in cruelty. On occasions when he was in charge of the PW he would compel them to perform the exercises at such a rate that they could not possibly continue and he would then bash them severely with a heavy stick . . . Even when some other guard was in charge of the PT exercises if HAYASHI considered that the exercises were not sufficiently severe he would come along and wield the stick in his usual manner.'

prisoner in the cage, he answered, 'Because they never did anything wrong'.

Hoshijima's evidence went on and on; the court did not sit on Friday but he kept talking throughout the weekend and into Monday. On the critical question of food he claimed to have argued with Colonel Suga about the prisoners' rations being inadequate and to have personally taken up the matter with 37th Army HQ at Jesselton and POW HQ at Kuching. While these protests came to nothing, Hoshijima maintained 'there were no deaths because of shortage of food':

> The biggest cause for their deaths was the shortage of medicines. The shortage of food caused them to lose their strength but did not cause their death. The second reason for deaths was the long confinement in a tropical area. That sort of a life affected them both physically and mentally. Another reason was that the bombings by the Allies, the progress in fighting made by the Allies, and the thought of an early Allied ending in Borneo was too much for them after the strain they had been living under.

Sworn statements by Sticpewich and three officers accused Hoshijima of forcing sick prisoners to work, a charge he strongly denied. Asked about the discrepancy by his counsel he snapped, 'They are all wrong.'

Hearing Hoshijima drone on for session after session convinced Moffitt 'it would have been better to have shot such people out of hand than to hear this exhibition which is almost an insult to those who died at Sandakan'. Finally, just before lunch on Monday, Moffitt stood up to begin his cross-examination.

Hoshijima agreed that in March 1945 prisoners were 'dying at the rate of ten or twelve a day' but held to his story that shortage of food had 'nothing to do with this'. When it was put to him that there were 'very many complaints . . . about the amount and condition of food from

June 1944 onwards' he replied, 'I never heard of such complaints.' When Moffitt raised the issue of medical treatment, Hoshijima tied himself in knots trying to defend his claim that POWs and Japanese shared medicines equally:

Q: Why did 1,000 PW while only one Japanese die at the compound if the medicines were the same? You said that medicine was the main cause of the deaths.

A: The Formosans were very strong in body.

Q: Is that your only answer?

A: Another reason is that the Japanese were receiving a bit more medicine than the PW. Also, because of their strength in body the Japanese did not use as much as the PW.

Q: But you just said to me that the medical treatment for the PW and the Japanese was the same. Which is true?

A: The medicine given to each of them was generally of the same quantity, but the PW had more patients than the Japanese and so used up their medicine quicker.

Q: Why did the PW have more patients than the Japanese if the medical supplies were the same? . . .

A: The white people are more vulnerable to a hot climate than are Formosans or Japanese.

While Hoshijima made some token expressions of regret for the actions of his guards he insisted that he himself was blameless. Asked by Moffitt if he had done anything wrong he replied, 'There were some bad things done in the camp but I never did any bad thing myself.' In his diary Moffitt made it clear that he had Hoshijima exactly where he wanted him. 'I feel sure now that H. is for the big jump,' he wrote after completing his cross-examination. 'I never had any doubt that he was guilty.'

A succession of unconvincing defence witnesses dutifully went back on statements they had previously made to Allied interrogators implicating Hoshijima in the starving and bashing of prisoners in the cage. On the contrary, they said, Hoshijima had given orders for prisoners to be treated with a 'strict and rightful attitude'. Moffitt queried whether they had been coached or pressured to change their evidence, but they denied it. When Hoshijima suffered a 'sudden turn of malaria' the trial had to be suspended for a day.

Efforts by the defence to portray Hoshijima as having only followed orders inevitably implicated both Colonel Suga, commandant of all the Japanese POW camps in Borneo, and the overall commander of Japanese forces in Borneo, Lieutenant General Baba Masao. The evidence was especially damaging for Baba, who was shown to have made little or no effort to find out the condition of the POWs at Sandakan before sending them on the death marches to Ranau. The first march had been planned before Baba came to Borneo, but he was responsible for implementing the plan and issuing the movement orders. He ordered the second march knowing that few if any prisoners would survive.

Although frustrated by what he termed the judges' 'fishing expedition' against Baba, Moffitt foresaw that Baba's 'attitude of non-inquiry and non-concern for the PW' would eventually be judged as either 'acquiescence in the crimes or criminal neglect of his duty'. Moffitt had returned to Australia before Baba stood trial, but he could see what was coming for the general. 'It seems probable,' he wrote in his diary, 'that HQ sent the PWs on the march for the purpose of disposing of them without mass slaughter.'

The third and most serious charge Hoshijima faced concerned the withholding of medicine and the systematic starvation of prisoners. Sticpewich provided a forensic account of how the prisoners' rations were steadily reduced, especially in the last twelve months of the war. Hoshijima claimed to have stood up for the POWs against ration cuts ordered by 37th Army HQ, but evidence from the quartermaster,

Lieutenant Arai, indicated the opposite: that it was Hoshijima himself who had suggested cutting the rations.

In a signed statement obtained by Moffitt five days before the trial began, Arai said that in March 1945 the quartermaster's department 'got wind' that the Sandakan POWs 'would be moved in the near future'. This news also reached Hoshijima. Concerned about the adequacy of rice reserves at the camp, Arai and Hoshijima discussed the idea of cutting out the prisoners' rice ration completely and replacing it with 'substitutes' (mainly tapioca and sweet potatoes):

> I asked Hoshijima if it was all right to give the PWs only rice substi-
> tute. Hoshijima could not decide that himself, therefore we wired HQs
> asking if it was all right. We . . . ourselves could not make up our mind
> if it was all right. HQs replied saying that it was all right. Hoshijima
> said that although the potato diet was not as good as rice . . . he was
> of the opinion that if it was all right with HQs it would be all right
> with him. He did not have any argument against it, however, he said to
> give more potatoes. Hoshijima also knew at that time, the PWs might
> be moving out.

Army headquarters authorised the cut by reply telegram and instructed Hoshijima to 'save rice to last till the end of the year'.

Arai's pre-trial declaration was so significant that Moffitt insisted on reading it back to him twice and getting Arai to initial any alterations he wanted to make. Confronted with his signed and initialled declaration in court, Arai was unable to disavow his evidence:

> Q: Do you remember saying in the declaration you made, 'He did not
>   have any argument against [the cut in rice imposed by HQ] but
>   said to give more potatoes'. Do you remember that?
> A: Yes, he said that after the answer to the telegram came back.

Q: Did you say in your declaration, 'Hoshijima said that although the potato diet was not as good as rice . . . he was of the opinion that if it was alright with HQ it would be alright with him'?

A: Yes.

The loss of even a reduced rice ration was effectively a death sentence for the POWs, since tapioca and potatoes were less nutritious and potatoes were subject to high wastage. By disclosing that it was Hoshijima who had initiated the cut and not army headquarters, Arai fatally undermined the commandant's case. 'He did not understand the Hoshijima defence and that what he said destroyed it,' Moffitt wrote 40 years later in a book about the Sandakan POWs.

Equally explosive was the revelation, made by Sticpewich and reluctantly corroborated by Arai, that while he was cutting the prisoners' rice ration down to starvation levels Hoshijima kept between 80 and 90 tons of rice contained in 800 to 900 100-kilogram bags stored under his house. Arai recalled seeing the rice there when he took over command of the field warehouse in January 1945 and again when he visited the camp in March. The only logical explanation for Hoshijima's personal stockpile was that he had been withholding rice supplied by army headquarters to feed the POWs.

The defence drew attention to Hoshijima having 'killed his own horse for the prisoners' consumption' and noted that Captain Cook had 'expressed his gratefulness', but Sticpewich pointed out that the emaciated animal was near death anyway. Character evidence given by fellow officers—Colonel Takayama called Hoshijima 'a very systematic man . . . a very deep thinker and an upright man', while Lieutenant Ogawa said he was 'very honest and upright'—was not enough to save him.

'It is impossible to make any punishment fit this crime,' Moffitt told the judges in his closing address. 'Even death by the ignominy of hanging, which I submit should be the penalty, is too good for this barbarian, ironically self-titled "cultured".'

Hoshijima was allowed to make a short statement in mitigation of his sentence. 'I think that Captain Cook was the only man who knew and understood the real me,' he told the judges. 'I would like you to imagine the bomb-torn Sandakan and think of the difficulties that existed there. I would like you to take this into consideration together with my many efforts to do all I could for the care of the prisoners. When I did these things I was thinking all the time of the happiness and protection of the prisoners. I ask the Court to try and understand all the difficulties that were in my path and to show mercy in your judgment.'

On 20 January 1946 the court found Hoshijima guilty on all four charges and sentenced him to death by hanging. Moffitt watched him carefully as the sentence was read out: 'There was not a sign of emotion on his face as he stood strictly to attention at his full 6' height,' Moffitt wrote in his diary. 'He saluted smartly and was marched out by the Gurkhas.'

Chapter 31

PERFECT MAN OF SENSE

Hoshijima's trial exposed a problem that would bedevil prosecutors in nearly every subsequent trial for crimes committed against Australian prisoners of war: the tendency of Japanese guards to change or disavow written statements they had previously made to war crimes investigators.

On 22 December 1945 the Formosan Nakano Ryoichi was interrogated at Labuan. Nakano was one of the guards on the second death march, although he was not accused of murdering any prisoners. During his interrogation he gave damning evidence about the treatment of prisoners in the cage: 'If the Australians were only to give me as much as those men [in the cage] received I would soon die,' he said. Nakano claimed to remember 'at least six occasions' on which men suffering from dysentery, malaria or beriberi were put in the cage. Many were wearing nothing but 'short trousers'. There were no mosquito nets and in most cases the prisoners had no blanket or covering despite the fact there were 'thousands of mosquitoes'.

In his statement Nakano confirmed that one prisoner 'definitely died in the cage undergoing his sentence' and claimed to be aware of 'two or three' other cases in which a man in the cage had to be taken out before his sentence was finished as he had become 'so ill that he would have died'. He said that 'five or six others died as a direct result of their ill-treatment while in the cage' and told the investigators that Hoshijima was 'fully aware' of the way the prisoners were treated in the cage. 'The cages were outside the camp on the side of the road and were visible to him as he passed along the road . . . Although to my knowledge he has never directly ordered a PW to be beaten, there were many occasions when PWs were beaten and ill-treated while Hoshijima was present.'

Less than three weeks later Nakano took the stand as a defence witness in Hoshijima's trial. By then he had completely changed his story:

Q: You said in your statement that 'At least on six occasions when men were put in the cage they were suffering from malaria, dysentery or beriberi before they were put in'. Did you actually see this or did you hear of it?

A: I have never seen or heard of it, I only thought it . . .

Q: Did you actually see sick PWs being put into the cage?

A: No, but I have seen PWs being put in the cage.

Q: In your statement you say that 'PWs were made to sit in the cage and if they moved from this position they were taken out and beaten'. Did you actually see this?

A: No, I did not see it.

Q: Did you hear of this?

A: Yes.

Q: And you also said in your statement that PWs put in the cage were not fed for two days. Did you see this?

A: No.

Q: And did you ever see their food being reduced?

A: No.

Q: You also said in your statement that 5 or 6 PWs died as direct result of their ill-treatment while in the cage. Did you actually see this?

A: No.

Q: You said that Capt Hoshijima was fully aware of the way PWs were being treated in the cage. How do you know this?

A: I only imagined that.

Q: Then why did you state all these things in your statement if you only imagined them?

A: At the time of my interrogation I was sick and cannot remember what I actually said.

The reluctance of Nagano and other guards to incriminate their officers was an ongoing source of frustration for Allied prosecutors, but in Sticpewich Moffitt had a witness who knew exactly what it took to obtain a conviction. In his closing address Moffitt mentioned Sticpewich by name 22 times; his evidence and the way he delivered it were critical to the case against Hoshijima. Privately, Moffitt applauded Sticpewich's performance under cross-examination: 'The little Jap had no idea of pinning down the tough Aussie S/Maj to the few facts in H's favour,' Moffitt wrote in his diary. 'He knew the camp and H so well that he found no trouble in putting a sting in the tail of each answer e.g. Q: Didn't H put up a POW sign at the compound? A: Yes, but it was for his protection as well as ours.'

It was not just Sticpewich's extraordinary memory for detail— especially on the subject of rations—that condemned Hoshijima but also the vehemence of his opinions. Sticpewich named several prisoners he believed to have died as a direct result of being kept in the cage, each time qualifying his assertion with the phrase 'in my opinion'. In his closing address Moffitt recast Sticpewich's opinions as statements of fact:

> Sticpewich states that the following among others died as a result of the cage treatment, namely, Weeks, taken out on a stretcher and died a week later; Clements, a Provost of big physique came out very sick and died 5 weeks later; Annear taken out unconscious and died 24 hours later; Anderson died four or five days later, and others died later as a result of their weakened condition from this vicious treatment.

A fortnight after the trial ended Hoshijima lodged a lengthy petition against both the verdict and the sentence, accompanied by several character references. The petition suggested the judges were guilty of a 'great mistake and a misunderstanding' in the way they had weighed the evidence, which had to be 'coolly and fairly measured . . . without any prejudice or partiality at all'. It complained about Sticpewich's 'deliberateness in producing unfavourable evidence against the accused' and Moffitt's insistence that 'all evidences produced by the accused are completely false'. While conceding that statements against Hoshijima were 'quite numerous', the petition maintained that when 'truth' was taken into consideration a 'good number' of these unfavourable statements could not be believed.

The petition described Hoshijima as a 'perfect man of sense' incapable of such a 'subtle and cruel' offence as the 'systematic starvation' of prisoners and as a 'bright and broad-minded' engineer with 'no savageous character as to approve such social evils'.

Lieutenant Colonel Sago Takuji found him 'highly educated and well-informed . . . a man of strong will, deep thinker, sound common sense, sympathy and self-sacrifice for others'. The relationship between

Hoshijima and his men was 'as if between father and sons. He has no habit of smoking but always had cigarettes with him and gave these to his soldiers and colleagues in [the] battlefield.'

Formosan guard Uemura Soichi, who worked as Hoshijima's batman and driver, also remembered his generosity with cigarettes: 'Capt. Hoshijima was fond of Japanese wine, but did never smoke. He always carried cigarettes with him and gave them to PWs whenever he made inspection or PWs came to his place':

> When Capt. Hoshijima was leaving Sandakan to be transferred to the Army HQ, Capt. Hoshijima and Capt. Cook took dinner together in his house. Capt. Cook brought some cakes made from tapioca, I brought sweet-potatoes, bananas and coffee, and Capt. Hoshijima brought some fishes caught by himself. Capt. Hoshijima opened a tin of butter which was the last one . . . and ate it with Capt. Cook and the tin with the remaining butter was brought back to the camp by Capt. Cook.

Among the Formosans, he said, 'some of them were scolded and some of them were beaten by Capt. Hoshijima, but in spite of that every guard without exception respected, praised and loved him'.

According to Sergeant Watanabe, Hoshijima was a 'good, trustworthy and humane officer' who 'loved his men as if a father loved his son, while he was divinely fair to others, very active, incorruptible, and upright'. So dismayed was Watanabe by the 'pitiful and regrettable' sentence imposed by the court on Hoshijima that it made him 'doubt if there is justice at all in the world'. In his own plea for mercy Hoshijima wrote that the guilty verdict and sentence of death by hanging were

> quite beyond my expectation and I still cannot understand at all why I was found to be so . . . I am afraid that the Court did not care

to take all my efforts [and] endeavours made for the benefit of PWs during the hardest times since about October 1944 into consideration . . . You can see how I had been worried about everything, especially in procuring food and medicine for them, and how I had done my best for the benefit of PWs . . . It is not an exaggeration to say that everything that had been given to PWs was the result of my efforts during day and night. To my great regret all persons in the camp had not been aware of my efforts which I had made outside the camp . . . Did the court really understand my sincerity which I concentrated for the protection of PWs? . . . Now confined in jail my only wish is that either Captain Cook or Captain Mills who had known me well could still be alive. [Cook and the younger British officer] appreciated a present of a horse which I gave them and [they] wrote me a letter of their gratitude by which I was much moved. To my great regret, I had burnt all of these letters before leaving Sandakan at the end of May 1945. Now that the court can hardly understand what I have done I wish I could have kept even one of these letters . . . But it is too late now.

Hoshijima failed in his appeal against both the finding and the sentence. The only authority with the power to commute death sentences was the Australian commander-in-chief, and there was little chance of Lieutenant General Sturdee exercising it on behalf of Hoshijima. Advised that the guilty verdict was 'justified on the evidence' and that the sentence was 'within the powers of the court', Sturdee confirmed the sentence and issued a death warrant on 27 February 1946.

At 9.15 am on 6 April Hoshijima was hanged at Rabaul, there being no scaffold at Morotai; Australian journalists were on hand to witness the execution. 'Hoshijima, elegantly dressed in a khaki jacket over a white silk shirt, grey riding breeches and polished leggings, gave a cheeky grin,' the Newcastle *Sun* reported on its front page. '[He] asked for morphia but was bluntly told none was available. He then asked for a pair of scissors to send a lock of his hair and toe-nail parings to his relatives in Japan, but this request was also rejected.' He was allowed to send ten farewell letters.

Before climbing the ladder to the scaffold Hoshijima began shouting '*Tenno heika banzai* [Long live the emperor]!' A provost officer immediately tried to silence him with a series of slaps across the face. 'The Japanese closed his teeth on the provost's hand, bit deeply into the flesh, and drew a steady flow of blood,' Sydney's *Daily Telegraph* reported. Hoshijima was then propelled up the thirteen steps to the platform, where the hangman settled the noose around his neck. The last words he heard were from the hangman: 'This is for the one thousand Aussies you killed at Sandakan.'

Chapter 32

THEY THOUGHT I WAS DEAD

—————

Sticpewich's standing as a POW at Sandakan and Ranau gave him unique authority as a witness in the war crimes trials, and he was determined to use it. As he wrote in his 'War crimes and events' statement:

> We now have all Japs concerned with the PWs throughout Borneo in custody, together with signed confessions of war crimes committed, in most cases. No court should allow any of these criminals to go unpunished. With this outline of facts of the darkest period of our prisoner-of-war life, no stone has been left unturned in bringing these inhuman Japs to trial.

Sticpewich went to great lengths to bring the worst of the Japanese and Formosan guards to trial. At the Labuan compound where suspected Japanese war criminals were interned after the surrender, he diligently identified the main abusers. He was often present at their interrogations and wrote detailed and damning 'notes' on statements made by Captains Takakuwa and Watanabe, implicating both officers personally in atrocities committed against POWs.

Nobody knew better than Sticpewich who was guilty of what: 'During the 2½ years or thereabouts in which I was a PW at Sandakan I became familiar with the habits and conducts of practically all the . . . Formosan guards,' he wrote in his statutory declaration. 'With few exceptions all . . . were very cruel in the treatment of PW and of their own initiative frequently carried out cruel beatings and assaults on PW to an excessive degree.'

In the 1947 radio broadcast *Six from Borneo*, Sticpewich claimed to have been able to 'interrogate and identify more than a hundred Japanese'. Their faces, he boasted, had 'gone green when I walked in. They thought I was dead in the jungle. They never expected me to come up with the evidence of how they had bashed and starved and killed our men.' Bill Moxham told Dick Braithwaite after the war that the Japanese guards held at Labuan were 'greatly shocked' when they saw him and Sticpewich. They 'didn't expect to see anyone', Moxham said.

Not all of the interned guards had cause to fear Sticpewich's retribution; there were many who had not mistreated the POWs or had done so only under direct orders. In his written comments on interrogation statements made by guards, Sticpewich was always careful to distinguish between those like the Gold Tooth Runt and the Black Bastard who bashed prisoners for their own amusement and those who used violence when ordered to but otherwise left the POWs alone. Kaneshige was an example of the latter: 'Usual type,' Sticpewich wrote in his statement. 'Carried out orders when NCOs and officers present. No ill-treatment when on his own.' On Nishikawa's statement he commented, 'Very easy going type; dodged as much of the bashing as he could; was an ordinary guard; did not ill treat unless forced to.'

Some guards such as Sticpewich's friend Takahara risked serious punishment by supplying food, medicine or information to the POWs; such acts of kindness were also acknowledged by Sticpewich in his written comments. Yamamoto Jiro, for instance, had the nickname 'Happy'. In his statement Sticpewich wrote: 'This man dodged as many beatings as he could & because of his being cheerfully disposed to PW was given the above nickname.'

Shoji was another guard who received a favourable comment from Sticpewich. 'This man's nickname was "Sparkles", he wrote:

On a few occasions he lost his temper and beat PWs but apologised afterwards. He realised he was wrong and gave them presents ... PWs undergoing sentence in cage were supposed to receive no food. He often brought food to them surreptitiously ... He warned us on several occasions when there were acts of bastardry to be put on on the orders of Moritake. They were given orders that on the least provocation they were to beat PWs. He was guard commander and restrained himself from many beatings.

Chapter 33

IT WAS AN HONOUR

Nothing better illustrated Sticpewich's ability to make himself indispensable to both sides than the trial of the guards on the second death march. Captain Takakuwa Takuo and Captain Watanabe Genzō had already been tried at Labuan for the murder of prisoners on the second march and simultaneously for the massacre of prisoners at Ranau. Both were found guilty on all counts. Watanabe was shot in March 1946 and Takakuwa was hanged in April.

Sticpewich had not arrived soon enough to give evidence in person against Takakuwa and Watanabe but the prosecution tabled an extract from his statement to Captain Ruse as well as the statement he had given a fortnight later to Justice Mansfield.

On 7 January 1946, two days after the officers' trial ended, 21 guards went on trial charged with the murder of 'numerous unknown PW' between Sandakan and Ranau. By then Sticpewich was busy giving evidence in the trial of Captain Hoshijima and the prosecution again had to rely on an extract from his statement to Captain Ruse along with the comments he had attached to the guards' interrogation statements.

By the time the trial began, the guards had had several weeks to reflect on the admissions they had made to the interrogators, and one by one they asked for permission to alter or add to their statements, usually with an anecdote about how they had shared food or cigarettes with a prisoner. Fukushima Masao complained about the 'unsatisfactory' comments Sticpewich had written on his statement: 'On being interrogated by Sgt. Maj. Sticpewich,' he told the judges, 'questions were forced on to me and if I denied it I was beaten. I wished to let Sgt. Maj. Sticpewich understand my effort [to improve conditions for POWs] during the last three years but he would not listen.'

Most of the guards admitted to killing one prisoner but insisted they were acting on orders or in some cases at the request of a prisoner begging to be shot. Nagahiro Masao recalled how 'one prisoner could not go on because of hunger and asked me to shoot him. I told him I could not do this but he begged me to and even saluted me so I killed him out of mercy.' Several told variations of the same story of prisoners saluting as they were mercifully dispatched with a shot to the head.

Late on the second day of the trial Sticpewich was called by the defence as a witness in reply, but this backfired when he was cross-examined by the prosecution and made fresh allegations that had not been in his statement to Captain Ruse. One allegation that emerged during his cross-examination was especially abhorrent:

Q: Do you think all of these wanted to kill PWs or do you think some did not want to?

A: From the talk I gathered it was an honour to kill a PW and they revelled in it.

Two guards unequivocally denied the allegation. Umemura Kenburō told the judges, 'Nobody thought it was an honour, everybody disliked that.' Asked whether it was 'considered an honour to be in the killing party', Takeuchi Yoshimitsu answered, 'No. It was an order.'

Despite these denials and despite the lack of corroborating evidence, the allegation that guards felt 'privileged' to murder Australian POWs became a central pillar of the case against the 21 guards on the second march, emphasised by the prosecutor in his summing up: 'Obviously, they gloried in these killings and considered it an honour to kill . . . The prisoners were simply murdered in cold blood and it is apparent that the accused considered it a privilege to be included in Tsuji's party.'*

The judge advocate general, when considering the guards' petition for mitigation, offered a pragmatic and even compassionate reason for the killings, arguing that while there was 'no doubt that the shooting of these prisoners of war amounted to murder . . . it must be . . . admitted that the only option that the Japanese had was either to murder them or abandon them to die on the track or in the jungle beside the track, and it is certain that it was more humane to shoot such prisoners of war'.

Urged by the prosecution to reject the guards' amended statements and accept instead the more damaging admissions they had made to war crimes investigators several weeks earlier, together with Sticpewich's damning evidence from the witness stand, the judges found nineteen of the 21 guards guilty of murder.

---

* The defence objected to the term 'killing party' to describe the squad led by Sergeant Major Tsuji. 'The said "Tsuji party" was not organised intending to kill the prisoners but to take in the prisoners who would drop out of the group during the march between Sandakan and Ranau . . . and that party was to be called properly "the struggler-receiving party" and not to be called "the killing party" as the prosecuting officer named it.'

Once he had completed his work for the prosecution Sticpewich immediately found himself enlisted as a witness for the defence, which used his comments about individual guards to plead for mitigation:

> As to the character and behaviour of the accused, WO Sticpewich stated—'Yokota treated us fairly well, he misappropriated foods and vegetables and gave them to the PWs'; 'Utsonomiya, good type, he always took care of stores and misappropriated some to our favour'; 'Kamimura, he is an inoffensive type and I have never seen him strike PWs'; 'Shoji often brought food for PWs', and even as to many others who had beaten PWs he said they struck only under the supervision of officers, and on their own were quite good. These comments prove their affection and goodwill towards the PWs.

Sticpewich's evidence was as effective for the defence as it had been for the prosecution: Utsonomiya was acquitted of murder while Yokota, Kamimura and Shoji were found guilty but sentenced respectively to only nine, ten and eight years—significantly less than Matsuda (twenty years) and Fukushima (fifteen years), who were both excoriated by Sticpewich. The judge advocate general recommended these sentences 'be reduced by half' but his advice was ignored. On 14 March 1946 Lieutenant General Sturdee confirmed both the finding and the sentences. Sticpewich was evidently satisfied with the twenty-year sentence imposed on Matsuda, but he was not finished with Fukushima.

Chapter 34

SKELETONS

———◦———

After his successful prosecution of Hoshijima, Athol Moffitt was given the job of prosecuting eleven Japanese—nine officers, a warrant officer and a sergeant—for atrocities committed during the first death march. Moffitt expected another 'difficult' case and worried that 'seven or eight may get off' due to lack of evidence. 'We all know what happened,' he wrote in his diary. 'PWs marched till they fell out and then shot. We can never tell they were shot except in a few isolated cases. The best we can do is prove murder by forced marching and rely on circumstantial evidence.'

The organisation of the marches militated against witnesses. As the men were divided into nine groups, a prisoner could only give first-hand evidence about what had happened in his own group. Even then, with prisoners in each group strung out in single file and long distances between those at the front and the stragglers, there was little chance of the two survivors, Botterill and Moxham, being able to say whether those who died were murdered by the Japanese or succumbed to disease or exhaustion, and if they were shot then by whom.

As Botterill and Moxham were still not well enough to come to Labuan to give evidence in person, the prosecution had to rely on sworn statements the pair had given to the war crimes commission in November 1945, together with evidence given by the accused before and during the trial. Sticpewich had not taken part in the first death march and did not appear as a witness, but on the day before the trial started he made a declaration stating things he had heard about the first march.

As well as being charged with the murder of POWs, the nine Japanese officers each faced alternative charges of forcing sick and starving prisoners to march long distances at great speed, causing the deaths of many. The trial was held at Labuan between 23 and 28 January 1946. Anticipating that the defence would attempt to use the excuse of 'superior orders' to mitigate responsibility for atrocities, Moffitt openly challenged the defence to 'prove in evidence any cases where Japanese officers or guards have really been seriously punished not just ridiculed, reprimanded or slapped for refusal or failure to murder . . . any PW'. Nearly all the evidence about killings was, inevitably, circumstantial: a straggler was seen in the company of an armed Japanese guard; a shot was heard; or the guard returned to the group alone and the prisoner was not seen again.

In their statements, effectively immune from contradiction due to the deaths of other witnesses, most of the accused claimed that the Japanese went to the aid of sick prisoners and even helped carry them on stretchers. They insisted that prisoners did not die on the track but were helped to rest houses and died there at night. But when Sticpewich arrived at Ranau in June 1945 he learned from Botterill and Moxham what had really happened. Nearly everything Sticpewich could say about events that took place on the first death march derived from these conversations and was therefore hearsay.

Japanese records—which at least in term of numbers were usually accurate—showed that 110 of the marchers had died by 22 February, when the last four groups were ordered to halt at Paginatan. Nearly all the deaths were attributed to illness but this was flatly contradicted by Botterill, who told the war crimes commission: 'Men dropped out from the march as they became too weak to carry on and they were immediately shot.'

Called as a witness for the defence, Captain Hoshijima described the condition of the 455 prisoners when they set out as 'good'. Reminded by Moffitt of his previous evidence that 'about 200' were not fit enough to go and that he had wanted to hold back a hundred of the sickest, Hoshijima blamed the interpreter for misrepresenting him.

Sticpewich's declaration broadly corroborated the statements made by Botterill and Moxham, although it sometimes deviated in detail or emphasis. For instance, he claimed to have been told not only that the POWs in the first march 'never received any assistance from the Japanese' but also that they were 'continually abused and hit with sticks and rifle butts if they lagged or looked like stopping'. While Moxham claimed to have been 'beaten along to get to our destination' on the last leg of the journey between Paganitan and Ranau, Botterill's evidence to the war crimes commission did not mention stragglers being beaten by the guards to keep up.

There was one point on which Sticpewich was able to give eye-witness testimony. The Japanese claimed to have buried dead POWs 'politely' and to have put 'roughly made crosses' on their graves. In his declaration, however, Sticpewich recalled seeing 'approximately 30 skeletons' lying beside the track when he came through on the second march. The skeletons, he said, had 'Aust. clothing and equipment covering them'. Moffitt made sure to mention Sticpewich's sighting of 30 skeletons in his opening address.

Given the lack of eye-witness testimony by prisoners, it was impossible in most cases to prove individual guards guilty of murder. Botterill, however, claimed that he 'saw four men shot when they fell out and this was done by the Japanese sergeant-major'. The sergeant major in Botterill's marching group was Gotanda Kiroku, who claimed to have always walked ahead of the group to look for food.

In his closing address defence counsel Colonel Yamada argued that Captain Yamamoto and his officers had no control over the conditions of a march they had been ordered to undertake at short notice by 37th Army HQ. They did not decide the speed of the march and they were not responsible for the provision of food and medicine along the route. 'The prosecutor's allegation that PWs were compelled to march under most inhuman conditions and kept moving with terrific speed is absolutely groundless,' he told the judges, and was based on 'imagination and rumours'.

Moffitt acknowledged in his diary that Yamada's address was 'clever and to the point—could easily lead a weak court astray'. As Moffitt had predicted at the start of the trial, Yamada repeatedly invoked the defence of 'superior orders' for seven of the nine accused officers while at the same time assuring the judges there was 'no trait of ill-treatment whatsoever' on the 'friendly march' from Sandakan to Ranau. On the contrary, there was 'not the slightest doubt' that Japanese soldiers had 'sacrificed themselves' in order to help the prisoners.

Moffitt conceded there was little direct evidence of the killing of prisoners but argued that facts such as the speed of the march and the number of deaths together 'may form circumstantial proof of the crime'. The defence, he said, had 'direct evidence' consisting of denials by the accused and of their claims to have acted kindly towards the prisoners, but it was all lies. It would be an 'insult', Moffitt told the court, for the prosecution to examine these lies in detail:

All the witnesses from the PWs except two have been killed off and the secret of what happened on the march . . . is locked in the minds of these Japanese accused now before the court . . . These men all in danger of their lives have formed a conspiracy to invent a story which each will corroborate to the last detail . . . Even Captain Hoshijima has been recruited to assist in the perjury.

Set against the 'pathetically weak' lies of the Japanese, Moffitt said, was the evidence of 'WO Sticpewich, Bdr Moxham and Pte Botterill'. The order in which he named the three men was telling since only the last two had been present on the march. But it was Sticpewich, by having 'spoken to' the six survivors of the first march, who tied the prosecution case together because those six 'must have known the full story of what really happened on the march': 'When they said generally "No Japanese assisted them" and that once a PW fell behind "We never saw him again", I submit that it was true of the whole joint march. It is only hearsay evidence but it is open to the court [to allow] such weight as it thinks fit and I submit that it is the truth.'

The judges agreed: they found Yamamoto, Abe, Gotanda and Sergeant Satō guilty of murder and the other seven group leaders guilty of the ill-treatment of prisoners. After listening to character references and claims by some of the accused to have shown kindness to the prisoners, the court handed down its sentences: death by hanging for Yamamoto, life imprisonment for Lieutenant Tanaka, who had sent two sick prisoners from group six back to Sandakan, and death by shooting for the rest. The lenient sentence given to Tanaka would have surprised Botterill, who claimed to have 'worked out No. 6 party was the worst of the lot'.

Moffitt was pleased with himself: 'I had to make sure they had no doubts and brought in the just penalty of death,' he wrote in his diary. 'The Japanese and the world must be taught that they cannot just subtly kill PWs by forced marching and get out of it with imprisonment only.' His closing address had been 90 minutes long: 'I had a job to do—a score to keep for the lads who died,' he wrote. 'I felt it was the best analysis of a circumstantial case I have done.'

The next day he learned that the eleven accused had been seen 'laughing and joking' as they waited to be led away, with one going up to Yamamoto and pretending to hang him and others putting on hand-kerchief blindfolds and 'shooting' each other.

Three days after the trial finished, news came through that the death sentences for seven Japanese guards found guilty of killing Australian POWs near Brunei had been commuted to ten years' imprisonment; only the officer in charge was to be executed. Moffitt was incensed, blaming the decision on the 'weak-kneed' Labor government's policy of opposition to capital punishment.

Ten days later Moffitt was sailing for Australia, and by the end of February 1946 most of the sentences he had fought so doggedly to achieve had been annulled. The findings and sentences related to the first death march were not confirmed; there would have to be a retrial.

Chapter 35

INVALUABLE SERVICE

On 22 March 1946, five weeks after Moffitt left Borneo, Lieutenant General Sturdee, acting commander-in-chief of the Australian military forces, approved the award of an MBE to Sticpewich for his services as a prisoner of war. The citation began with a three-line summary of his time as a prisoner of the Japanese, while the remaining twenty lines described his exploits in the months after his escape:

> From Temaliau village he sent police boys with a message giving the history of Sandakan [POW] camp and enemy strength and dispositions. These boys got in touch with an SRD party and on 10 August 45 WO Sticpewich joined the SRD where he reported that 4 AIF personel [sic] had escaped on 17 Jul 45. They were located on 14 Aug 45. During the period 10 Aug to 20 Sep 45 WO Sticpewich carried out patrols with the SRD.

He was evacuated to Morotai and there assisted in the war crimes investigations. Later he voluntarily proceeded on foot from Keningau to Ranau, Borneo, with a prisoner of war contact party and located a number of graves which would probably not have been found without his assistance. He then proceeded on foot to Jesselton, inspected all Japanese and identified about one hundred who had been concerned with the brutalities in the camp and the deaths of nearly two thousand on various death marches. He then returned to Labuan and rendered invaluable service in the interrogation of these Japanese. Without such assistance it is most probable that many Japanese would not have been brought to justice.

Throughout the period from his escape to the present date WO Sticpewich has shown devotion to duty of a very high order and has been most unselfish and co-operative in assisting authorities and the next of kin of his former fellow prisoners of war.

That Sticpewich immediately after his escape was capable of spending six weeks 'carr[ying] out patrols' with fit and highly trained SRD agents was confirmation of how little his health had suffered relative to the other survivors. Moxham and Botterill, by comparison, had to be carried in on stretchers, while Short could barely walk unassisted. Two months after he was brought in, Campbell was described in his interrogation report as 'still a patient at 2/5 AGH [Australian General Hospital] and . . . progressing satisfactorily'. Braithwaite was so weak after his escape that after weeks of medical care, during which he was fed up to six times a day and plied with vitamins and supplements, he could handle no more than two hours' daily interrogation. Sticpewich, however, was well enough to retrace the route of the death marches to find the graves of dead comrades and to walk from Ranau to Jesselton (a distance of around 100 kilometres) to point out the Japanese guards who had bashed and murdered them.

Sticpewich's service and casualty form shows him flying to Sydney from Labuan on 15 December 1945, then returning to Morotai from Brisbane in the new year. During January and February he flew back and forth between Brisbane, Morotai and Labuan. Correspondence during this period shows his eagerness to remain involved in the search for war graves.

On 4 March, described as 'an ex PW at present on leave in NSW', he was the subject of a reinforcement direction that 'anticipated that WO Sticpewich will volunteer with HQ Aust War Graves Gp (Central Pacific)'. The unit had specifically requested his assistance in the 'recovery of deceased members of the Forces on the Sandakan–Ranau trail', an area of which he was known to have 'an intimate knowledge, being one of the survivors of the march over that route'. His posting would go through on the condition of his being 'prepared to serve through the demobilisation period, and being medically fit to return overseas'.

Sticpewich's efforts to return to Borneo paid off, and his service and casualty form confirms that on 29 March 1946 he was on his way back to Morotai to take up his posting with the war graves unit. It had been almost eight months since his escape from Ranau, and during that time he had been almost perpetually on the move. He appeared indefatigable, a man with unfinished business and no time to lose.

Chapter 36

A BIT DOUBTFUL

⸺⸺◆⸺⸺

The retrial of Captain Yamamoto and others for atrocities committed on the first death march was scheduled for 20–27 May at Rabaul, and this time Sticpewich, Moxham and Botterill gave evidence in person. Sticpewich was the odd one out, a hearsay witness testifying about a march in which he had not taken part.* During a break in his evidence he was allowed by the defence to 'refresh his memory' by referring to a statement he had made during a previous interrogation.

---

* Sticpewich was on the second march that left Sandakan at the end of May, not the first, which left at the end of January, yet the transcript of evidence recorded the following statement by Sticpewich: 'We left as far as I can remember on 28th Jan 45 and left the camp at about 5 o'clock in the morning.' Was it a slip of the tongue or a stenographer's mistake that caused him to include himself among the first group of marchers?

What followed was largely a recapitulation of evidence he had already given at Hoshijima's trial and in various written statements. Some of it related directly to his own experience on the second march, and some was hearsay based on information he claimed to have been given by the six survivors of the first march when they reached Ranau.

In the three months between the original trial and the retrial, Sticpewich's recollection of the march had markedly improved. He was able to help the prosecution with the kind of detail it needed to prove that prisoners had been killed rather than simply left to die. He remembered a lot more about the '30 or more skeletons' he had seen beside the track:

> Some days we saw 4 or 5 but sometimes we only made 1 . . . we could see webbing, Aust boots and hats and throughout the march we knew we were following another party as we would pick up soldiers' personal gear such as a letter or paybook. There was only one proper grave and en route we could not go off the track to inspect these remains . . . at night at rest camps we would sneak away and scout around for evidence . . . there was one place with 5 bodies together. The bodies' bones were scattered around as though they had been mauled by pigs and there were 5 skulls.

Sticpewich could not say for certain whether any of the prisoners whose skeletons he had seen had been shot, but Botterill could. One or two men in his group (group three) were left behind 'every second or third day', he told the court. Each morning those who were too sick to move would tell the Australian officer in charge that they 'could not move with the party and the Japanese sgt or officer would count us and move us off and we would get along the road about ¼ mile and we would hear shots'. According to Botterill, the Japanese officer would tell the POW officers they 'had to shoot the men who were left behind'.

As well as the prisoners who fell out at the start of the day, others attempted to march but were too weak to keep up; these, too, were killed. 'The way I know the Japanese shot these men,' Botterill told the judges, 'was that the Japanese officer told us at night.'

Moxham marched in group seven, one of the last to leave. He claimed to have seen bodies on 'quite a few occasions' at resting camps, and once he heard 'quite a lot of shooting' coming from the camp 'about a mile' away. Moxham also remembered 'definitely human smells' at a number of places along the road, although he 'never saw the bodies'.

The second trial largely followed the course of the first, except in the findings against Sergeant Major Gotanda and Sergeant Satō, both of whom had initially been found guilty of killing prisoners and sentenced to death. This time the defence argued successfully that the evidence against the pair was flimsy. The case against Gotanda depended on evidence from Botterill, whose allegations had always seemed questionable. In the second trial Botterill accused Gotanda of going back from Paginatan to shoot a sick prisoner despite admitting that he 'may have been a bit doubtful' when the same question had been put to him the previous morning.

It emerged that after giving evidence Botterill had confronted Gotanda outside the latrine and made 'certain hand gestures' towards him. 'I caught the word Paginatan . . . and after that he held up one forefinger and then with it made a motion similar to pressing a trigger,' Gotanda told the court. 'From Pte Botterill's gestures and expression I thought he was going to ask me a question. I used my hand by waving it sideways, backwards and forwards in front of my face which meant I did not do it.'

Apparently the encounter outside the latrine jogged Botterill's memory, enabling him to make the accusation he had been 'a bit doubtful' about the day before. Seizing on the discrepancy, the defence wondered how his memory could have been 'so mysteriously reinforced' after seeing

Gotanda's gesture of denial. It was the duty of the prosecutor, he argued, to 'ask him in re-examination to explain his certainty in order to clear the matter up as to why he had become positive overnight'. The reason why the question had not been asked was, he suggested, that the prosecutor was 'fearful of what the answer might be'.

In his closing address the defence counsel argued that in the absence of any other evidence against him Gotanda could not be convicted and the judges agreed, finding both him and Satō not guilty. Yamamoto and Abe were not so fortunate; both were found guilty of murder and sentenced to hang. The other group leaders were convicted of ill-treatment of POWs and given ten years. This time Lieutenant General Sturdee confirmed both the findings and sentences. Captains Yamamoto and Abe were hanged at Rabaul on 19 October 1946.

But Sticpewich's job as a witness was far from done. He had played a small part in the conviction of Yamamoto and Abe, and was a decisive witness against Hoshijima, but there were other scores still to be settled.

Chapter 37

I GOT HIM HUNG

In the final week of May 1946 three separate war crimes trials were held at Rabaul. Sticpewich, Moxham and Botterill gave evidence for the prosecution in all three.

The first trial was of three guards accused of having murdered Gunner Albert Cleary in February or early March 1945. The three guards were Kitamura, Kawakami and Suzuki Saburō. The first two were already serving fifteen-year sentences as a result of previous trials, while Suzuki was serving a twelve-year sentence. All three had been among the most hated guards at Sandakan, and Sticpewich had attached incriminating comments to their written interrogation statements.

Kitamura used to trip prisoners ju-jitsu style, and 'when the PW went down he would kick him. He was always most cruel.' In a statutory declaration dated 26 January 1946 Sticpewich described Kitamura as a 'flash show-off type' who 'excelled in cruelty on the slightest pretext'.

Sticpewich had personally interrogated Kitamura in the Japanese prisoners compound at Labuan, where Kitamura 'admitted to me that he had kicked the English doctor—Capt. Daniels—in the testicles. The reason for this was that Capt. Daniels had seen Kitamura kick another PW in the testicles and said he was going to report Kitamura to the Commandant.'

Kawakami, the 'Gold-toothed shin-kicking bastard', was 'the guard commander on many occasions and used his powers cruelly. His beatings and ill-treatment of PWs are too numerous to mention. His special delight was kicking and particularly if he kicked PWs in the testicles. He was implicated in ill-treatment of PWs in cage and working parties in general.' Suzuki was notorious for bashing prisoners, especially those confined in the cage.

The prosecution case was that Kitamura, Kawakami and Suzuki had tortured and bashed Cleary to death as punishment for having escaped. Of the three prosecution witnesses, only Botterill was at Ranau when the incident took place: Moxham was at Paginatan with other survivors from the seventh group and would not arrive at Ranau until late March, and Sticpewich, who gave evidence in the form of a statement, was 260 kilometres away at Sandakan.

Botterill had already given a succinct account of Cleary's ill-treatment to the war crimes commission:

Two Australians, Crease and Cleary, attempted to escape from Ranau but were recaptured and tortured. Logs were put under their legs or behind their knees and then the Japanese would tread on them and make them scream out in pain. These men were also starved and the Japanese put the point of the bayonet between their eyes. Cleary was just about dead when the Japanese sergeant told us to take him into the hut, where he died about ten minutes later. He had a chain around his neck and had no clothes. He was out in the open for two weeks with very little food and was in full view of all the natives who passed. During this time, he went down and down in health.

Moxham's mention of Cleary to the war crimes commission was even briefer. Cleary and Crease, he said, 'were stripped and tied at the guard-house to a post, without food; the weather was very cold, much colder than at Sandakan. They kept Cleary there until he was practically dead; he died a few hours after being returned to camp. He was badly beaten.'

By the time he came to give evidence in the trial of Kitamura, Kawakami and Suzuki, Botterill's recollection of events had improved. He was in the witness box for two days, describing in graphic detail a prolonged and savage assault on Cleary that he had neglected to mention to the war crimes commission just six months earlier. He saw the guards kick Cleary 'viciously all over his body, the face and mouth and everywhere possible; holding his head up and hitting him in the throat with the bare knuckles. They were charging at him with a rifle and fixed bayonet, stopping about an inch from his face.' Botterill gave an especially vivid account of the log torture, telling the judges: 'I have suffered this treatment myself.' He saw Suzuki, Kitamura and others jumping on the ends of the log, sometimes with one foot and sometimes with both feet, making Cleary 'squeal':

> Every half hour they would make him get to his feet . . . After being on the log for about a quarter of an hour the legs are paralysed . . . After half an hour you can't feel them as they go numb altogether. Then they stand you up and that causes more pain for about 5 minutes. The effect of standing up is worse. You can feel the pain in your legs for the rest of the day.

Cleary's torturers, Botterill said, were the 'best condition I have ever seen them in; they could hit strong and hard . . . The beating was continu-ous, and there was always someone there to hit him. I was in the hut most of the time . . . and Cleary was in my full view . . . and when he was not I could hear him.'

According to Botterill, Cleary was beaten continually for several days. During this time Botterill went on one or more rice-carrying trips to Paginatan, returning once to find Cleary tied to a tree, naked except for a loincloth. Eventually he was released, but by then 'Cleary weighed about 3½ stone and we knew he was going to die, from the look of his eyes'. After feeling his pulse Captain Jeffrey, the Australian medical officer, allegedly murmured a single word, 'Murdered', before adding, 'If any of you ever get out of this, don't forget to tell the authorities about it.'

Although many guards had joined in the beating of Cleary, Botterill only named three: 'In the treatment given to Cleary,' he told the court, 'Kitamura was the worst by a long way, Kawakami was next, and Suzuki and the rest of the guards did their fair share of it.'

The guards denied everything. Kitamura swore that he had not given Cleary the log torture and had never seen or even heard of it being carried out in the Japanese army, nor had he seen or heard of any 'rough treatment' given to Cleary or any other escapee. Both Kitamura and Kawakami stated that Suzuki was at Paginatan, not at Ranau, when Cleary was supposed to have been beaten. The court rejected a request by the defence to call five more witnesses, all willing to testify that Suzuki was at Paginatan at the time. Suzuki swore that he was at Paginatan and did not return to Ranau until 25 or 26 March—several weeks after Cleary's death. 'Moxham should know that I returned at that date,' he told the court. Moxham, however, gave a much earlier date for Suzuki's return to Ranau, a date early enough for him to have taken part in the bashing.

Compelling as it was, Botterill's testimony created problems for the prosecution. Under cross-examination he was forced to admit that he had 'difficulties with dates' and had 'got the dates a bit mixed up'. He was unsure about when Cleary and Crease had escaped and about the dates of the various rice-carrying trips to Paginatan. In the end, however, none of this mattered: the judges believed Botterill and Moxham and rejected the evidence of all the guards. Kitamura, Kawakami and Suzuki Saburō were found guilty and sentenced to death. The sentences were confirmed and the trio were hanged at Rabaul on 18 October 1946. Botterill must have had this in mind when he told Tim Bowden in a taped conversation that he had 'no grudge against the Japanese myself . . . I went back to the War Crimes [trials] . . . and got all the revenge I wanted.' Asked specifically what he remembered about Kitamura, Botterill replied softly: 'I don't want to talk about him. Because I don't remember that much about him. He was a mongrel and a pig. He really bashed me plenty of times. I got him hung.'

There is no doubt that Cleary was brutally mistreated over many days but did he die as a result of dysentery and, as Botterill told the war crimes commission, of being beaten, starved and left almost naked in the open, or was he murdered? And if he was murdered, by whom?

In her book Silver accuses Moxham and Botterill of having 'stitch[ed] up' Suzuki Saburō. Moxham, she writes, 'was prepared to lie under oath' to get Suzuki hanged. Botterill, meanwhile, was determined to punish Kawakami, who had boasted of killing his best mate, Richie Murray.

Misguided attempts to secure a posthumous Victoria Cross for Cleary prompted Silver, in 2011, to write to the Defence Honours and Awards Appeals Tribunal with more detailed allegations of perjury by Botterill, who had died in 1997. She described Botterill as a 'close friend' to whom she had been a 'trusted confidante'. In all his interviews and conversations, she told the tribunal, Botterill 'always identified the dysentery, poor food, exposure and lack of medical treatment as the cause of Cleary's death'. According to Silver, Botterill confessed to having 'lied to make sure [he and Moxham] "got" the guards responsible for the murders of the sick [at Ranau] and his friend Murray. Although Suzuki took no part in Cleary's torture, [Botterill] and Moxham were out for revenge for his other misdeeds and put him in the frame with the others.'

Chapter 38

ADDITIONAL INFORMATION

Sticpewich could not claim credit for the convictions of Kitamura, Kawakami and Suzuki, although his comments on the trio's interrogation statements probably helped convince the judges of their capacity to commit the crimes Moxham and Botterill had accused them of. He played a more significant role, however, in the trial of the Formosan guard Fukushima Masao for the murder of Sapper Arthur 'Dickie' Bird at Ranau. The trial was held immediately after the Cleary trial, on 28 and 29 May.

Fukushima, aka the 'Black Bastard', had a reputation for being one of the most vicious and sadistic guards at Sandakan. In January 1946 he had been sentenced to fifteen years for murdering prisoners on the second death march.

In his statement to the war crimes commission Botterill mentioned Fukushima by name, saying he 'used to force sick men out to work and sometimes even drag them from their beds; he used to bash dozens of men every day on the working parties'. Sticpewich noted his habit of picking out a prisoner and kicking him on his bandaged leg to see if there really was an ulcer beneath. 'It might be mentioned this is the most cruel thing that anyone could witness,' Sticpewich said, 'as anyone who has had an ulcer knows the severe pain one has to endure without having an animal kick it.' He added an unusually long comment to Fukushima's interrogation statement:

> He would walk along the line and pick out PWs [for working parties] . . . irrespective of their condition. If any comment was passed he would bash them with a stick and kick them on their ulcers . . . he watched the condition of the PWs undergoing sentences in the cage. When the condition of these men became so low that they looked like dying he would report to Moritake and have them sent back to camp. He . . . bashed the cage personnel and also those on outside working parties. He 'stood over' the other Formosans as he was a favourite with the officers.

Moxham and Botterill had particular cause to hate the Black Bastard, who confessed to having beaten prisoners both at Sandakan and later at Ranau. Having seen Fukushima escape the death penalty for murders committed on the second march, they now saw a second opportunity to put a noose around his neck.

Moxham was the first to give evidence, telling the court that 'early in the month of July 45 . . . about 5th July' he was detailed to join an afternoon work party. When Fukushima saw the work party was short, he went to fetch more prisoners from the group deemed unfit by the medical officer. One of these was Sapper Bird, who had an ulcer on his leg and was suffering from malaria. When the party set off Bird collapsed, saying he was too sick to go on. Fukushima slapped him 'about 15 or

20 times' across the face while Bird pleaded to be allowed to go back to the lines, then Fukushima started kicking him. When the interpreter Private Lance Maskey tried to intervene he was slapped. Fukushima was wearing Japanese army boots, Moxham said:

> The first time the kicks appeared to me to be landing around his neck and head . . . Then I saw the accused become very excited swearing in Japanese at Private Bird to make him get up and go on the party. Private Bird did not rise and the accused then put the boots into him in a very ungodly fashion. The kicks landed all over his body, stomach, testicles, legs, head. Standing there a minute seemed like hours, I should think it would be at least ten minutes that the kicking lasted.

When the working party returned around 5pm Bird was still lying where they had left him. They carried him back to the lines, where medical officer Captain Picone looked at him. '[A]t this time he was coughing and vomiting blood,' Moxham told the judges. 'Capt Picone shook his head and then went away.' The next morning Bird was dead.

Botterill gave a similar account of the bashing:

> The accused kicked Bird in the chest and stomach. The accused then lost his head and he started kicking Bird and shouting out at him. He kicked him all over the body, the more he kicked, the more he worked himself up. I remember him kicking him in the testicles a few times, we spoke about that during the afternoon. He also kicked him in the face, head, mouth, chest and body. The accused was wearing Japanese Army boots.

When it was Fukushima's turn to take the stand he said his job was doing paperwork in the office and he left it to Captain Cook and Private Maskey to organise work parties. On the afternoon of 5 July no work parties went out, he said, as all guards had to listen to an address by Captain Watanabe about the killing of Lieutenant Suzuki by a Formosan guard. He denied even knowing Bird, but he knew Botterill and Moxham. Their motive for giving evidence against him, he suggested, was that the pair 'have been bearing a grudge against me because I had punished and struck [them] often . . . when they stole food or did some wrong while we were situated at Sandakan'.

After listening to the judge advocate general's advice on points of law the court found Fukushima not guilty, but he was immediately rearrested and committed for trial for the same offence on the grounds that 'additional information' had come to light. The source of the new evidence was Bill Sticpewich, who had been in Rabaul throughout the first trial but was only now called on to testify. According to Silver, Botterill and Moxham had been 'outraged' by the not guilty verdict in the original trial and 'briefed' Sticpewich on what to say in the second trial, which would take place on 30–31 May.

Moxham and Botterill had little time to rehearse their evidence, but their recollections about the bashing of Sapper Bird aligned perfectly:

[Moxham:] On about 5th July in the afternoon about 2 o'clock I was detailed to a work party cutting cane . . . the accused swearing and cursing at Bird tried to make him rise to his feet. Bird did not rise and then he gave him a very unmerciful kicking about the head, face, body and testicles . . . the accused was wearing Japanese Army boots . . . I saw Pte Bird the next morning dead . . . I thought that the bashing that he received contributed mainly towards his death. From my observations Bird definitely would not have died when he did had he not received the bashings.

[Botterill:] On the 5th July at 2 o'clock in the afternoon I was on a cane collecting party . . . [The accused] kicked him and then motioned to the party and Bird made no attempt to move. This made the accused wild . . . The accused seemed to lose control of himself and kicked him all over the body on the testicles, on the mouth and head . . . the accused was wearing army boots . . . I saw Bird again the next morning. I passed him about 7 o'clock in the morning going to roll call and he was dead . . . From my personal observations I formed the opinion that he died because of the beating he had received.

Cross-examined by the defence on whether anyone other than Bird had died as a result of 'beating or kicking' by Fukushima, Botterill said that at Sandakan Fukushima used to pull sick men out of the line and beat them and they would die 'four or five days later'. Asked how many men had died from this, Botterill answered: 'I should say about twenty men.'

The third and final witness for the prosecution was Sticpewich, who by his own account 'knew [Fukushima] from about Oct 42 up to the time I escaped' and who 'practically had connections with him daily in the matter of being detailed for work and since his apprehension as a prisoner'. Sticpewich's evidence about the death of Sapper Bird exposed an array of contradictions. In court he gave a typically meticulous account of the events surrounding Bird's bashing, but his version of the assault deviated significantly from Moxham's and Botterill's, especially in the timing of the incident. 'I am speaking of 8 o'clock in the morning,' he told the judges, although the other two had both put the time of the beating at 2 o'clock in the afternoon.

As Bird lay dying from the bashing he had received, Captain Oakeshott allegedly told Sticpewich, 'If anybody is fortunate enough to escape this camp or live it out, this incident with others should be brought before the authorities and see that justice is brought about'—a speech remarkably similar to that allegedly made by Captain Rod Jeffrey after the fatal bashing of Gunner Albert Cleary.

The gruesome description by the three Australians of Fukushima's assault on Bird raised awkward questions for the prosecution. If the beating was ferocious enough to cause Bird's death, why had the medical officers been so reluctant to treat him? Why had Bird's fellow prisoners not made more effort to intervene? And why, especially given Oakeshott's impassioned plea for justice, had Moxham, Botterill and Sticpewich remained silent about the killing of Bird until now?

Sticpewich was asked directly by the defence whether he 'had the intention of reporting this incident of Pte Bird to the higher authorities'. He answered, 'Yes, with many other incidents which have been dealt with in the past.' However, it had been nine months since the war had ended, and although Sticpewich had made several statements to Australian war crimes investigators this was the first time he had mentioned the killing of Sapper Bird.

In the long statement he gave at Morotai in October 1945 Sticpewich described meeting the five Australian survivors (the sixth survivor was British) of the first march, including Bird, soon after his arrival at Ranau:

> Within a couple of days I had an opportunity to have a conversation with two of these five, Spr Bird and Sgt Stacy. They told me that all the others had died from malnutrition and from exhaustion brought on by the rice carrying from Ranau to Paginatan . . . Both these men have since died of dysentery, malnutrition and the effects of their bad treatment.

This was hardly the ringing denunciation of the killing of Sapper Bird called for by Captain Oakeshott. Nor had Sticpewich mentioned the fatal bashing of Bird when he gave evidence against Fukushima in the second death march trial, and nor did he mention the incident in his comment on Fukushima's statement, although he described Fukushima's brutal treatment of POWs in general terms.

Sticpewich told the court that at the 6.30 am sick parade on the day after the bashing he saw Bird lying 'in approximately the same position as I had seen him the night previous'. There were marks on the ground 'where it could be seen that he had been writhing during the night'. Four hours later Bird had been 'stripped of all his clothes' and Sticpewich 'assisted with the carrying of the body down to the cemetery. There were bruises on the face and abrasions on the chest and shoulder'.

No prisoner, he said, 'not even myself, being one of the fittest at that time, could survive any sort of a belting whatsoever let alone a kicking', but when asked by the defence when exactly Bird had died, Sticpewich answered that '[t]he actual hour could not be ascertained because he died during the night as there were many sick and no-one could attend to them personally'.

Q: You mean to say that no POW took care or looked after him?
A: They had a full time job looking after themselves.

With some assistance from Sticpewich the defence was able to show that after allegedly seeing an Australian soldier bashed to within an inch of his life his own medical officers had simply walked away, that other prisoners had not come to his aid during the night and that Moxham, Botterill and Sticpewich had not seen fit to raise the matter until now. 'I cannot understand,' the defence counsel told the judges, 'why such an incident, which was said to have given such a deep impression upon the minds of POWs, has not even been taken up by the court of Labuan when the accused was tried there in another matter.' As far as the defence was concerned there was no evidence to prove Sapper Bird was murdered: Bird was obviously very sick, and none of the three Australians had the medical knowledge to say what had caused his death.

Sticpewich was the difference between Fukushima's first trial and his second. Silver suggests that Moxham and Botterill, having failed in their first attempt to have Fukushima convicted, 'decided to enlist the aid of Sticpewich'. The pair had no love for Sticpewich but regarded him as 'a consummate performer in the witness box . . . the best liar Botterill had ever met'. Sticpewich 'could argue black was white', Botterill told Silver, 'and he would be believed'.

Yet Sticpewich's performance as a prosecution witness was ambiguous, his evidence a curious mix of the helpful and the unhelpful. His pointed remark that he was 'speaking of 8 o'clock in the morning' as the time of the bashing he witnessed did not necessarily contradict the pair's evidence that the bashing they saw occurred at 2 o'clock but nor did it corroborate it, and he must have known that the more horrifying his account of Bird's injuries the more the judges would wonder why he had kept quiet about them before now. Given his own experience of legal proceedings at his court martial in Brisbane, did Sticpewich also have an inkling that the decision to retry Fukushima might not survive legal scrutiny?

The defence attempted to have the trial discontinued on the grounds that the 'additional evidence' on which the second trial was premised had not materialised; however, disregarding the many inconsistencies in the prosecution case, the court found Fukushima guilty. Reviewing the case, the judge advocate general, W.B. Simpson, expressed his disbelief at the decision to acquit Fukushima in the first trial as '[i]t appears to me that the accused was undoubtedly guilty'. His review, though, was based not on whether or not Fukushima committed the crime but on the validity of the second trial. Simpson argued that under common law Fukushima could not be tried twice for the same offence, thus as he had been found not guilty the first time the court had no jurisdiction to try him a second time. Lieutenant General Sturdee accepted his advice and Fukushima was acquitted.

Silver states as fact that Moxham, Botterill and Sticpewich committed perjury in Fukushima's second trial: 'Sticpewich had been out of the camp on a work detail when Bird was attacked,' she writes. 'However, by the time the other two had filled him in on the fine details, to which Sticpewich had added his own little touches, he was able to recount a blow-by-blow account of the incident.'

The court transcripts show, however, that Sticpewich told the judges he 'did not see what happened that afternoon'; the 'blow-by-blow account' he gave the court was of a bashing he claimed to have witnessed in the morning. Was Sticpewich playing both sides, hedging his bets, testifying as asked for the prosecution while giving evidence that in the crucial matter of when the bashing took place must have muddied the picture? Did the 'new evidence' Sticpewich was supposed to supply, and which was the sole justification for the second trial, help the prosecution or did it actually hinder it?

And what of Sticpewich's remark that he 'practically had connections with [Fukushima] daily in the matter of being detailed for work and *since his apprehension as a prisoner* [my italics]'? Was Sticpewich merely telling the court he had often seen Fukushima in the prisoner compound when he, Sticpewich, was identifying Japanese soldiers accused of war crimes, or was there something more to the 'connections' between Sticpewich and Fukushima?/ Or between Sticpewich and other Japanese war criminals?

Chapter 39

LIEUTENANT STICPEWICH

It was not until mid-August that Sticpewich was able to put his local knowledge to use in the search for bodies. Arriving from headquarters at Macassar, he found that 31 Australian War Graves Unit (AWGU) had almost completed its work on the Sandakan–Ranau track. The wet season was closing in and the unit's efforts over the previous two months had worn out most of its equipment and trucks. 'All MT [motor transport] requires a thorough overhaul,' the unit's CO, Captain Johnstone, advised war graves HQ in Macassar. 'It is very difficult to maintain MT in as good condition owing to continual usage and very poor roads.'

Sticpewich was highly critical of 31 AWGU's results. During a search for remains on the section between Boto and Paginatan he clashed with Lieutenant Brazier over what he considered to be the latter's failure to properly supervise the local workforce. Johnstone's weekly report for 17 August 1946 noted that a total of 94 bodies had been recovered from the Sandakan–Ranau track. 'It is considered that this is a reasonable figure,' Johnstone advised war graves HQ. A week later he had changed his mind: 'The OC has decided to recall the whole party to Sandakan for reorganisation and refitting,' he wrote. 'This is also necessary as the OC is not satisfied with the number of recoveries.'

A party under Sticpewich's command was sent to re-search a section of track between Sapi Island and Paginatan, but problems with the local workers continued. 'Having trouble with coolies,' the unit diary for 30 August 1946 recorded. 'Rubber planters offering double our wages. OC decided to increase wages 20 cents per day. Have lost 20 coolies from our compound this week.' The following day Sticpewich took the entire track search party to Beluran to cover sections 'not covered to satisfaction of the OC or Lt. Brazier'. In his weekly report for 31 August Johnstone expressed his confidence that 'this party will complete the track task'.

As well as searching for remains, Sticpewich collected evidence from local villagers who had information about Japanese atrocities. A cable from Captain Russell Brereton suggested that Sticpewich 'try contact native RANAU MENGAU area who witnessed killing of survivors from RANAU camp about 12 August (45). If possible get signed statements from them.'

Vehicle breakdowns continued to plague 31 AWGU, whose work was further hampered by the arrival of the wet season. In mid-October Sticpewich was busy 'check[ing] over all the recoveries so far completed and supply[ing] additional information if possible', work that was interrupted for more than a week when he became ill. A request came through for him to provide assistance to 8 AWGU, which was working in the Ranau area and having trouble reconciling its finds with information previously supplied by him. But where exactly was Sticpewich? Nobody seemed to know. His whereabouts around this time was the subject of a string of increasingly impatient entries in 8 AWGU's war diary. There was speculation that he was in Sandakan or even Singapore.

Sticpewich was finally sighted on 1 November 1946. The 8 AWGU diary recorded that 'Captain Johnstone and WO Sticpewich arrived from Sandakan . . . with stores for this unit. Included was a second-hand refrigerator, but not in working order.' The broken refrigerator was much smaller than the crate it came in; 8 AWGU concluded that a 'newer, larger refrigerator' had been on its way to them before being 'intercepted and replaced by 31 AWGU'. In addition 31 AWGU had helped itself to a large consignment of paint meant for 8 AWGU, leaving only 'one gallon of white'.

On 4 November a conference was held 'between all members of the unit and WO Sticpewich re all locations in the Ranau area. Existing figures were checked and altered where necessary.' The total number of deaths at Ranau was revised down to 537, of which the unit had recovered 435 or 81 per cent. This was the 'highest recovery figure of any PWs as far as is known'. After listening to Sticpewich's advice 8 AWGU decided to re-search the track to Paginatan, as Sticpewich had 'pointed out several probable locations which were a mile or so off the track, and not noticeable previously'.

With 8 AWGU still struggling from a lack of essential provisions—the whisky ration had to be 'cut down on the grounds of insufficient supplies'—Sticpewich departed on 8 November by flying boat for Singapore en route to Tokyo, where he was required to give evidence in another war crimes trial. According to his service and casualty form, while in Tokyo he spent some time in hospital for an unspecified ailment. In early 1947 he was again lobbying to return to Borneo but by then 31 AWGU had had enough of him, and he was ordered back to general headquarters at Macassar. While he had no choice but to follow these orders, he was determined to return to Sandakan.

The army's decision was made in the belief that Sticpewich had already gone over the entire length of the Sandakan–Ranau track, re-searching the sections that had been inadequately searched the first time, but this was not true: he had re-searched some but not all of the track. When he pointed this out he was told he could return after all, but the terms no longer suited him and he went back to Australia, where he set to work on a statement outlining all his grievances.

In a scathing letter to the director of the war graves commission Sticpewich noted there had been 'no personal supervision over the native searchers by a European, natives have to be strictly supervised, or else they will take the line of least resistance meaning, instead of a strict pattern search they will go where its [sic] easy travelling if they are not checked and kept in line'.

Sticpewich's complaints were also personal. On several occasions, he wrote, he had 'expressed to Capt Johnstone, the fact he was not giving me a fair go, and not treating me right as I came up here to help and search and he was placing every obsticle [sic] in my way . . . he was treating me as an interloper . . . I was told I was of no consequence, a W.O.1, and only attached and I was under his orders.'

While adamant that he 'would not tolerate any of the past treatment', Sticpewich insisted that 'its [sic] our duty to those who were not as fortunate as I to leave no stone unturned to do everything possible . . . The way I feel is that some one has been responsible for wasting some of my time and taxpayers money, in the face of so many next of kin demanding to know what is being done and want information.'

There was more than a hint of menace in these words. Sandakan had become a hot potato for both the army and the government: distraught relatives of Sandakan POWs were clamouring for information about the fates of their husbands, sons and fathers, and many had written to Sticpewich himself seeking help. Any perceived lack of will or effort in the recovery operation would only deepen the tragedy of their deaths.

In his 'Confidential Report re Sandakan–Ranau area' dated 27 March 1947, Major Harry Jackson noted that only five bodies had been recovered

from the track between Paginatan and Ranau, the section searched by 8
AWGU. To him this seemed a 'very low figure': Jackson had walked the
track and he knew the story of the rice-carrying trips to Paginatan. He
suspected 'many more bodies' were to be found along this section of the
track 'in view of the fact that the Japanese used PW as "coolies" carrying
rice between Paginatan and Ranau, and that the condition of the PW
would be abnormally low on the last difficult stage of the march from
Paginatan to Ranau which no doubt caused many stragglers who were
always killed by the Japs'.

The original search by 8 AWGU had only extended about 20 metres
either side of the track, a distance that had been cleared by the Japanese
themselves. It seemed logical to Jackson that if the Japanese were going
to dispose of the murdered prisoners they would hide them beyond the
cleared area. By widening the search to 40 metres either side of the track he
believed more bodies could be found. 'The country is extremely difficult to
search,' he wrote, 'but my opinion is that many deaths must have occurred
between Paginatan and Ranau, certainly more than the five recovered.'

Jackson had spent time with Sticpewich, although he never learned
how to spell his name, and had seen something of his personality—enough
to know what he might be capable of if his wishes were not granted. In his
'Confidential Report' Jackson wrote that the 'likelihood of WO Stipewitch
[sic] causing trouble if he does not return to Borneo should be seriously
considered'. The problem for Sticpewich was that others involved in the
search for remains were now sceptical or even openly dismissive of his
advice. In his 'Confidential Report' Jackson commented:

> This WO was able to give me a considerable amount of information
> which enabled me to successfully complete my mission, on the other
> hand he also gave me information that was incorrect. From what has
> been told me I know that neither the OCs 8 AAWGU [Australian
> Army War Graves Unit] or 31 AAWGU place much reliance on . . . the

information given by Stipewitch [sic] in view of the fact that so many of his statements were proved to be false. I consider that the OCs of the war graves units in Borneo [should] be given the opportunity of answering the complaints made by Stipewitch. I also believe that the other survivors of the death march can give enlightening information on the activities of WO Stipewitch.

Given the context of this remark it seems possible and even likely that Jackson was alluding to the kind of 'activities' that caused Owen Campbell to tell Don Wall that if the war had ended before the first death march the Australians 'would have killed' Sticpewich as a collaborator.

By the time Jackson submitted his 'Confidential Report' the war graves commission's director had decided that Sticpewich should, after all, return to Borneo, but the paperwork for the transfer bore little resemblance to the glowing citation that accompanied Sticpewich's MBE a year earlier. The adjutant general included two remarks with his approval of the posting:

1. No other suitable officer is available for posting to undertake special duties in the Sandakan–Ranau area.
2. Appointment considered necessary and in the best interests of the Service.

Despite the obvious reservations Sticpewich was given the temporary rank of lieutenant under strict conditions:

He is to be informed that his appointment as lieutenant will be terminated by his demobilization at the end of this period of duty and that, consequently, the rank of lieutenant is granted to him for the duty he is to perform in North Borneo, and is to be retained only whilst he is performing that duty.

The new commanding officer of 31 AWGU, Captain Burnett, was briefed in writing before his arrival. Sticpewich had been detailed to 'carry out a complete re-search of the Sandakan–Ranau Track' and was to come under Burnett's command. Burnett, however, would have to 'make arrangements for provision of stores and personnel required by Lieut. Sticpewich'. The extent of the search on both sides of the track 'will be determined by you after consultation with Lieut. Sticpewich'. It was 'imperative', Burnett was reminded, that 'every assistance and full co-operation be extended by your unit'. Jackson was not hopeful of success:

> I consider that further searches on the *rentis* [track] are essential but whether WO Stipewitch [sic] can do any better as an officer is a matter that Capt Johnstone of 31 AAWGU, Capt Collins OC 31 AAWGU or Lieut Brazier can speak with more authority than I, except that from what I have learned from them I would say that their answer would be "No". What WO Stipewitch said he knew and what this alleged information produced in the form of bodies were apparently different matters.

If Major Jackson's intention was to block Sticpewich's return to Borneo he was too late. Sticpewich was given instructions to 'embark by US Catalina aircraft . . . leaving Sydney on or about 31 March 1947'.

It was in Sydney that, according to Lynette Silver, Sticpewich 'ran into Mo Davis' in a pub. Private Eric 'Mo' Davis was another Sandakan survivor, but unlike Sticpewich he had got out before the death marches. A larrikin who made trouble equally for his own officers and the Japanese, Davis had been part of a group of officers and assorted miscreants transferred to Kuching in June 1943 after the escape of eight prisoners from Berhala Island. 'On learning that Sticpewich was returning to Sandakan,' Silver writes, 'Mo mentioned that a search of the hollow trunk of the Big Tree, where POWs . . . had cached their valuables, might be in order.'

Keeping any personal motives to himself, Sticpewich rejoined 31 AWGU as lieutenant (special duties) and immediately began preparing for a comprehensive search of the track. His diary for the period shows him struggling to manage an often refractory local workforce while diligently pursuing information about Japanese killings:

At the 10¼ mile a native led us to a location where he stated . . . he was working on the rentis for the Japs. He saw 6 Japs 4 ORs and two officer types with swords with a white man (soldier) they put a rope round his neck and strangled him then dragged him into the jungle about 12 yds where they left him. He later saw where they left the PW stating he covered the body with the PWs ground sheet, but said the Japs stripped the cloths from the victim. All that he could produce was the top of a skull . . . This man came out of hospital to guide us to this location . . .

Our hands are full handling this bunch of wild men. Both [Sergeant] Bunter and myself horse [sic] shouting at them and chasing them up . . .

Had conference with Orang Kia he knew nothing what went on here while the Japs were here. He is a liar he was their head native man in the interior. Natives are now beginning to spill any information required . . .

Have decided to divide the rewards for finding remains between those who dig them in the cemetery plus a $10 bonus for the one who gets the most recoveries . . . A bulldozer could not shift as much dirt as this gang has been doing. I would be here a month on the ordinary terms of employment and costs would be higher.

Sticpewich's efforts resulted in the discovery of more than a hundred bodies that had been missed during previous searches. Although his information did not always prove reliable, he made an invaluable contribution to the recovery operation. Of the 2428 Australian and British prisoners known to have died at Sandakan, Ranau or somewhere between, the remains of 2163 were recovered. One of these was of particular significance to Sticpewich.

Chapter 40

A VERY TROUBLED MAN

———⟶●⟵———

In the statement he made at Morotai on 7 October 1945, Sticpewich described the last days of his friend Herman 'Algie' Reither thus:

> On the 2nd August after a lot of adventures I had contacted a kampong chief and prevailed upon him to help us as the Allies were close and he did feed and help us . . . After I escaped that is the last I saw of anybody in the Ranau camp. Reither died due to exhaustion from dysentery on the morning of 8 Aug out from the kampong.

He appears to have given a similar account of Reither's death to Major Jackson. In his report Jackson wrote that the two Australians were 'found by a native named Ginssas', and that while they were hiding in a hut owned by Ginssas 'a Japanese came but the men were hidden from his view under a grass mat'. Sticpewich and Reither then 'found their way to the house of a man named Dihil [also known as Adihil]' where 'Reither became seriously ill with dysentery and eventually died on 8 August'.

Silver introduces a further element, suggesting that by the time they reached Dihil's house 'Reither had sustained injuries to his stomach, arms and legs'. Dihil had heard shots the previous night and 'thought the wounds had been caused either by a bayonet or bullet'. Neither Sticpewich nor Reither offered any explanation for the wounds.

News of Reither's death took some time to reach his family in Australia. A family notice published in the Bacchus Marsh *Express* on 1 September referred to Reither as 'previously reported prisoner of war, now presumed dead'. A week later two more notices in the same newspaper stated conclusively that Algie Reither 'died while a prisoner of war'.

Sticpewich avoided contact with the Reither family for several years but in February 1951 he wrote a letter to Reither's sister, Bessie Clissold, in which he said that Algie died on 8 August and had been suffering from dysentery and malaria. The letter, a copy of which is among a small folder of documents relating to Reither at the Australian War Memorial, also described how he and Algie reached the kampong:

We struck out from our hold up the following evening and took all that night to travel a mear [sic] 2½ miles and had to rest him up the next two days of which he wandered into near trouble and I happened to be along after doing a Reccie. By luck we managed to save the situation as I was fortunate in speaking some Dusun, and malay, and managed to have travelled over the mountain the following day helped by two colaberators [sic] to the Samong Kampong.

The letter implies that Sticpewich rescued Reither from some kind of confrontation with locals and suggests that dysentery and malaria were the cause of his death.

Another account cited by Richard Braithwaite gave a different version of events. It came from a Formosan guard who was interviewed in 1995 for a Film Australia documentary called 'Return to Sandakan'. The guard, Karoshima Toyashuge, said that after Sticpewich escaped 'the next day the whole camp, all of us guards searched. I searched too, but couldn't find him. But . . . a man called Takahara found Sticpewich, but made as if he hadn't. I heard afterwards that he had found him.'

Takahara was the guard who had been transferred from 8 Mile Camp in June 1944 'under suspicion of being too easy' with POWs and who warned Sticpewich to escape before the remaining prisoners were massacred. Michele Cunningham gives a similar account of the escape but identifies the Formosan guard as 'Takata'. Whether it was Takahara or Takata, the implication seems clear: Sticpewich survived because the Japanese allowed him to get away. Sticpewich, already under a cloud for his perceived collaboration with the Japanese at Sandakan and Ranau, would not have wanted such a story told and might have gone to some lengths to keep it secret.

What of the wounds mentioned by Silver: had Reither been injured in some kind of scuffle with a Formosan guard? In her book she writes simply that '[w]eakened by dysentery and his injuries', Reither died on 8 August.

In his interview with Tim Bowden, Don Wall offered yet another version of the incident. According to Wall, Sticpewich claimed to have left Reither in the hut while he went out 'bandicooting'* in a nearby vegetable garden. When he returned to the hut he found Reither dead with 'three or four' stab wounds, which he claimed were self-inflicted. Wall told Tim Bowden, 'Sticpewich wanted people to believe that Reither had killed himself.' Wall investigated this theory and tracked down a 'native' who told him that Reither had been stabbed in the back.

---

* 'Bandicooting' was cutting a plant beneath the ground in order to steal the tuber and then replanting the stem.

'Reither couldn't have done that,' Wall told Bowden, 'and they pointed the finger at Sticpewich.'

Asked by Bowden why Sticpewich would have wanted to murder his mate, Wall replied, 'He wanted to be the only survivor. He didn't want witnesses around.' Witnesses to what, Bowden asked. Wall answered, 'His friendship with the Japanese.'

At the time of his escape Sticpewich would not have known there were five other survivors, although if the Japanese had caught or shot Botterill's group he would have been quick to hear of it.* It is possible that Sticpewich believed he and Reither might be the only survivors, and with Reither out of the way there would only be him.

Bessie Clissold's son Alan (Algie's nephew) told Richard Braithwaite of a visit to Borneo in 1995 during which he met Adihil, the man who had hidden his uncle from the Japanese. Adihil told of Algie 'dying in his arms' and made a 'vigorous stabbing motion', which Clissold apparently understood to indicate the stabbing from which Reither had died. However, the meeting was cut short and Clissold confessed to being 'unable to establish [from Adihil's gestures] who was stabbing whom'.

Braithwaite writes that Adihil's youngest son Apin 'seemed to know his father's story well' and claimed that Reither 'had been shot by a Japanese in the upper leg and side by two or three bullets':

According to Apin, there were no stab wounds. Reither was talking, and he and Sticpewich seemed good friends. Sticpewich was not wounded but had scratches on his body. Reither's wounds became infected. He told Sticpewich to leave him behind. However, they moved him to greater safety at night on an improvised bed on the back of a water buffalo . . . Sticpewich promised he would return and

---

*   While Sticpewich was aware that others including Botterill's group had escaped, he would have had doubts about their ability to survive in the jungle.

build Adihil a fine house, which Apin says never happened. However, Stipewich did pay for Adihil's two older sons to attend school in Sandakan.*

Two decades later Apin changed his story—or, rather, added to it. Through his 'fluent English'-speaking son, Apin told Lynette Silver that when Adihil encountered the two Australians Reither was suffering from 'lacerations to the backs of his calves' and a 'deeper wound, which had punctured his abdomen, just above his hip'. Adihil risked being tortured to death by the Japanese for harbouring escaped POWs, but despite this he hid the pair and fed them, each day bringing food 'concealed in lengths of hollow bamboo'. Reither's wounds became infected, and although Adihil treated him with local herbs the infection worsened.

Reither's injuries would have made it impossible for him to keep up with Sticpewich as he attempted to make contact with Allied forces on the west coast, but there was another reason why Sticpewich came to consider his friend a liability: Reither was delirious with a fever and began crying out. Worried that someone would hear him and inform the Japanese, Sticpewich allegedly convinced Adihil that in order to save himself and Adihil and his wife they had no choice but to kill Reither. However, as Sticpewich had sent a runner to try to contact Allied forces in the area his friend's death had to 'look like an accident'. According to Apin, Sticpewich persuaded Reither to move from the hut and shelter inside a cave hidden from view by a slab of overhanging rock. Adihil, Silver writes on her website, 'was waiting nearby with two stout and heavy

---

* Laniam binte Baranting told Kevin Smith in 1997 that 'After the war we heard from Adihil's family that Sticpewich had offered to educate the children in Australia, but they did not accept.' Smith went on to say that Adihil's son 'proudly keeps a large photograph of his father as a young man with Sticpewich who is wearing a green beret. That beret was later given to Adihil . . . by Sticpewich as a memento.'

poles, made of belian or iron wood, which were used by his wife to pound rice . . . Standing on the bank above Reither's hiding place, the pair used the poles to collapse the overhang, suffocating him.'

Pigs discovered the body and Adihil later buried what was left of Reither's remains in a spot close to the original Ranau POW camp, where they were found some months later by an Australian war graves unit. The discovery of his friend's body in a different place to where he had left it would presumably have surprised the meticulous Sticpewich, if nobody else.

Did Apin tell Silver the truth? In the film documentary *Return to Sandakan* Adihil told the story in his own words. Recalling how he helped Sticpewich, Adihil said, 'The white man [Sticpewich] had been attacked by the Japanese, but he managed to escape. He came to me at night for help. I pitied him and took him in. I gave him food and hid him.' Had Adihil forgotten all about Sticpewich's companion, or was there a more sinister reason for leaving Reither out of the story?

Sticpewich's interrogation records and witness statements reveal nothing more about the fate of Algie Reither, but eight years after the war Sticpewich returned to Labuan for the dedication of the cemetery where Reither and nearly 4000 other Commonwealth servicemen were buried. A photograph published on 10 June 1953 in the Adelaide *Chronicle* shows Sticpewich crouching beside a grave. The caption reads: 'LT. W. H. STICPEWICH, one of six survivors of the infamous Sandakan death march, represented the Eighth Division P.O.W. Association. He pays his respects at the grave of a death march comrade, Herman Reither, of Victoria, who later died of illness.'

Father Brendan Rodgers, a former POW who was at Sandakan and became a kind of confessor to Sticpewich after the war, told the Reither family that Sticpewich was a 'very troubled man'.

Chapter 41

ALWAYS BEST FRIEND

———————

According to Don Wall, Sticpewich murdered Algie Reither in order to keep his 'friendship with the Japanese' secret. There was one Japanese in particular whom Sticpewich had worked hard to befriend: Captain Nagai Hirawa.

Nagai arrived at Sandakan in April 1943 and became Hoshijima's second in command. Dick Braithwaite described him as 'very cunning', a quality Nagai would surely have recognised in Sticpewich and vice versa. Although Nagai purported not to speak English, it turned out that he spoke it very well. Braithwaite told Tim Bowden that Nagai had been spotted sneaking under the Sandakan huts at night, eavesdropping on the prisoners' conversations. This, Braithwaite thought, was how the Japanese found out about the secret wireless.

Botterill's assessment of Nagai was much harsher: he described him as 'one of the worst guards'. In his statement to Captain Ruse, Sticpewich accused Nagai of more than doubling the size of the aerodrome work force from 300 men to 800 men despite the growing list of prisoners unable to work due to dysentery and malnourishment: 'I often heard Capt. Nagai and Lieut. Moritake when the guards were drawn up, instructing them to be more hard on us for breaches of rules . . . After [Nagai's] appearance the beatings increased.'

In his 'Notes on interrogation of Nagai', Sticpewich alleged that after a prisoner lost an eye as the result of being beaten with a stick, an Australian doctor, Major Eddey, took Nagai to task, promising to hold him personally responsible for the injury. Nagai 'then said "Mind your own business as this is a matter for our governments to settle, and don't mention any more such incidents or I will have you sent to Sandakan", meaning to the Kempai-Tai'. Nagai insisted on prisoners being cremated, put a stop to burials and banned padres from funerals. 'He definitely did NOT like the Aussie manner or spirit, which he tried to break,' Sticpewich wrote.

None of this, apparently, prevented Sticpewich from cultivating a personal relationship with Nagai. According to Dick Braithwaite, Nagai had the technical section build a pressure gauge for a small launch he owned. As a qualified engraver, Braithwaite was seconded to Sticpewich's crew. 'Sticpewich requested he engrave some Japanese script on the pressure gauge he made for Nagai's boat,' Richard Braithwaite writes. 'Dick initially refused but then did the job in exchange for a billy can made by the technical group and the use of a good quality engraving tool.' The tool was later retrieved.

Nagai left Sandakan in mid-1944 to take charge of 300 POWs building an airstrip at Labuan. In February 1945 he took over as commanding officer at Ranau, but he was gone by the time Sticpewich arrived with the survivors of the second march. After mid-1944 Sticpewich and Nagai did not meet again until Sticpewich saw him at the Japanese prisoner compound on Labuan.

Following their rescue by SRD agents, Sticpewich, Moxham, Short and Botterill had all been questioned about the roles of individual Japanese officers at Sandakan and Ranau. Captain Mort's interrogation report noted that Nagai was 'well educated and spoke fluent English' before singling him out as being 'responsible for most of the atrocities and starvation endured by PW'.*

At the Labuan prisoner compound Sticpewich identified Nagai to Captain Brereton as an officer at Sandakan from April 1943 but, crucially, he did not denounce him, enabling Nagai to be repatriated to Japan without facing trial—a quite extraordinary outcome for him given the allegations made in Mort's interrogation report just weeks earlier.

When Keith Botterill, who was back in Australia and too sick to go to Labuan, found out that Nagai had given investigators the slip, he drew up a list of Nagai's crimes and asked Sticpewich to deliver it to war crimes investigators and bring the matter to the attention of the International Military Tribunal for the Far East in Tokyo, where Sticpewich was to appear as a witness. After being given to Sticpewich the list was never seen again. Botterill told Silver about Sticpewich's sarcastic remark 'What do you want to do: hang every Jap in Japan?' and said he found this comment 'rather odd'. It did not occur to Botterill that Sticpewich might have his own reasons for letting Nagai go.

After Sticpewich and Nagai met in Tokyo at the end of 1946, the two men began a correspondence; there were even plans for them to write a book together. On 16 January 1952 Nagai wrote to Sticpewich:

---

*   As Botterill held a deeper grudge against Nagai than the other three, it seems likely he was the principal source of this rather wild allegation. By contrast, Mort's assessment of 'Capt. Osojima' (that is, Hoshijima) consisted of only two points: 'OC Sandakan camp prior to Capt. Takakuwa' and 'Left Sandakan for Jesselton'.

Dear Bill Sticpewich,

Many many thanks for your Christmas and New Year greetings. Really I was so much pleased to receive a card from you, that the memories of my life in Borneo and a day in Tokyo with you kept me doing nothing for a couple of days . . .

I have to count five years passed since you left me in Japan and those five years were too long for me because I lost a card with your address on it . . .

According to your proposal when you were in Tokyo, I wrote a rough stories [sic] of my life in Borneo Camp. Do you still have some idea to write a book with me? If you do still, please let me know your plan . . .

Yours always best friend,

Peter H. Nagai

Did the pair make a pact at Labuan in 1945 that led to this remarkable post-war friendship? Sticpewich's critique of his interrogation statement demonstrated the power he held over Nagai: 'Beatings of Australians was [sic] much more intense in Nagai's stay,' he wrote. 'He had a better feeling for the [British] than the Australians.' Such allegations, repeated in an Australian court, might have put Nagai in prison for a long time. But Nagai also held something over Sticpewich: knowledge of his collaboration with the Japanese. When it came to identifying the worst Japanese war criminals, Nagai's name was not on Sticpewich's list.

Sticpewich was a gambler; Billy Young told Silver that Sticpewich controlled the gambling at 8th Division's base depot at Johor Bahru and at Sandakan. If a deal was done to ensure Sticpewich kept quiet about Nagai's war crimes, what was Sticpewich's price? Was Nagai's silence enough, or did Sticpewich also demand money from his 'always best friend, Peter'?

Chapter 42

TREASURE

———⇒●⇐———

Unlike his fellow death march survivors, Sticpewich did not leave the army after the war. He served for a time with the regular army supplementary reserve before being seconded to the Department of Supply as a technical officer. His army report for 1954 listed the following qualifications:

(a) Command of Malay language.
(b) Full member Australian Welding Institute.
(c) Qualified supervisor of Welding.
(d) General engineer.
(e) Instructor in blacksmithing and oxy and electric welding.
(f) Qualified meat and foods inspector.

The skills that had kept him alive in Borneo continued to make him useful to the Australian Army.

In the late 1960s Sticpewich married and had two daughters. Braithwaite writes that Sticpewich was 'subject to paranoia and lived in a rather well-secured house in Melbourne'. According to Sticpewich's great-nephew Ben, the grandson of his brother James, it was a 'nice house in a nice area'—nicer, perhaps, than a soldier of his modest rank might normally have been able to afford.

Sandakan left deep psychological scars on all six survivors. Bill Moxham probably spoke for all of them when he told Justice Mansfield in November 1945: 'This is all something I will never be able to forget. I cannot get to sleep now—I cannot sleep until 3 or more in the morning. It's all buried somewhere inside me. I am having some treatment. I am out now on 14 days' sick leave which ends next Friday.'

After the war Moxham drank heavily and underwent electric shock therapy for psychosis before taking his own life in 1961. Braithwaite writes that his own father contemplated suicide.

Sticpewich was promoted to captain in December 1966 and retired in June 1970, aged 62, after 30 years service in the Australian Army. In retirement he was granted the title of major. A commendation signed by the adjutant general noted that he 'has proved loyal and trustworthy and has performed all his duties in a capable and efficient manner'. His experience in the field of equipment development would, the commendation said, be 'greatly missed'.

Seven years after Sticpewich retired from the army he was killed while crossing a road; apparently he was hit by two cars. It is not known whether his death was an accident or whether, like Moxham, he committed suicide.* Like so many other veterans, he struggled to

---

* Don Wall believed that Sticpewich was murdered by or on behalf of Nagai or one or more of the other survivors. 'Sticpewich was murdered,' he told Tim Bowden in 2004. 'A hit and run job.' Wall admitted that he had no evidence from the police to support his assertion, and the idea has been rejected by both Silver and Richard Braithwaite. Other than the unusual circumstance of being

obtain the compensation he felt he deserved as an ex-POW. Perhaps the fight depressed him.

While he knew he was disliked by his fellow survivors, Sticpewich was always confident they would not denounce him in public. He told his nephew Keith Sticpewich, Ben's father, 'Those bastards will never say anything while I'm alive.' Whatever reasons he might have had for that confidence, he took them to the grave.

Six years after his death other former prisoners of war, including Braithwaite, Botterill, Campbell and Short, began speaking to Hank Nelson and Tim Bowden for their radio documentary series *Australians Under Nippon*. In the course of these conversations a picture of Sticpewich as a 'white Jap' began to emerge. According to Richard Braithwaite, Owen Campbell accused Sticpewich of having given away prisoners who ventured outside the wire—an unforgivable act, if true. Silver personally witnessed Nelson Short telling Sticpewich's widow in front of others 'your husband, madam, was nothing but a collaborator'.

Whether or not it was fair to call Sticpewich a collaborator, Short's assertion that he was 'nothing but a collaborator' was untrue. After September 1943, when only three doctors were left at Sandakan, Sticpewich acted as a medical orderly.* He also 'assisted', as he put it, 'in the improvisation of instruments, making them and splints to hold the decayed legs of the prisoners, many of them to be able to get around

---

struck by two vehicles, there is no evidence whatsoever to support the theory that Sticpewich was murdered. The fact that Wall and possibly others believed it is indicative of the antipathy he aroused and also, perhaps, of a lingering belief among fellow survivors that Sticpewich was capable of anything: of collaborating, of murder and of being murdered.

* His medical qualifications were unorthodox, to say the least. He told the judges at Captain Yamamoto's second trial, 'My training as a medical orderly was [as] a student apprentice in an abattoir, which covers veterinary degree and also Army training qualified nurse.'

had to have their own leg reinforced with wood, their own bones not being strong enough to carry their weight'.

Dick Braithwaite tolerated rather than liked Sticpewich, although he might have felt differently had he been at Ranau, where Sticpewich effectively took over command from Captain Cook and where, according to Botterill and Short, he ingratiated himself with the Japanese by cooking their meals. Botterill, Short and Moxham carried secrets of their own— for instance, about how Andy Anderson, the fourth man in their escape party, really met his death*—but so long as they kept quiet their secrets were safe.

Time did not diminish Sticpewich's notoriety: he was a constant background presence in tape-recorded interviews conducted by Bowden, Nelson and Don Wall. References to 'Stippy' by other prisoners of war were rarely complimentary.

---

* Keith Botterill was interviewed by Tim Bowden in March 1983 for *Australians Under Nippon*. When asked about his escape he told Bowden: 'We were going downhill fast . . . we were in this hut for approximately a month when Anderson died of dysentery and malaria'. A note on the transcript described the interview as 'very hesitant and stilted'. Twelve years later Botterill took part in the Film Australia documentary 'Return to Sandakan'. Refusing to look at the camera, Botterill said in a halting voice, 'He just died there one night and the next day, uh, we buried him'. Lynette Silver believes that he, Moxham and Short agreed to kill Anderson, who was suffering from severe dysentery and whose delirious cries threatened to give them away. In her article 'The death of Private Herman Reither' she states that they beat Anderson over the head with a piece of wood and that Botterill was haunted by nightmares, often crying out in his sleep 'We had to kill him'. Without trying to justify Anderson's murder, Silver characterises it as a 'spur of the moment' killing, contrasting it with what she calls the 'ruthless, premeditated and very cunningly planned' murder of Reither by Sticpewich. It could be argued, however, that the circumstances and motivations behind both killings were remarkably similar: in each case a very sick and delirious man appears to have been killed by his companion(s) out of fear that he might give them away to the Japanese.

One of the many unresolved questions about Sticpewich concerned the valuables said to have been hidden inside the trunk of the Big Tree. According to Silver, Private Howard Hewitt, a notorious black marketeer who was nicknamed the 'Turk', had brought a cache of gold and diamonds with him from Singapore and hidden them inside the Big Tree. Sticpewich would have had opportunities to search the tree when he returned to Sandakan with 8 AWGU in 1946 and with 31 AWGU the following year. Silver notes that soon after his arrival at Sandakan in 1947 Sticpewich 'burn[t] the Big Tree to the ground'. Did Sticpewich find the Turk's loot?

Dick Braithwaite died in 1986. In 1995 his widow Joyce travelled to Sandakan with Sticpewich's widow Chris and others to attend a memorial service. Joyce and Chris shared a room. Joyce later told Don Wall that Chris Sticpewich confided to her that after the war she and her husband had lived well on the proceeds of the hidden treasure Sticpewich had recovered from Sandakan and smuggled home to Australia. Wall repeated the story in his tape-recorded conversation with Tim Bowden but made Bowden promise not to publish the material until after his death (he died in 2004). He also asked Bowden to deposit a copy of the recording with the Australian War Memorial, which Bowden did. Was this recovered treasure the reason why, after returning to Australia, Sticpewich was able to afford a 'nice house in a nice area' and to keep sending money to Adihil, the man who had kept him hidden from the Japanese?

Chapter 43

PROJECT KINGFISHER

———⟫●⟪———

Athol Moffitt intended to hold Captain Hoshijima personally to blame for the nearly 2500 prisoners of war who had died at Sandakan or Ranau or along the route of the death marches. 'I want to lay direct responsibility at his foul door for the 1100 [who had died at Sandakan while Hoshijima was commandant],' Moffitt wrote in his diary, 'and indirect responsibility for the other 1250.'

The case had been presented to Moffitt as a mass of written statements that under the War Crimes Act 1945 could be used as evidence. Some of the evidence contained in these documents and in the courtroom testimony of Sticpewich and other witnesses implicated Hoshijima personally, but much of it did not. To Moffitt the distinction was academic: Moffitt wanted Hoshijima to pay for *all* the atrocities perpetrated by the Japanese on Australian prisoners at Sandakan.

After seeing him for the first time Moffitt described Hoshijima's face as being 'more sadistic than I expected', but the war criminals he had seen among the surrendered Japanese soldiers at Lawas in November 1945 were also 'fat and sadistic'. Hoshijima represented every sadistic Japanese guard, and although Moffitt could not hang them all, with Sticpewich's help he could—and did—hang Hoshijima.

Moffitt's anger at Japan's treatment of Australian prisoners of war never abated, but in time he began looking for others to blame for the grim toll at Sandakan and Ranau. One question in particular haunted him: why had the Australian Government made no attempt to rescue the Sandakan POWs?

Years after the war ended Moffitt spoke to Private John 'Lofty' Hodges at a memorial service for those who had died at Sandakan. Moffitt had been deeply affected by the story of how Hodges found Moxham, Botterill and Short all near death and helped bring them to safety. It was an encounter, Moffitt wrote later, that 'graphically and emotionally tells the inner story of the hearts, minds and sorrows of the Sandakan POWs as a whole'. For Moffitt, the rescue of those three men would be a perpetual reminder of a larger rescue that never happened.

Hodges had parachuted into British North Borneo on 18 August 1945 as part of a reinforcement party for an SRD operation codenamed Agas III, one of whose objectives was 'making a reconnaissance for the rescue of P'sW at Ranau'. As a legal officer in the Australian occupation force in North Borneo, Moffitt would have known nothing about the operational objectives of Agas III, but he certainly knew something about the SRD's activities in North Borneo.

The source of his information was another Australian, Major Rex Blow, the SRD officer who in November 1945 had marched more than 300 Japanese prisoners to the village of Lawas, where Moffitt was working as a prosecutor. Blow and another SRD officer, Captain Jock McLaren, were among the group of eight Australians who escaped from Berhala Island in June 1943 just hours before they were due to be transferred to Sandakan.

From his conversations with Blow, Moffitt learned that the SRD had been running covert intelligence operations in Borneo since well before the Allied landing at Tarakan on 1 May 1945. Some of these reconnaissance missions had been in the Sandakan area. During a personal interview with General Blamey near the end of April 1945, Rex Blow and Jock McLaren had raised the question of a mission to rescue the prisoners at Sandakan. The pair gave slightly different accounts of that meeting but both recalled asking to be part of a paratroop assault on the POW camp, after which the prisoners would be taken off by boat. According to McLaren, Blamey told them: 'If it can be fitted in with the other operations we'll do it, and you two will be in it.' Blow and McLaren appear to have been taken in by the last part of Blamey's carefully worded promise without fully recognising the implications of the word 'if'.

Blow was later given permission to go to Sandakan with the aim of infiltrating the camp or at least communicating with some of the prisoners. Sometime around the end of May or the beginning of June 1945 an American patrol boat dropped Blow at a spot on the coast near Sandakan, where he was met by a local man with a canoe. After paddling upriver Blow was to make his way on foot to 8 Mile Camp.

While walking to the camp Blow and his companion stumbled upon what appeared to be the route of the second death march, the state of the trail suggesting that men had only recently passed through. Blow told Athol Moffitt by letter in 1988, 'I would say that I got onto the Death March trail not more than 48 hours after the PWs went through.' As they walked towards the camp they met locals who told them that the compound was now deserted; of the roughly 2100 prisoners at Sandakan at the start of January 1945 not a single one was left alive.

Blow was picked up by patrol boat and flown back to Australia to report his findings. Five months later he told Moffitt what he had seen, and for the rest of his life he remained convinced that he had missed the prisoners on the second death march by only a few days.

What neither Blow nor Moffitt knew when they met at Lawas was that when General Blamey made his qualified promise of a rescue operation he was aware that the mission—for which detailed plans had been drawn up—had already been shelved. In other words, he was offering to mount a rescue mission he knew would not happen. It took Moffitt more than 40 years to get to the bottom of this tragic story of broken promises and conflicting military priorities.

The seeds of a rescue plan were planted in early 1944 with the return of three of the Berhala Island escapees to Australia. The senior officer was Captain Ray Steele but the most valuable intelligence about Sandakan came from Walter Wallace, the only one of the eight who had actually seen the inside of 8 Mile Camp. Wallace was in some respects a similar character to Sticpewich. Like Sticpewich he had been able to avoid the worst of the physical labour by running a small maintenance party at the aerodrome. Richard Braithwaite writes that his father regarded Sticpewich and Wallace as 'highly skilled craftsmen who were somewhat envied . . . [for] their extra rations'. While neither was popular with fellow prisoners, both were 'smart operators' whose intelligence and practical skills brought benefits for the prisoner group as a whole; both were involved in the construction and operation of the secret wireless.

When Steele, Wallace and Sapper Jim Kennedy made their intelligence report in March 1944 the information they could supply about the condition of Australian prisoners at Sandakan was nearly a year out of date, but it told a shocking story. Wallace reported:

Bashings of all sorts soon commenced, both with canes and pick handles. Even though perspiration was pouring hard from the men, bashings continued hard and fast, many being crippled . . . Sickness spread, especially dysentery, averaging one death per week . . . rain or sunshine, Sundays included, work had to continue. Ju-jitsu was practised on the prisoners, a lot of men becoming nervous wrecks,

always fearing a bashing for no reason . . . The gang bashings, at least
six guards would take part . . . Food was still bad, sugar and salt was
never heard of . . . Clothes were wearing out, boots also, men were
going to work bootless, shirtless and in lots of cases just a piece of
cloth around the waist . . . Sickness increased at one stage to over
300 bad cases with little treatment and even patients were bashed
from time to time.

Wallace's account of Sandakan comprised only a small part of the
report, but it prompted the SRD to begin planning a rescue operation.
The mission, codenamed 'Kingfisher', had a single objective: 'to evacuate
and rescue all prisoners of war from the PW camps in the Sandakan area
of British North Borneo'.

Before detailed operational plans could be drawn up for the rescue,
an SRD party consisting of '2 officers, 2 W/T [wireless] operators and
2 natives' was to be inserted into the area to gather up-to-date intelligence on such subjects as the suitability of the chosen dropping zones,
the position of enemy anti-aircraft defences, the position, number and
routine of the camp guards and the times when prisoners would be
concentrated in the camp. In addition, detailed information was sought
on 'local topography, collaborators, vital installations, fuel dumps etc'.

The final draft of the 'outline plan' for Kingfisher, dated 3 December
1944, called for the SRD party to be in place 'at least six weeks' before
'D' day—the day of the rescue—in order to obtain and transmit the vital
intelligence not later than D-10 (that is, ten days before the rescue).
During that time the party was expected to 'contact a senior P/W officer'
from whom much of the necessary information could be 'extracted' and
who would be able to organise selected prisoners inside the camp to
'receive arms dropped from the aircraft' on the day of the rescue. How
this was to be achieved in the face of resistance by armed Japanese guards
was not explained.

The outline plan canvassed three options for the insertion of the SRD reconnaissance party: by Catalina flying boat, submarine or parachute from a B-24 Liberator bomber. Insertion by Catalina was deemed 'feasible' but 'less secure'. The parachute option, although used for other SRD missions in Borneo, was rejected on the grounds that the chance of members of the party being able to find either each other or their storpedoes (equipment containers dropped by parachute) after a night drop in the heavily wooded and unsurveyed Sandakan hinterland was 'extremely small'. In the end it was decided that insertion by submarine was the safest way to avoid 'compromising the main attack'.

After completing its reconnaissance tasks the SRD party was to remain in the area to help with the rescue operation, which would be carried out by an Australian parachute battalion dropped from C-47 transport aircraft. The paratroops, an elite force led by Lieutenant Colonel John Overall, were undergoing intensive training on the Atherton Tablelands in north Queensland. The reconnaissance party would place homing devices on the drop zones to guide in the paratroopers and lead them to the camp, where they would rout the Japanese guards and evacuate the prisoners to a landing ship lying offshore.

By late 1944 it was known that the prisoners at Sandakan were in a desperate physical state. This alone reduced the chances of a successful evacuation. There was also the risk that at the first sign of a rescue operation the Japanese would remove or, more likely, massacre the prisoners. Nelson Short told Justice Mansfield of being warned that 'if there were any landings by the Americans we would be shot. One of the guards told us that. He said that if the Americans landed all the prisoners would be done away with.'*

---

* In December 1944 at the approach of an American convoy the Japanese incinerated nearly 150 US prisoners of war at Palawan in the Philippines. News of this massacre had reached US intelligence by early 1945.

Some have dismissed Kingfisher as little more than a pipe dream—Paul Ham, for instance, writes that 'a whiff of fantasy permeates the whole scenario'—but the 'outline plan' was a thorough piece of work. It included annotated aerial photographs and detailed maps of the town, harbour and aerodrome, seaborne approaches and beaches suitable for landing craft as well as a sketch plan of the POW camp indicating single- and double-row barbed-wire fences along with the location of the guard house, sentry boxes, hospital and the camp's most striking landmark, the Big Tree. Technical data covered everything from offshore tides, topography, climate and vegetation to 'flying obstructions', known POW routines and even the names of Japanese officers. However, detailed as it was, it was not an operational plan, and without the last-minute intelligence to be obtained from the SRD reconnaissance party it could never become one.

In December 1944 GHQ approved the Kingfisher plans, although there is some disagreement over whether this approval related to the SRD's intelligence-gathering mission or to the rescue operation itself.

While planning for Kingfisher continued the SRD was busy with the first phase of Operation Agas, the purpose of which, according to the operations report, was to establish an intelligence network along the north-east coast, to organise guerrilla forces and harass enemy forces and to obtain information about the 'location and condition of Allied PWs in the Sandakan area'. But as early as August 1944 SRD chief Colonel Chapman-Walker had been advised by the controller of the Allied Intelligence Bureau (AIB) that Agas would not be approved by GHQ unless it prioritised the setting up of a military intelligence network.

A month later the SRD redrafted the Agas plan, shifting the area of operations to the west coast of Borneo, too far away to be able to help the prisoners at Sandakan. It was then modified again, this time with no reference to POWs at Sandakan or anywhere else. Its focus became creating intelligence networks, sabotage and organising guerrilla resistance against the Japanese. These priorities reflected a broader change in the role of the SRD as the Pacific War moved towards its endgame. By the end of 1944 the Allies had reconquered much of the Philippines. Other islands were falling faster than General MacArthur had expected and SRD operations on the drawing board risked being overtaken by events. The SRD had its hands full supporting Australian landings in Borneo.

Preparations for Operation Agas were not ideal. The party's leader, Major Gort Chester, wanted aerial photographs of the area around the insertion point but bureaucratic bungles meant these were never taken. The Agas I party left Darwin on 16 January 1945 aboard the American submarine *Tuna*, arriving off the designated entry point on Bisa Island twelve days later. A periscope surveillance of the area revealed what looked like buildings, 'whitish' smoke and two tall poles 'whitish in colour, about 100ft high with a cable (aerial) connecting them'. Chester interpreted these as evidence of 'enemy installations and . . . activity ashore'. Deciding it was too dangerous to land, Chester aborted the mission and returned to Australia. Reconnaissance later showed that the 'radio masts' Chester thought he saw were actually burnt trees.

At the same time, Allied advances were putting the Sandakan POWs in grave danger. Intelligence discovered after the war indicated the existence of orders from Tokyo to 'dispose' of prisoners of war before they could fall into enemy hands. A policy memorandum from the Japanese Ministry of War dated 1 August 1944 and found in the journal of the Formosan POW camp headquarters gave advice on how prisoners should be treated if the situation became 'urgent'. An English translation of the document was listed among the exhibits at the Tokyo war crimes trials. The translated memorandum urged camp commandants to take 'extreme measures' on their own initiative to suppress POW 'uprisings' and to prevent escaped prisoners from becoming a 'hostile fighting force':

Whether they are destroyed individually or in groups, or however it is done, with mass bombing, poisonous smoke, poisons, drowning, decapitation, or what, dispose of the prisoners as the situation dictates. In any case it is the aim not to allow the escape of a single one, to anni-hilate them all, and not to leave any traces.

By the time the Agas I team was ready to go again in late February the whole picture had changed. Kingfisher had been scrapped as a stand-alone project and was folded into Agas I, with Gort Chester in charge of both. According to another member of the party, Chester had deep misgivings about the combined operation, 'ranting and raving' about being given responsibility for Kingfisher. The party left Darwin aboard the *Tuna* on 24 February 1945, almost a month after the first death march set out from Sandakan.

With the planners envisaging a six-week reconnaissance mission, any rescue of the POWs still at Sandakan could not be carried out before the end of April. While its primary objective was to build a wireless station on the east coast of British North Borneo, the Agas team was also expected to set up an intelligence network to provide 'detailed informa-tion on the P.W. camp at Sandakan'.

By the time Chester's party landed on the night of 3 March, 'military developments' had extended the Agas target area west towards the Sarawak border and inland to Ranau, the destination of the death marches. Chester quickly identified Jambongan Island, just off the north-east coast and well over 100 kilometres from Sandakan, as a suitable spot for stores to be dropped by parachute. For the next six weeks, while Chester went exploring on his own, his comrades led attacks on Japanese soldiers as well as 'teach[ing] the natives to hide food from the Japs, who in most cases are extremely short of food'.

Any hopes the POWs had of being rescued depended on Chester's party obtaining accurate, up-to-date information about Sandakan as stipulated in the original Kingfisher plan, but with Chester preoccupied with intelligence and guerrilla activities further along the coast, none of the Agas/Kingfisher party went near it. The radio reports Chester sent back about the condition and whereabouts of the POWs were based not on first-hand information but on unconfirmed sightings—or rumours of sightings—passed on by local 'agents'.

The Agas files in the National Archives of Australia record numerous POW sightings, the cumulative effect of which was to obscure rather than clarify the true picture. Chester sent a report that was forwarded to AIB headquarters on 4 April 1945 advising that information had been supplied by a 'native chief' in the Sugut area, some 200 kilometres from Sandakan, that the Sandakan prisoners had been moved 'in groups' overland to Jesselton via Ranau. Many of the prisoners were said to be suffering from beriberi and 'those who were unable to travel were shot'. Chester described the information as 'reliable'. The gist of the report was, of course, true: more than 450 POWs had been sent to Ranau on the first death march and many had beriberi, but the implication that *all* prisoners had been moved was false.

On 20 May Chester was extracted from Borneo by Catalina flying boat and flown to Morotai for debriefing. The record of his interrogation dated 22 May and captioned 'Intelligence report No. 1', stated: 'All PW have now been moved from Sandakan to Ranau, where they now are. Many were killed or died on the way. NO estimate can be given, at the moment, of their numbers or their location at Ranau.'

The faulty information received and passed on by Chester had calamitous consequences for the 900 POWs still precariously alive at Sandakan. Seven days after Chester's debriefing at Morotai, the Allies launched an air and sea bombardment of Sandakan that killed several guards and more than a dozen POWs, convincing the Japanese that a landing was imminent and directly precipitating the second death march. In mid-June two 'natives' were picked up from the Labuk Bay area, around 30 kilometres from Sandakan, and flown to Morotai for questioning. As well as giving detailed reports of enemy troop dispositions, the pair said there were '300 Australian PW at Sandakan'. According to the interrogation summary the informants were 'intelligent' and their information was 'reliable'. But conflicting information continued to be sent back to SRD headquarters in Australia. A memorandum dated 30 June stated that most POWs had left Sandakan and were seen 'about 12 June at Mile 23 from Sandakan marching in the direction of Ranau. Many of the PW were shot when too weak to march further'. According to the memorandum, 'all reports' now indicated that there were 'NO PW in the entire area'.

The recovery of Dick Braithwaite sparked panic at the SRD when he confirmed that several hundred POWs had been at Sandakan when the camp was bombarded by Allied boats and planes. Braithwaite told his interrogators that around 150 very sick POWs had been left behind on 1 June when the second march set out. It was clear that any POWs who survived the march were beyond the reach of a Kingfisher-style rescue operation and that most were, in any case, too sick to be moved.

A report dated 19 July compiled by 'an SRD party in North Borneo' stated that 32 Australian POWs had been seen 'carrying stores from Boto . . . NE of Ranau a few days ago'. A fortnight later another report stated that 'some' Australian prisoners 'said to have come from the east coast' had been seen in early July working '300 yds east of the Tambunan road [near Ranau] in groups guarded by 3 Japs with rifles . . . They are in poor condition'.

With the evidence now pointing towards the surviving POWs being at Ranau, another SRD party, Agas III, was inserted by submarine with instructions to '[make] a reconnaissance for the rescue of P'sW at Ranau'. A reinforcement party would arrive later tasked with 'setting up a field medical post in the Ranau area for treatment of P'sW; to search for surviving P'sW; and to arrange PW evacuation'.

Bypassing Japanese outposts, Agas III pushed inland towards Ranau.

In early August a villager brought news that two Australian prisoners, Sticpewich and Reither, had escaped from the camp at Ranau. Sticpewich told his rescuers that four others—Short, Moxham, Botterill and Anderson—had also escaped. From local information Agas III estimated that on 10 August approximately 20 prisoners were left alive at Ranau, guarded by around 80 sickly Japanese. The condition of the prisoners was said to be 'very bad'. Two days later they called in an air strike on Ranau, which resulted in the death of one Japanese soldier.

The seven-man reinforcement party, including Lofty Hodges, was dropped by parachute from B-24 Liberators on 18 August. Six days later Agas III made contact with Short, Moxham and Botterill; Anderson had died and the remaining three were described as being in an 'extremely grave condition'.

The official report stated that Agas III had been 'unable to rescue the remaining 20 odd P'sW at Ranau. They were all known to be in a very weak condition, many were actually dying and all were entirely dependent upon each other for food, sanitation etc. Any attempts at rescue necessitated the removal of all survivors as rescue of the fitter would have meant the death of the remainder.'

Unable to rescue the surviving prisoners, the SRD party arranged instead for a 'large white arrow' to be placed on the hillside in a jungle clearing to indicate the POW camp for 'possible rescue by paratroops'. All it could do now was report the dreadful fate of the rest. A report dated 2 September noted the discovery near mile 110¾ of 'a number of discarded Australian hats with prisoners' numbers on wooden tags': 'There are graves nearby but no estimate of their capacity is given. These graves were not there 20 days ago. The tags are being collected, but the location of any survivors is unknown.'

The next day another report stated that the 'PWs who moved from Ranau on 27 August 1945 have all been murdered'. A further report confirmed that the camp at Ranau 'has been dismantled and five number tags have been collected . . . There is no trace of the PWs.' SRD Information report No. 377, dated 7 September, stated: 'Approx. 660 PWs are known to have died at Ranau, and AGAS have the only four survivors. 700 Australians and 480 British died at Sandakan before the movement to Ranau in June, and 250 mixed Australians and British PWs were left at Sandakan owing to their inability to walk.'

The final death toll was 2428, the majority of whom had never left Sandakan.

Months had been spent preparing for a rescue operation, but had Project Kingfisher collapsed under the weight of its own intelligence failures or had it been stymied by outside forces? Had the Sandakan prisoners died because it was too difficult to save them or because, in the larger picture of the Pacific War, they were deemed expendable?

After the war, covering up the story of the rescue mission that never was became a priority for the SRD and for its ultimate head, the commander-in-chief of the AIF, General Sir Thomas Blamey. There was little risk that senior figures in the organisation—those implicated in the conception and planning of Kingfisher—would tell what they knew. As for the SRD operatives on the ground, the one man who knew enough to expose the logistical failures and confused priorities that bedevilled Kingfisher from the start, the Malay-speaking Englishman Gort Chester, died of blackwater fever in Jesselton in 1946.

The clandestine culture of the SRD and Blamey's own secretiveness ensured that the Australian Government was kept in the dark about its activities. Disasters such as the Timor operation in which dozens of men died while gold, guns and other supplies were dropped into the laps of waiting enemy soldiers were never to be made public.

After the war Major Harry Jackson travelled to Sandakan to honour the government's pledge to reward locals who had risked their lives to help Australian prisoners. Japanese war criminals were tried and, in some cases, hanged. Revelations that a plan to rescue the Sandakan POWs had been bungled—or, worse, vetoed—would have hurt the government, Blamey and the SRD.

No one breathed a word about Kingfisher until November 1947, when Blamey stood up to speak at the second federal conference of the Royal Australian Armoured Corps Association in Melbourne. Blamey stunned his audience, which included Australian paratroopers who had spent a year on the Atherton Tablelands training for a 'secret mission' that never took place, by revealing the existence of a plan to rescue the Sandakan POWs:

> We had high hopes of being able to use Australian parachute troops. We had complete plans for them. Our spies were in Japanese-held territory. We had established the necessary contacts with prisoners at Sandakan, and our parachute troops were going to relieve them . . . [But] at the moment we wanted to act, we couldn't get the necessary aircraft to take them in. The operation would certainly have saved that death march of Sandakan. Destiny didn't permit us to carry it out.

Some historians have wondered why Blamey said what he did, but the timing of his speech provides a clue. During the war Blamey and the supreme Allied commander, General MacArthur, had been at loggerheads over issues including the latter's sidelining of Australian troops in the campaign to retake the Philippines. In 1947 the unpopular MacArthur, safely out of the way overseeing the post-war Allied occupation of Japan, made a handy scapegoat for the failure of Project Kingfisher.

After Blamey's comments were reported in the press there were demands for the Labor government to set up an inquiry, but a year earlier the government had resisted calls for investigations into 'past operations' on the grounds that 'no good purpose would be served by seeking to

allocate blame for the reverses sustained during the early part of the war',
and it was in no hurry to reverse that decision. The secretary of the army
received advice, however, from the chief of general staff that there was
'no record of any official request being made to General MacArthur'
for aircraft to be used for the rescue of the Sandakan POWs and that
Advanced HQ, Allied Land Forces had explored the possibility of a rescue
mission and found it 'quite impractical from all aspects'. With archival
records of SRD operations closed and Blamey refusing to elaborate on his
claims, Chifley's government was able to ride out the controversy.

Athol Moffitt became a barrister and Supreme Court judge after
the war but the question of why no attempt had been made to rescue the
Sandakan POWs continued to rankle with him, as it did with the death
march survivors. In 1983 Owen Campbell told Tim Bowden, 'I reckon
they could have saved them all. If they'd come in early in the piece.'

After retiring from the bench in 1984 Moffitt decided to write a
book about his wartime experiences. His research in the now-unlocked
wartime archives of the SRD confirmed that a plan to rescue the
prisoners—Project Kingfisher—had existed. Convinced that a rescue
'was practicable and would have substantially succeeded', Moffitt set out
to discover 'why a rescue . . . was never carried out'.

Nelson Short showed Moffitt a press cutting of Blamey's 1947 speech
to the Royal Australian Armoured Corps Association in which Blamey
was reported to have said that aircraft and ships needed for the Sandakan
rescue mission 'were required by the higher command for another operation'. To Moffitt, the reference to higher command 'could only refer to
General MacArthur or his HQ virtually under his command'.

Sir John Overall, commander of the Australian parachute battalion
that was being trained in far north Queensland to carry out the rescue,
told Moffitt 'there had been a plan to rescue the Sandakan prisoners.
We were asked by Army HQ . . . to undertake the rescue in the belief
there were only third-class Japanese troops there . . . I understood

General Blamey wanted it, but the US would not release the planes to make the drop.'

After studying the Kingfisher plans Moffitt deduced that the 'comparatively few' American C-47 transport aircraft needed for the rescue operation could have been provided at any time between March and early May 1945 'if there had been the will and interest to do so'. As far as Moffitt was concerned all the evidence pointed to MacArthur having withheld the planes needed for the rescue of the Sandakan POWs, but the source of much of this 'evidence' was Blamey himself. Lynette Silver quoted an irate Gort Chester telling one of his SRD comrades: 'You know what they're going to do? Blamey's going to shift the blame for all their bungling onto MacArthur.' Moffitt argued that MacArthur did not supply the necessary aircraft because

> to do so would not have been consistent with MacArthur's culti-vation of his personal image and the prestige of the US forces he commanded . . . A spectacular success by non-American paratroops would have raised questions at home for MacArthur . . . If US aircraft were used to rescue British and Australian prisoners, why had they not been used to rescue Americans in a similar situation?

US aircraft had been used with MacArthur's blessing to rescue American prisoners in the Philippines, albeit in different circumstances to those at Sandakan. It seems unlikely that MacArthur would have shied away from claiming credit for a successful operation using US aircraft to rescue the Sandakan POWs. In any case, records show that MacArthur *did* authorise at least the intelligence-gathering phase of Kingfisher. So if he was not to blame for Kingfisher's failure who or what was?

Lieutenant General Sir Leslie Morshead, commander of Australia's 1 Corps, commented ruefully that SRD parties 'provided a wealth of information on enemy movements and strengths, but uncertainty as to the reliability of most of the information provided materially lessened its value'. Michele Cunningham suggests that as much as 90 per cent of SRD intelligence 'ranged from unreliable to totally inaccurate'.

Kingfisher was effectively dead from the moment the AIB interpreted Chester's signal of 4 April 1945 to mean that all POWs had been moved from Sandakan. But accurate information concerning the routine and whereabouts of the POWs, without which there could be no rescue, had never been supplied. In the absence of such intelligence it was impossible for Kingfisher to progress from an 'outline plan' to an 'operational plan', let alone to an actual mission.

If Chester had verified his intelligence before sending it, or if he had worded his 4 April message differently, would a rescue mission still have been possible? Probably not. The Pacific War in early 1945 was not the war the Allies had anticipated when Kingfisher was first conceived. The rapid collapse of the Japanese defence of the Philippines caused the Allies to rethink their objectives and accelerate the timetable for a possible invasion of Japan.

If Sandakan had been a significant military objective the case for an operation to rescue the POWs would have been compelling. In February 1945 MacArthur had given orders for the rescue of Allied prisoners who lay in the path of advancing US troops in the Philippines. But Sandakan had no real military importance aside from its aerodome, which Allied bombers had made unserviceable by the beginning of 1945. Nor did Sandakan have any real strategic value as a place from which to launch or consolidate other attacks.

Rescuing the Sandakan prisoners would have had to be a stand-alone operation, peripheral to the main thrust of the Allied advance. As David Sissons has written, this made Kingfisher a more difficult logistical exercise than any of the three operations undertaken by MacArthur's forces to free internees in the Philippines. Only one of these—the rescue of 2000 civilian prisoners from Los Banos—involved a parachute drop, and the distance over which the internees had to be evacuated to reach the American lines was only 80 kilometres. A seaborne evacuation of the Sandakan POWs would have been far more hazardous over a far greater distance.

Don Wall believed it would have been possible to evacuate the POWs by air. By the start of 1945 Allied air superiority over Borneo was so complete, he argued, that once the camp and surrounding area had been secured, prisoners could have been evacuated in an orderly way using Hoshijima's airfield.

In a tape-recorded conversation in 1989 Owen Campbell told Wall there had been two periods during the day when the camp was vulnerable to attack: late afternoon when the guards turned out for roll call, and early morning when they exercised on an oval 100 metres down the hill from the barracks. Campbell told Wall that during afternoon fitness parade only four guards were left on duty, one at the main gate and three in towers around the camp perimeter. Each guard was armed with a .303 rifle and a single magazine holding a maximum of ten rounds.

Once the four guards on duty had been dealt with, Campbell said, the unarmed guards on the oval would have been trapped, since the nearest Japanese reinforcements were either at the aerodrome 1.5 miles (2.4 kilometres) away or 8 miles (13 kilometres) away at Sandakan. Asked by Wall how many paratroopers he thought would be needed to carry out the attack, Campbell replied, 'Fifty good armed men.'

As Wall and Campbell envisaged the rescue, a four-man infiltration party would slip into 8 Mile Camp during the night ahead of an early-morning assault coinciding with the guards' fitness parade. Once the assault was under way more paratroopers would attack the aerodrome while Allied fighters strafed targets outside the camp and on the road between Sandakan and Ranau: 'Old Hoshijima was there too, you know [at the oval during fitness parade] . . . he was down there or sittin' on his horse watching what was going on . . . They would have got the lot.

By the time anyone could have got back to the huts . . . they could have been strafed, the huts, and set . . . on fire.'

In an earlier interview with Tim Bowden, Campbell spoke of the prisoners having weapons stashed close to the camp. He boasted of having 'a machine gun and seven hundred rounds':

> We had enough ammunition and equipment. We could have took the place in the early stages. But we could not have held it. That was the trouble. We knew we couldn't have held it because they could have brought reinforcements in faster than we could have done anything . . . Even if we'd have gone to the jungles we wouldn't have survived.

In Campbell's view the removal of the final group of Allied officers in October 1943 made the Japanese 'very lackadaisical' about security. To the end of his life he remained convinced that a rescue mission was feasible but did not happen because 'we were expendable, and I reckon that was it'.

History proved Owen Campbell right. Insofar as rescuing them was not a sufficiently high priority to demand action the Sandakan POWs *were* expendable. In *War by Stealth*, his study of the AIB, Alan Powell asserts that 'Wars are essentially cruel and brutal and in the execution of the principal object no activity which does not contribute to the achievement of that objective can be entertained.' After years of bloody fighting, defeating the Japanese and bringing an end to hostilities were the overriding concerns for Allied high command. These goals had to take precedence over competing objectives such as the rescue of prisoners and even the capture of enemy-held territory and raw materials.

If Chester and his party had been able to supply the intelligence demanded by Kingfisher's planners, and if the will had been there, the 30 or so aircraft required to transport Overall's highly trained paratroopers could have been found. Athol Moffitt was surely right about that. The Kingfisher archives confirm that for a few months towards the end of 1944 there was interest at the highest levels of the Allied command in an operation to rescue the Sandakan prisoners. Six months later Allied objectives had changed and the opportunity was lost. By the time the full horror of Sandakan became clear it was too late.

How many of the POWs who died at Sandakan or Ranau or on the track might have survived the war if a rescue operation had gone ahead? We will never know. But if Owen Campbell was right there was one Australian who might have had cause to fear his liberation. Campbell said that if the war had ended before the first death march Bill Sticpewich would have been killed by his fellow prisoners as a collaborator. As things turned out, he outlived all but four of them.

Chapter 44

THEY GOT GAMER

—⟫●⟪—

Although Dick Braithwaite was the first of the death march survivors to reach safety, the first name to reach the Australian public was that of Owen Campbell. Rupert Charlett, war correspondent for Melbourne's *Argus* newspaper, was in hospital at Morotai when army public relations circulated the story of Campbell's amazing escape on 7 June 1945. Since the *Argus* man was not well enough to leave his bed, he typed up his story straight from the press handout, then army PR staff took his copy and cabled it to Melbourne.

His hastily written report, datelined 'Morotai August 31', described how Australian soldiers had been taken prisoner at Singapore and forced to load Japanese ships with

loot including thirty-three thousand sewing machines and large quantities of silk and woollen goods . . . Gunner Campbell said quote if the Jap guards didn't think you were working hard enough they hit you with shovels lumps wood and even pieces of iron. Sometimes they thrashed our men with dog whips and once lined up all the officers to wi[t]ness [a thrashing]. Although at first the Japs seemed frightened of us they got gamer as time went on and in the finish were like savages unquote.

Charlett described how Campbell made his break from the second death march when American fighters strafed the track. Campbell, he wrote:

... struggled through the jungle for some days eventually his companion collapsed and pleaded with Campbell to go on and leave him. Campbell refused and went to a stream to get water. When he came back he found that his companion had cut his throat. Campbell buried him and went on for eleven days with nothing to eat but fungus from the trunks of trees. Eventually he was found by natives who tendered [sic] him and then took him to an Australian unit.

Two months earlier Charlett had landed with the Australian 7th Division at Balikpapan; now he was incensed by the sight of Japanese wounded receiving treatment in the same hospital as Campbell. The Japanese, Charlett wrote, were 'well nourished, well housed and well treated ... [they are] given tobacco and cigarettes as well as being clothed with Australian army issue even to slouch hats'. Departing from the handout he had been given by the army's PR unit, Charlett declared that he

happen[ed] to be a patient in the same hospital and have seen some of the emaciated victims of Japanese prison camps brought in. It is a grim contrast that makes it difficult to remain calm and dispassionate in ones [sic] judgment of how far our humanitarian ideals should be given scope in our treatment of men of whose brutality and inhumanity there is now incontrovertible evidence.

Reports of Campbell's escape and of the mistreatment and starvation of Australian POWs at Sandakan were published in newspapers all over Australia on 31 August and 1 September 1945. In some papers Campbell's story ran alongside a report filed by the Australian Associated Press from Rangoon in Burma. It began: 'One of the greatest mercy missions of the war began on Tuesday, when RAF planes began carrying messages of freedom to more than 100,000 war prisoners in scattered camps ranging from Singapore to Saigon and from Bangkok to Sumatra.'

The story, attributed to the 'Air Ministry news service', reported that Liberator bombers were 'parachuting down supplies and scattering leaflets' on POW camps in Siam 'where the greatest number of prisoners is concentrated'. Promising that 'supplies will be brought quickly', the leaflets advised prisoners to remain in camp and warned against 'eating large quantities of food if they have been starved or underfed'. The message ended with the words, 'We want to get you home quickly, safe and sound.'

Allied planes were also said to be dropping another set of leaflets for Japanese guards 'tersely telling them what to do and how to do it and sternly warning them against taking any unauthorised action'. By the time those admonitory leaflets were dropped it was too late for the Australians who had been clinging to life at Sandakan and Ranau, the last of whom, Ted Skinner's brother John, was executed on 15 August.

Chapter 45

YOUR POOR FRIEND

———⟐———

Captain Nagai was not the only Japanese guard to correspond with Sticpewich after the war. Among Sticpewich's personal papers at the Australian War Memorial are two handwritten letters by Takahara, the Formosan guard who had surreptitiously supplied Sticpewich with anti-malarial drugs and extra food and who precipitated his escape by warning him that the remaining prisoners at Ranau were about to be massacred.

But there was more than one Takahara at Ranau. Takahara Koji was a member of the killing squad commanded by Sergeant Okada that murdered seventeen POWs at the cemetery. In their interrogation statements some of his fellow guards accused Takahara Koji of joining in the shooting while others named him as having been present but not having shot anyone. According to several guards, Takahara Koji 'escaped', either at Keningau or Tenom. Paul Ham seems to be alluding to this when he

writes: 'Two Formosans, one of whom is Takahara,* Sticpewich's informant, are so disgusted by their actions they will try to escape the jungle
camp'. There is no evidence, however, of Takahara Koji corresponding
with Sticpewich.

Takahara Mizuō was part of a four- or five-man search party sent by
Captain Takakuwa to hunt down Sticpewich after his escape. According
to evidence from other guards, he was not at Ranau when the massacres
took place. It was Takahara Mizuō, not Takahara Koji, who corresponded
with Sticpewich after the war. The first letter, written entirely in capitals
and dated '28/5 1946', says:

Dear Sticpewich
How are you I hop you are well
    I am many many thanks for you are kindness
    I am at the 26/4 1946 safet arriv my home as pleas take your ease
    I am tell my family and he's many thanks for your kind
    I am return home jst now as I can't tell you so many but I will send
you a photograph of my and write again next month
    My name Chenes [Chinese] call Fan Shui Eng
    Jponnes [Japanese] call Takahara Mizuō
    English call Fan Water Cherry
    If you want send me litter please use my Chines nama
    Good bey from your frind Water Cherry

Takahara's second letter, three pages long and apparently written in
response to one from Sticpewich, is more perplexing. The date is unclear
but a reference to his having 'return[ed] home . . . eleven months ago'
suggests it was written around February or March 1947:

---

*   Confusingly, Ham refers to the Takahara who escaped into the jungle as
    'Takahara Nisu'. In interrogation statements by other Ranau guards the fugitive
    guard is always identified as 'Takahara Koji'.

Dear Sticpewih

I am many tanks for your letter and I well know it is your vary busy I am also and you hope will finish the busy time and got holiday as soon as possible

I am return home a eleven months ago and I am can not gat my good job and my property is lost by the war and now in Formosn day by day the goods of price is up very high therefore I am everyday work is vary hard but the pay me mony is only for my daily I can not leave the mony up, in the reason I am is anxiety now

And now Formosn the goods of price compare to the before-war is up hundrefold centuple and America or England mony one dollar can to exchange seventy Formosan dollars

Now I am to began to leare to read and wright English to well as soon as I can

I am plan if may I trade with you. Now is best chance I am can got Formosan of tea and sugar or products of Formosan for you which and how many you want you letter me know I can get many for you

And when your ship to cam Formosan I will ask you to got products of Australia for me

I am had savings 2000 dollar in the Japan army I think it vary difficult to got the money I think better if I can get the new job and I will see you again

Now I send you photograph of me and my wife and my child . . .

Goodbye for now from your por friend F. S. Eng

What had transformed Takahara in a matter of months from 'your frind Water Cherry' to 'your por friend F. S. Eng'? The letter is essentially a catalogue of Takahara's financial woes: was he hoping Sticpewich would take pity and send him money? What did he mean by telling Sticpewich 'I can not leave the mony up': was he sending money to Sticpewich and explaining why he could not afford to pay more?

If, as Ham suggests, it was Takahara Koji who befriended Sticpewich and tipped him off about the impending massacre, then what was the reason for his correspondence with Takahara Mizuō? As the prosecution's most energetic and persuasive witness Sticpewich was in a uniquely powerful position to identify, not identify or even deliberately mis-identify guards as war criminals; at one time or another he did all three. He was capable of being both a benefactor and a blackmailer: which was he to Takahara Mizuō?

Another handwritten letter by a man named H.K. Hasegawa attests to Sticpewich's ongoing power over his former enemies. Posted from Japan and dated 7 February 1947 it begins:

Dear Sgt-Maj,
How are you sir? Over a year have passed since I had the good fortune of meeting you. I returned in March last year and am employed by the Occupation Forces . . . Mr Takahara and I could not return together but I am sure he returned to Formosa straight after.

Hasegawa asserts that he is eager to return to the 'Hawaiian islands' but needs a 'certificate or letter' from Sticpewich to the 'American Consul, Foreign Service Officer, Yokohama, Japan' stating that he 'was found to be OK' and had 'assisted' the Australian authorities in prosecuting Japanese war criminals:

Please send me a copy of this certificate. I am sure my passport will be okayed [as] soon as they hear from you. Please also put in a good word [be]cause I want to return to the Islands very much. I will appreciate it very, very much and will be waiting and praying to hear from you.

I read your articles (Dec 1946) to the Press* and I am wondering if you are still in Tokyo. If you are I pray that this letter will be forwarded to you quickly as possible.

I pray this letter will find you and all concerned in the best [health?]. With my best of wishes for your wellbeing, happiness and success I beg to remain

Sincerely yours

H. K. Hasegawa

Hasegawa's near-fluent command of English gives a clue to the nature of the 'assistance' he had provided to the Australians: he acted as interpreter in at least twenty prisoner interrogations, including that of Captain Yamamoto, and his name ('Herbert K. Hasegawa') and signature can be found on numerous witness statements. This work would likely have brought him into contact with Sticpewich, who was himself assisting in the interrogations and whose 'comments' on individual guards could (as we have seen) significantly influence the outcome of their trials. Did the pair strike up a friendship or was their relationship more pragmatic? What was the connection to 'Mr Takahara'? And why did Hasegawa believe Sticpewich would be willing to do what he asked? If Sticpewich ever responded to Hasegawa's 'prayers' for a certificate stating that he was 'OK', there is no evidence of it in the Australian War Memorial's files.

---

* In December 1946 Sticpewich gave evidence to the International Military Tribunal for the Far East in Tokyo that was widely reported in the newspapers.

Chapter 46

I USED HIM

—⊶⊷—

Personal traits and habits instilled and valued by the army and by society as a whole—for example honesty, obedience and self-sacrifice—were no guarantee of survival at Sandakan. The selfless did not survive.

Bill Moxham was born into a wealthy Sydney family. After an expensive private education he spent a decade managing the family's rural properties, describing himself on his attestation form as a 'station overseer'. Silver's description of him as having a 'wild, almost reckless streak' is borne out by the string of offences and reprimands recorded on his service and casualty form. On hearing that Sticpewich had survived, Moxham threatened to 'kill him with my bare hands', yet Moxham had been able to escape only because he stole Captain Oakeshott's boots. Without boots Oakeshott was doomed to die.

Nelson Short had joined the army hoping to be a cook, the occupation he noted on his attestation form. Instead he was sent to the infantry.

Short's service record, like Moxham's, lists a string of offences, and his transgressions continued—and even increased—after he became a POW at Changi. In a bid to escape the fighting at Singapore Short feigned madness, inventing an imaginary dog that he took everywhere with him on an imaginary leash and even conversing with his imaginary wife. Various accounts suggested Short was widely disliked; Don Wall described him to Tim Bowden as a 'known liar' with a 'bad reputation' while Paul Ham, citing an unnamed 'reliable source', writes that Short 'offered news about the death of a prisoner to the latter's bereaved family in exchange for money'. This was the same man whom Silver witnessed telling Sticpewich's widow that her husband was 'nothing but a collaborator'.

The rat cunning that helped Keith Botterill survive his upbringing in a tough working-class suburb of Sydney also enabled him to survive Sandakan. Like Moxham and Short, he was regularly punished for such offences as being absent without leave and using 'insubordinate language' to an officer. Botterill had no hesitation denouncing Captain Cook for collaborating with the Japanese in return for extra rations—he described Cook to his confidante Silver as being 'as fat as a pig'—but he was more circumspect in his comments about Sticpewich.

While he told the war crimes commission that he 'asked a lot of men' to escape with him, he told Bowden he had kept his plans secret from Sticpewich, presumably out of fear that the latter might betray him. At Fukushima's trial, however, Botterill was willing to suspend his personal antipathy to secure Sticpewich's cooperation. When it came to lying on oath to ensure Fukushima was hanged, Botterill saluted Sticpewich's superior ability: he 'could argue black was white', Botterill told Silver, 'and he would be believed'.

Self-sacrifice was an alien concept for Sticpewich, but he was far from alone in that. He survived because he was resilient,* because he was lucky** and because he put his own survival ahead of that of every other man in the camp. Others did so too, but they did not have his luck or the practical skills that made his survival useful to the Japanese.

While Sticpewich's first priority was always his own interests, that doesn't mean he acted only for himself. As a member of the prisoners' committee he regularly pressed Cook to take up prisoners' grievances with Hoshijima. On the second death march he was a resourceful and sometimes courageous group leader: he saved his group's valuable sugar and salt ration by immediately distributing it while other groups had theirs confiscated by guards. At Sandakan and Ranau he found ways of obtaining medical supplies, including Atebrin and quinine, for the treatment of sick prisoners. At Ranau he shared information he had winkled out of the guards about the likely fate of the remaining prisoners.

Sticpewich's record as a prisoner at Sandakan shows the efforts he made to communicate both with the Japanese and with the local population. He taught himself enough Japanese and Malay to be able

---

* Before enlisting in the army Sticpewich worked at an abattoir. One day his co-workers locked him in the cool room, and when they let him out he was covered in ice. On another occasion he was put in a bullpen and had to kill as many bulls as he could with a hammer. Both stories, which were told to Ben Sticpewich by Bill's brother Arthur, corroborate the image of Sticpewich as a loner who was unpopular with his colleagues and forced to prove himself through physical toughness. Dick Braithwaite, of course, recalled Sticpewich having 'fancied himself as a bit of a wrestler . . . he used to pick on the young blokes and throw them around a bit'.

** Luck seems an inadequate explanation or part-explanation for Sticpewich's survival, yet he was surely lucky never to have suffered the kind of accident that might have resulted in a tropical ulcer, and lucky too in having escaped serious disease. Some of his luck was self-made: Ben Sticpewich recounts a story his father Keith told him about Bill's time at Sandakan: when it rained he used to take off all his clothes and wash himself with gravel. Such fastidiousness about personal hygiene must have improved his chances of staying healthy.

to cultivate relationships with the guards as well as to negotiate with outsiders for the supply of food and contraband. Paul Ham suggests that Sticpewich '[chose] a different course to the rest because he [saw] that only by understanding the Japanese [could] the prisoners hope to exploit them, and survive'. He understood, perhaps, that unrelenting hostility and refusal to cooperate with the Japanese could only, in the end, have one outcome.

Although never popular, Sticpewich was evidently respected and tolerated enough to be a member of the prisoners' committee and to have some responsibility for protecting the secret wireless. At some point, however, under the pressure of brutal labour, harsh discipline, sickness and starvation the dynamics of the camp changed and he—more or less untouched by all the above—became a pariah, a so-called 'white Jap'.

While giving evidence at the Tokyo war crimes trials, Sticpewich was asked to nominate any 'guards or officers that showed you any kindness'. He mentioned just three: the 'quartermaster sergeant', the 'interpreter' and 'the guard that give me the tip to escape'. The latter was Takahara who, Sticpewich said, 'had always been good to us right throughout'.

He was then asked about the Japanese medical orderly at Ranau who told him of having seen a written order that said all prisoners were to be killed. The soldier was 'just a private', Sticpewich said, and he could not remember his name. Asked by the defence counsel, Mr Shimanouchi, whether he and the medical orderly had an 'intimate' relationship, he replied, 'Not what you call intimate relationship. I was out to get any information I could receive from any of the Japanese.' Pressed on whether the pair were on 'intimate or friendly terms', Sticpewich answered bluntly, 'I used him.' Even as a prisoner, he was the user, rarely the used.

Sticpewich was not satisfied simply to survive the war. More than any of his fellow survivors he carried the burden of obtaining justice and a proper burial for his murdered comrades. Without his knowledge and energy the remains of many POWs would never have been recovered. Without his phenomenal memory and painstaking evidence some of the most brutal guards might have walked free.

After the camp records were lost it was Sticpewich who took on the responsibility of ensuring the collective story of the Sandakan POWs was told. His tendency to report things he had been told by other prisoners as first-hand evidence could be problematic in trials, but it made him a kind of everyman, a repository of the camp's shared memory.

Bill Sticpewich returned to Australia in far better physical shape than the other five death march survivors, but he too had suffered: from dysentery, pneumonia, cerebral malaria and other diseases. Braithwaite, Campbell, Moxham, Botterill and Short in their own different ways suffered more than Sticpewich; all of them bar Braithwaite despised him as a collaborator and resented his survival. By the time the war was over all those who might have judged Sticpewich less harshly were dead. The Manichean perception of Sandakan after the war did not allow for the possibility that cooperation or apparent cooperation with the enemy might achieve a more subversive outcome than resistance.

Ben Sticpewich concedes that his great uncle Bill 'could have been a murderer, a blackmailer, a thief of what was under the Big Tree—he could have been all these things'. But there is no proof he was any of them.

On 14 December 1963 Sticpewich stood as a by-election candidate for the east ward in the city of Fitzroy in Victoria. Two years earlier, Bill Moxham, the most tormented of the Australians who escaped from Sandakan, had taken his own life. Sticpewich's voting card stated that he was running 'For reform and progress with honest and efficient local government'. Written in pencil on the back of the voting card are two names along with addresses and telephone numbers. They belong to Dick Braithwaite and Owen Campbell, the pair Tim Bowden considered the 'most reliable' of the four death march survivors he interviewed.

Almost two decades had passed since the end of the war. In that time Sticpewich's prediction that 'Those bastards will never say anything while I'm alive' had largely held true. He was 55 years old and had another fourteen years to live: had the time come for him to confide in his two former comrades?

CITY OF FITZROY

COUNCIL BY-ELECTION — EAST WARD

SATURDAY, DECEMBER 14th, 1963

VOTE ☐1 STICPEWICH

W. H., M.B.E.

RESIDENT OWNER RATEPAYER

FOR REFORM AND PROGRESS WITH HONEST AND EFFICIENT LOCAL GOVERNMENT.

Authorised by F. E. Ritchie, 193 Smith St., Fitzroy.

Perfection Press Pty. Ltd., 237-239 Gertrude St., Fitzroy, Vic. — JA 2762.

Chapter 47

UNHAPPY CAPTIVES

In late July and early August 1945, the Allies considered sending a proposal to Japan's 37th Army Command in Borneo for the release of Allied POWs and civilian internees. Among the papers of Athol Moffitt at the Australian War Memorial is a letter dated 4 August 1945 and marked 'CONFIDENTIAL' that was written by the commander of I Australia Corps, Lieutenant General Leslie Morshead, to MacArthur's GHQ in Brisbane:

Subject—Allied PW and internees in Borneo

1. We have been examining the feasibility of negotiating with the Commander Japanese 37th Army in Borneo for the release of British, Australian and other Allied Army PW and civilian internees.

2. The total number of Allied Army PW in Borneo is assessed at 2,700 of whom 1,200 are in the Ranau–Boto area and 1,500 in the vicinity of Kuching. There are also some hundreds of civilian internees in the Kuching area and about 2,250 Indian and NEI [Netherlands East Indies] PW mostly in the Balikpapan area.

    Attached is a review of the situation.

3. It is suggested that a personal letter be addressed to the GOC 37th Army by GOC I Aust Corps, and that several identical letters in English with Japanese translation be dropped by aircraft at different places, these letters to be marked 'Personal and Confidential. To be delivered to HQ 37th Army'.

4. It is thought that the text of the letter should be in the form of a frank request for the compassionate release of PW and internees who, on account of sickness and poor physical condition, are of little use to the Japanese Commander for labour and whose part in the war is over.

5. In the PW compound at Morotai we have an intellectual Japanese officer, 1st Lieut. Takeda, who has given us a good deal of interesting and valuable information. We have obtained his views on this proposal and he considers it well worth trying, and he made the following points—

    (a) The appeal should be a direct one as from one Commander to another and should be in the best formal style of Japanese etiquette.

    (b) There should be no 'psychological nonsense' (as he expressed it) included.

    (c) The appeal should treat the Japanese Commander as a gentleman, fully appreciative of the normal humanitarian qualities.

    (d) There should definitely be no bargaining, and negotiations or a truce should be avoided at all costs as these will place too great a responsibility on the Japanese Commander, and he would be almost certain to refer it to higher command.

(e)   The appeal should imply that we consider the Japanese Commander of adequate importance to decide the question.

(f)   The appeal should be made in the form of several identical letters formally addressed to the Japanese Commander, dropped at several different places, stating where they were dropped, to eliminate the possibility of a subordinate destroying the letter and not forwarding it.

(g)   The whole proposition and the implementing of it should be made in the one letter to reduce to a minimum the necessity for inter-communication, from which it is considered the Japanese Commander would fight shy.

(h)   The proposal should require the minimum and simplest action on the part of the Japanese Commander and should merely request the Japanese to leave the PW at some point or points near the coast where we could go in and take them out without interfering or affecting the tactical situation in any way.

6.   In regard to the implementing of the request, it is considered that a simple plan might be acceptable by which the Japanese are requested to concentrate the PW at each of Beluran, Tuaran and Trombok Beach, north of Kuching, on the coast where we could put in landing craft, rescue the PW and withdraw without any effect on the tactical situation.

7.   The question of inter-communication might be met by requesting the Japanese to make a simple reply by light signal to an Allied ship which would stand off, say, Jesselton, or some other point at a specified time on four consecutive days or nights and make a signal to the shore.

The reply could be couched simply as
'Yes', 'Beluran 24 stop 95
Tuaran 12 stop 161
Trombok 18 stop 3580'
indicating that 24 days after date of signalling 95 PW may be picked up at Beluran, etc

8. I should be glad to have your approval of the proposal in which case I should welcome your guidance generally, and particularly on the procedure and on the composition of the letter.

The form that such a proposal might have taken is suggested by another document, marked 'TOP SECRET' and addressed to the 37th Army commander, Lieutenant General Baba Masao:

On my instructions as commander of all Allied forces in Borneo, one copy of this letter addressed to you is being dropped today at each of the following places:
RANAU airfield
KENINGAU airfield
SAPONG ESTATE
Further copies of the letter will be dropped at these places on each successive day for 10 days unless an acknowledgement that the letter has actually reached your hands is made before the expiration of this time. It is suggested that this acknowledgement might take the form of a large white cross displayed for at least 24 hours on the ground in front of the Keningau airfield. If no acknowledgement is made in the first ten days then reconnaissance aircraft of my command will observe the Keningau airfield for a further ten days or until your acknowledgement is made, whichever is the sooner.

This acknowledgement in itself will not constitute a rejection or acceptance of the request which I wish to make to you.

I ask you to release into my care the Allied prisoners of war and civilian internees at present in your keeping.

I ask this because, as a soldier, I believe that they are no longer capable of bearing arms against your forces. I further believe that their usefulness to you as labourers has been impaired by illness to such an extent that you may be willing to adopt this humane course in preference to permitting the death of further of their number, not on the field of honour but as unhappy captives.

On the seventh day after the day upon which you acknowledge receipt of this communication, an Allied vessel carrying my representative and flying the Australian flag and a white flag of truce will anchor a mile off Jesselton wharf at 0300 hrs GMT. For a period of one hour this vessel will endeavour to communicate with your shore station by visual signals using the International Morse Code.

In the event of failure to enter into communication with your shore station, the Allied vessel will return at the same time each day for a week and renew the attempt. If no reply is received during this period, then I will understand that you are not willing to grant my request.

If however you answer that you will release these prisoners then it will be necessary that your message should also contain your decisions on the following points:

(a) Places at which PW should be picked up by Allied vessels.

(b) Dates on which PW will be assembled at these embarkation points.

(c) Numbers of PW to be picked up.

(d) Points at which supplies of food* and clothing should be dropped from Allied aircraft to provide for PW during movement from PW camps to embarkation points.

I appeal to you to give this request the full benefit of your mature deliberation.

---

*   Here someone has inserted the handwritten words 'medical stores'.

The logistical detail contained in both documents eerily echoes the fastidious planning that went into the abortive Kingfisher rescue mission, but the handwritten correction to point (d), along with the absence of a date or signature, indicates that the second letter was a draft only and was never dropped. In any case, time had long run out for any attempt to save the POWs at Sandakan and Ranau, most of whom had little hope of surviving 17 hours, let alone the 17 days envisaged in the second letter.

By the time Morshead wrote his letter only a handful of prisoners were left alive. Two days later, on 6 August 1945, the Americans dropped an atomic bomb on Hiroshima, and three days after that a second bomb was dropped on Nagasaki.

With their combination of doomed implausibility and desperate optimism, the two documents somehow encapsulate between them the entire tragedy of Sandakan. Whether or not Baba received the Allied proposal and would have consented to release his 'unhappy captives' will never be known.

In May 1947 Lieutenant General Baba was tried as a war criminal for his command role in the two death marches and the subsequent massacre of prisoners at Ranau. The first two charges stated that Baba had ordered POWs to march from Sandakan to Ranau in January and May 1945 'at a time when the said Prisoners of War were in such a condition that the said march would necessarily cause them great pain and suffering'. Exhibit (e) for the prosecution was a copy of Sticpewich's evidence at the trial of Captain Yamamoto. In his summing up the judge advocate characterised Sticpewich's evidence about the first death march as 'largely hearsay', but on the crucial issue of the prisoners' fitness to undertake both marches he accepted Sticpewich's description of the men as 'very worn, starved and practically physical wrecks'.

According to a report in the *Sydney Morning Herald*, the court deliberated for just twelve minutes before finding Baba guilty. Sentenced to death, he was hanged at Rabaul at 8 am on 7 August 1947.

BIBLIOGRAPHY

—▸◄—

Australian War Memorial

Affidavits by Japanese personnel in connection with charges arising from Sandakan–Ranau with comments by Warrant Officer W.H. Sticpewich, AWM 54 1010 4/174

Papers of Athol Moffitt, PR01378

Papers of W.H. Sticpewich, PR00637

'Prisoner of War Days', Maj Hugh Rayson, AWM 2019.22.136

Report by Capt Steele, WO Wallace & Spr Kennedy, AWM 226 [9/2]

Sound recording of Dick Braithwaite by Tim Bowden, S03006

Sound recording of Dick Braithwaite by Tim Bowden, S03025

Sound recording of Keith Botterill by Tim Bowden, S02949

Sound recording of Keith Botterill and Nelson Short by Don Wall, S04095

Sound recording of Keith Botterill by Don Wall, S04080

Sound recording of Nelson Short by Tim Bowden, S02907

Sound recording of Owen Campbell by Tim Bowden, S02906

Statement by Bdr Braithwaite to war crimes commission, AWM 54
    1010/4/19

Statement by Gnr Campbell to war crimes commission, AWM 54
    1010/4/27

Statement by L-Bdr Moxham to war crimes commission, AWM 54
    1010/4/107

Statements by Lt Wells and Lt Weynton to war crimes commission,
    AWM 54 1010/4/146

Statement by Lt-Col Alf Walsh to war crimes commission, AWM 54
    1010/4/144

Statement by Pte Botterill to war crimes commission, AWM 54 1010/4/17

Statement by Pte Short to war crimes commission, AWM 54 1010/4/129

Summary of proceedings and petitions, messages and correspondence
    re Japanese war criminals, Labuan 1945–6, AWM 54 1010/6/1

Trial of Baba Masao, AWM 54 1010/3/88

Trial of Takakuwa Takuo and Watanabe Genzo, AWM 54 1010/3/94

Unit Diary, 8 Australian War Graves Unit, Jan–Dec 1946, AWM52
    21/2/9/3

Unit diary, 31 Australian War Graves Unit, Jan–Dec 1946, AWM52
    21/2/32/1

National Archives of Australia

Agas I, copy I (British North Borneo, February–September 1945), NAA:
    A3269, A1/A

Agas V, copy II (British North Borneo, February–September 1945),
    NAA: A3269, A5/C

Agas (Projects) Intelligence Reports (British North Borneo, February–
    September 1945), NAA: A3269, A5/A

Awards to helpers British North Borneo—Major Jackson's report, NAA: MP742/1, 328/1/32

Botterill, Keith, service record, NAA: B883, NX42191

Braithwaite, James Richard, service record, NAA: B883, NX45378

Burns, Tom, diary, NAA: B3856, 144/14/140

Campbell, Owen Collin, service record, NAA: B883, QX14380

Court martial of William Hector Sticpewich, NAA: A471, 22870

Kingfisher, copy I (Sandakan), NAA: A3269, A22/A

Kingfisher, copy II (Sandakan), NAA: A3269, A22/B

Moxham, William Dick, service record, NAA: B883, NX19750

Platypus Intelligence Reports (Balikpapan, March–August 1945), NAA: A3269, A6/A

Python Copy I (British North Borneo), NAA: A3269, A7/A

Second trial of Yamamoto Shoichi, NAA: A471, 81029 PART B

Services Reconnaissance Department (SRD) (HQ) Correspondence, NAA: A3269, H1

Short, Nelson, service record, NAA: B883, NX58617

Statements by WO1 Sticpewich, NAA: B3856, 144/1/372 PART 3

Sticpewich, William Hector, application for a commission, Australian War Graves search—Sandakan Ranau Track, NAA: MT885/1, S/8/2541

Sticpewich, William Hector M.B.E, service record, NAA: B2458, 1905032

Trial of Beppu Yoichi, Yamamoto Jiro, Hashimoto Masao et al., NAA: A471, 80913

Trial of Fukushima Masao, NAA: A471, 81060

Trial of Hoshijima Susumu, NAA: A471, 80777 PART 1

Trial of Kitamura Kotoro, Kawakami Koyoshi and Suzuki Saburō, NAA: A471, 81213

Trial of Matsuda, Fukushima and others, NAA: A471, 80772

Trial of Murozumi and others, NAA: A471, 80776

Trial of Sugino Tsuruo, NAA: A471, 80716

Trial of Yamomoto Shoichi, NAA: A471, 81663 PART B

War Crimes Borneo—Lieutenant General Baba Masao, NAA: MP742/1, 336/1/1180

Books and articles

Braithwaite, Richard Wallace, 2016, *Fighting Monsters: An intimate history of the Sandakan tragedy*, Australian Scholarly Publishing, North Melbourne, Victoria

Cunningham, Michele, 2013, *Hell on Earth: Sandakan—Australia's greatest war tragedy*, Hachette, Sydney, New South Wales

De Graaff, Bob, 'Hot Intelligence in the Tropics: Dutch Intelligence Operations in the Netherlands East Indies during the Second World War', *Journal of Contemporary History*, vol. 22, no. 4, October 1987

Firkins, Peter, 1979, *From Hell to Eternity*, Westward Ho Publishing, Perth

Fitzpatrick, Georgina, McCormack, Timothy L.H. and Morris, Narelle (eds), 2016, *Australia's War Crimes Trials 1945–51*, Brill Nijhoff, Netherlands

Followill, Gary, 2020, 'Necessary chicanery: Operation Kingfisher's cancellation and inter-Allied rivalry', Masters thesis, University of New South Wales, Sydney, New South Wales

Ham, Paul, 2013, *Sandakan: The untold story of the Sandakan death marches*, Random House, Sydney, New South Wales

Japanese War Ministry, 'The order to murder all the POWs', doc. 2701, Exhibit 'O', Box 2015, http://www.mansell.com/pow_resources/Formosa/taiwandocs.html, accessed 6 April 2021

Meale, Katie Lisa, 2015, 'Leadership of Australian POWs in the Second World War', PhD thesis, University of Wollongong, https://ro.uow.edu.au/theses/4620, accessed 6 April 2021

Moffitt, Athol, 1995, *Project Kingfisher*, ABC Books, Sydney, New South
     Wales

Moffitt, Athol, 2003, transcript of interview, Australians at
     War Film Archive, University of New South Wales,
     http://australiansatwarfilmarchive.unsw.edu.au/archive/799,
     accessed 6 April 2021

Moffitt, Athol, unpublished memoir

Morris, Dr Narelle, 2019, 'Japanese war crimes in the Pacific: Australia's
     investigations and prosecutions', National Archives of Australia

Ooi, Keat Gin, 2002, 'Prelude to invasion: covert operations before
     the re-occupation of Northwest Borneo 1944–45', *Journal of the
     Australian War Memorial*, Issue 37

Powell, Alan, 1996, *War by Stealth: Australians and the Allied Intelligence
     Bureau, 1942–1945*, Melbourne University Press, Melbourne, Victoria

Silver, Lynette, 1998, *Sandakan: A conspiracy of silence*, Sally Milner
     Publishing, Sydney, New South Wales

Silver, Lynette, 2019, The murder of Private Herman Reither,
     https://lynettesilver.com/investigations/the-murder-of-private-
     herman-reither/, accessed 6 April 2021

Sissons, D.C.S., 'The Australian War Crimes Trials and Investigations
     (1942–51)', https://www.ocf.berkeley.edu/~changmin/documents/
     Sissons%20Final%20War%20Crimes%20Text%2018-3-06.pdf,
     accessed 6 April 2021

Smith, Kevin, 1999, *Borneo: Australia's proud but tragic heritage*,
     self-published

Tamura, Keiko and Stockwin, Arthur (eds), 2020, 'Bridging Australia
     and Japan, Volume 2: The writings of David Sissons, historian and
     political scientist', Asian Studies series monograph 15, ANU Press,
     Canberra

Tanaka, Yuki, 2019, *Hidden Horrors: Japanese war crimes in World
     War II*, Routledge

Taucher, Paul, 2016, 'Command Responsibility at the Sandakan–Ranau war crimes trials', BA Hons thesis, Murdoch University, Perth, Western Australia

Wall, Don, 1990, *Abandoned? Australians at Sandakan, 1945*, self-published, Sydney, New South Wales

Wall, Don, 1997, *Sandakan under Nippon: The last march*, revised 5th edn, self-published, Sydney, New South Wales

Wallace, W., 1958, *Escape from Hell: The Sandakan story*, Robert Hale, London, United Kingdom

Young, Bill, 1991, *Return to a Dark Age*, Allawah, Sydney, New South Wales

Young, Bill, 2006, 'Outward Bound B Force to Borneo', http://www.borneopow.info/young/billyoung.htm, accessed 6 April 2021

INDEX